The Overeducated Worker?
The Economics of Skill Utilization

The Overeducated Worker?

The Economics of Skill Utilization

Edited by

Lex Borghans and Andries de Grip

Research Centre for Education and the Labour Market
Maastricht University, The Netherlands

EUROPEAN LOW-WAGE EMPLOYMENT RESEARCH NETWORK
(LoWER)

Edward Elgar
Cheltenham, UK • Northampton, MA, USA

Published by
Edward Elgar Publishing Limited
Glensanda House
Montpellier Parade
Cheltenham
Glos GL50 1UA
UK

Edward Elgar Publishing, Inc.
136 West Street
Suite 202
Northampton
Massachusetts 01060
USA

A catalogue record for this book
is available from the British Library

Library of Congress Cataloguing in Publication Data

The Overeducated worker? : the economics of skill utilization / edited by Lex Borghans and Andries de Grip.
    Includes bibliographical references (p.) and index.
    1. Underemployment. 2. Labor supply—Effect of education on. 3. Unskilled labor—Supply and demand. I. Borghans, L. II. Grip, A. de.
HD5709.O94 2000
331.13—dc21
99–087189

ISBN 1 84064 155 X

Printed in the United Kingdom at the University Press, Cambridge

Contents

Contributors   *vii*

List of Tables   *xi*

List of Figures   *xv*

INTRODUCTION

1. The Debate in Economics about Skill Utilization   3
   Lex Borghans and Andries de Grip

PART ONE: UNDERUTILIZATION OR UPGRADING?

2. Technology and the Demand for Skills   27
   Edward Wolff

3. Has the Finnish Labour Market Bumped the Least Educated?   57
   Rita Asplund and Reija Lilja

4. Are British Workers Becoming More Skilled?   77
   Francis Green, David Ashton, Brendan Burchell, Bryn Davies
   and Alan Felstead

PART TWO: CAUSES OF UNDERUTILIZATION

5. Overeducation and Crowding Out of Low-skilled Workers   109
   Joan Muysken and Bas ter Weel

6. Overqualification makes Low-wage Employment Attractive   133
   Thomas Zwick

7. Overeducation and Crowding Out in Britain   157
   Harminder Battu and Peter Sloane

8. The Effect of Bumping Down on Wages: an Empirical Test   175
   Ides Nicaise

PART THREE: CONSEQUENCES OF UNDERUTILIZATION OF SKILLS

9. Low Wages, Skills and the Utilization of Skills   191
   Lex Borghans, Allard Bruinshoofd and Andries de Grip

10. Do More High-skilled Workers Occupy Simple Jobs During   203
    Bad Times?
    Pieter Gautier

11. Job Competition in the Dutch Labour Market   231
    Loek Groot and Albert Hoek

Index   253

Contributors

David Ashton is a Professor of Sociology and the Director of the Centre for Labour Market Studies at the University of Leicester. His research interests include the origins and effects of education and training systems, and the role of work-based learning.

Rita Asplund is Research Director at the Research Institute of the Finnish Economy ETLA and is responsible for the institute's research programme Technology, Competence and Competitiveness. Her research interests are interactions between technology and competence particularly from the perspective of the labour market success and exclusion of individuals, educational economics and wage determination.

Harminder Battu is a Lecturer in the Department of Economics at the University of Aberdeen. His main research interests are in labour and regional economics.

Lex Borghans is Principal Researcher at the Research Centre for Education and the Labour Market (ROA), Maastricht University. His research concerns the acquisition of human capital, the measurement of skills and the way in which these skills are utilized in the labour market.

Allard Bruinshoofd is a Ph.D. student at the Department of Economics of the University of Maastricht. His research interests include a number of topics from both labour economics and the economics of financial intermediation.

Brendan Burchell is a Lecturer in the Faculty of Social and Political Sciences at the University of Cambridge. His research interests include job insecurity and atypical employment.

Bryn Davies is a Consultant in occupational psychology.

Alan Felstead is Reader in Employment Studies at the Centre for Labour Market Studies, University of Leicester. His research interests include the growth of non-standard forms of employment, the process of skill formation and training policy.

Pieter Gautier is a Post-doc at the Erasmus University Rotterdam and the Tinbergen Institute Amsterdam. His research interests include: search, matching, and assignment models of the labour market.

Francis Green is a Professor of Economics at the University of Kent at Canterbury. His current research interests include the measurement and analysis of skills, the role of education and training systems in the economy, and the sources of changing work effort.

Andries de Grip is Professor of Economics at the Faculty of Economics and Business Administration, Maastricht University and Head of the Division of Labour Market and Training of the Research Centre for Education and the Labour Market (ROA). His current research interests include various aspects of the relation between training and the labour market.

Loek Groot is Economist and Philosopher and is now working as a Grotius post-doctorate research fellow at the Amsterdam School of Social Research (ASSR), University of Amsterdam. His research activities centre around the interaction between social security arrangements and the labour market, the educational and occupational segregation of men and women and the economics of superstars.

Albert Hoek is Junior Researcher at the department of Social Sciences at the University of Utrecht and interested in labour market and education topics.

Reija Lilja is Research Director at the Labour Institute for Economic Research. Her research interests cover different aspects of individual behaviour in the labour market and applied labour market research in general.

Joan Muysken is Professor of Economics at the Faculty of Economics and Business Administration, University of Maastricht. His research interests include unemployment, matching problems, skill formation, wage formation and endogenous growth.

Ides Nicaise is Research Manager at HIVA (Higher Institute for Labour Studies, University of Leuven) and lecturer of labour economics at the Vlaamse Economische Hogeschool (Flemish Business School, Brussels). His research covers issues relating to poverty, the economics of education and the evaluation of labour market policies.

Peter Sloane is Jaffrey Professor of Political Economy, Vice-Principal and Dean of the Faculty of Social Sciences and Law, University of Aberdeen. His research interests cover various aspects of labour economics and the economics of professional team sports.

Bas ter Weel is a Ph.D. student at the Maastricht Economic Research Institute on Innovation and Technology (MERIT), Maastricht University. His research interests cover the broad range of theoretical and empirical studies on the impact of technological change on employment and economic growth, mainly focussing on skill-biased technical change and (human) capital development and investment.

Edward Wolff is Professor of Economics at New York University and Senior Scholar at the Jerome Levy Economics Institute of Bard College. He also serves as Managing Editor of the Review of Income and Wealth, Associate Editor of Structural Change and Economic Dynamics, and Council Member of the International Input-Output Association. His principal research interests are productivity growth and income and wealth distribution.

Thomas Zwick is a Research Fellow at the Centre for European Economic Research (ZEW) in Mannheim, Germany. His main research interests are in the economic aspects of human capital formation, the microeconomics and econometrics of labour markets and personnel economics.

List of Tables

Table 2.1	The distribution of employment by occupational group, 1950–1995	33
Table 2.2	Annual rate of change of workplace and workforce skills, total economy, 1950–1995	36
Table 2.3	Mean skill scores by major industry in 1970 and change over 1950–1990	39
Table 2.4	Distribution of employment by major industry, 1950, 1970 and 1995	42
Table 2.5	Decomposition of the change in overall skill levels into an occupational composition and an industry employment shift effect, 1950–1990	44
Table 2.6	Regressions of skill change on technology and other variables	49
Table 3.1	Transition probabilities of all employees, separately for the 1975 and 1985 samples	61
Table 3.2	The relative risk of transition of the least educated as compared to the more educated (more than 9 years of schooling)	62
Table 3.3	Dependency between the occupations' share of overeducated and selected features	65
Table 3.4	Propensity to remain overeducated, based on a constant and a changing definition of overeducation	66
Table 3.5	Average transition probabilities	67
Table 3.6	Transition probabilities by education	68
Table 3.7	Transition probabilities by overeducation	70
Table 3A.1	Multinomial logit estimation results for labour market transitions between 1975 and 1985	72
Table 3A.2	Multinomial logit estimation results for labour market transitions between 1985 and 1995	73
Table 4.1	Qualifications required in Britain, 1986 and 1997	84
Table 4.2	The demand for qualifications in Britain, 1986 and 1997	85
Table 4.3	'Overeducation' of workers in Britain, 1986 and 1997	86

Table 4.4	Further measures of job skill trends	88
Table 4.5	Skill trends by age	89
Table 4.6	Occupational structure in Britain, 1986 and 1997	90
Table 4.7	Skill trends by occupation	91
Table 4.8	Skill trends by industry	92
Table 4.9	Type of work skill changes in Britain 1992 to 1997	95
Table 4.10	Exclusion from skill rises	97
Table 4.11	Changing skills of the lowest paid quintile, males and females	99
Table 4A.1	Comparison of SCELI with LFS 1986	102
Table 4A.2	Comparison of data on qualifications held	105
Table 5.1	Percentages of workers with excess education in the Netherlands	110
Table 5.2	Education and unemployment in 1990	110
Table 5.3	Returns to human capital in the Netherlands	111
Table 7.1	Qualification levels across the three data years	164
Table 7.2	Extent of mismatch	165
Table 7.3	Mean Hope-Goldthorpe score across education groups	167
Table 7.4	Educational qualifications of the unemployed	169
Table 7.5	Logit equations for over-education	171
Table 8.1	Sample selection effects on the earnings function (Belgium, 1985)	184
Table 8.2	Direct and indirect earnings effects of education (two-stage model, Belgium 1985, in thousands BEF – men only)	185
Table 9.1	Wage equation for school-leavers in the Netherlands, total group and by category of utilization	196
Table 9.2	Wage equation for school-leavers in the Netherlands, total group and by level of education	197
Table 9.3	The mean and standard deviation of the wages for Dutch IVE graduates (in Dutch guilders)	199
Table 9.4	Predicted incidence of low wages, Netherlands and US	200
Table 9.5	Predicted incidence of low wages for different educational groups	201
Table 10.1	Unemployment rates for different education classes	204
Table 10.2	Labour market conditions in 1993 and 1995	214
Table 10.3	Allocation of workers with a certain education over different jobs for 1993 and 1995	215
Table 10.4	Allocation of workers with a certain education over different jobs based on the 1992–1993 sample	216

Table 10.5   Allocation of workers with a certain education over   217
different jobs based on the 1994–1995 sample

Table 10.6   Gross hourly wages (including overtime payments, etc.)   218

Table 10.7   Estimation results: ordered logit estimates with and   219
without wages 1993/1995

Table 10.8   Simulated probabilities of being employed at a   220
certain job complexity level

Table 10.9   The relevance of crowding out; probabilities based on   221
ordered logits for different years and different education
groups

Table 10.10   Crowding out; different probabilities based on stocks   222
of the 1995 sample

Table 10.11   Hiring and firing rates for different job complexity   226
levels

Table 11.1   The main differences between the human capital   233
theory and the job competition theory

Table 11.2   The equilibrium wage levels according to the human   237
capital theory

Table 11.3   The distribution of workers and jobs over wage levels   238
according to the job competition theory

Table 11.4   The equilibrium wage levels according to the job   238
competition theory

Table 11.5   Indexed educational participation between   240
1975–1993 (1975=100)

Table 11.6   Shares in the labour force and in the unemployed by   245
educational level, 1990 and 1994, %

Table 11.7   Estimation results of the indirect test on job competition   248

List of Figures

Figure 1.1   An occupational productivity profile and a wage   7
curve, together determining the optimal skill level for
a specific occupation

Figure 1.2   A shift in the optimal skill level of an occupation due   8
to a shift in the education–wage profile, caused by
changes in demand or supply

Figure 1.3   A shift in the optimal skill level of an occupation due to   9
a change in the occupational productivity profile, caused
by the introduction of new technology

Figure 2.1   Mean skill score by type and year, 1950–1995   34

Figure 2.2   Actual educational attainment and skills, 1950–1995   35

Figure 2.3   Growth in workplace skills by period, 1950–1995   37

Figure 2.4   Growth in workplace and workforce skills by period,
1950–1995   38

Figure 2.5   Growth in skills, education and productivity by   47
decade, 1950–1990

Figure 3.1   Labour force and employment, 1975–1995   58

Figure 3.2   Comparison of average schooling years in 1975 and   60
1995, by occupational category

Figure 3.3   Share of the overeducated in 1975 and 1995, by occupa-   63
tional category, changing definition of overeducation

Figure 3.4   Share of the overeducated in 1975 and 1995, by occupa-   64
tional category, constant definition of overeducation

Figure 5.1   Determining the relation between labour market tight-   117
ness, wage and duration

Figure 5.2   What happened in the 1970s?   125

Figure 6.1   First-best equilibrium   142

Figure 6.2   Monopolistic competition   147

Figure 6.3   Reduction in the minimum wage   149

Figure 7.1   Cumulative percentage of unqualified workers against   166
the Hope-Goldthorpe scale

Figure 7.2   Cumulative percentage of workers with apprenticeship   167
              level or commercial qualifications
Figure 7.3   Cumulative percentage of workers with other   168
              qualifications
Figure 7.4   Cumulative percentage of workers with O-level   169
              qualifications
Figure 7.5   Cumulative percentage of workers with A-level   170
              qualifications
Figure 7.6   Cumulative percentage of workers with professional   172
              qualifications
Figure 8.1   Upward bias in OLS-regression: the reservation wage   176
              (or opportunity cost) hypothesis
Figure 8.2   Downward bias in OLS regression: the bumping-   177
              down hypothesis
Figure 8.3   Earnings profiles by level of education: men (Belgium,   182
              1985, corrected for selection bias)
Figure 8.4   Earnings profiles by level of education: women   183
              (Belgium, 1985, corrected for selection bias)
Figure 10.1   Labour market flows   207
Figure 10.2   Shifts in job complexity distributions based on   224
              ordered logits for different education groups
Figure 10.3   Shifts in job complexity distributions for employment   225
              inflow based on ordered logits for different education
              groups
Figure 11.1   The main difference between human capital and job   237
              competition theory
Figure 11.2   Relative wages (compared to the average wage of all   241
              workers) by educational level, 1969–1993
Figure 11.3   Relative wages of higher compared to lower educated   242
              workers, 1969–1993
Figure 11.4   Number of unemployed and number of vacancies by   243
              educational level

Introduction

1. The Debate in Economics about Skill Utilization

Lex Borghans and Andries de Grip

1 OVEREDUCATION OR UPGRADING?

In many OECD countries, one may observe the tendency for highly skilled people to be employed in jobs that used to be occupied by people with a lower level of education. This phenomenon is often directly interpreted as under-utilization of skills or overeducation, and concerns in many cases substantial fractions of people with a certain skill level, varying from 20 to 50%. One of the first studies that focused on this phenomenon, was Freeman's (1976) *The Overeducated American*. Freeman suggested that students invest too much in education. On the basis of dated information about the labour market, students expected good labour market prospects after graduation. In reality, however, the increasing supply of higher educated people could not be absorbed by the market and many school-leavers were forced to accept a job that required fewer skills than they actually obtained. For these reasons, it is often suggested in policy debates that the employment of higher educated workers in jobs that were traditionally held by lower skilled people, implies a waste of skills and harms lower educated people. When people accept jobs below their educational level, it is claimed, they start competing with skilled labour at lower levels, and as a consequence these lower educated will also be forced to accept jobs below their level of skills, or even become unemployed, a process that is generally referred to as *bumping down* or *crowding out*. The policy conclusion from this interpretation is that at the social level, investments in education are too high. If students stay at school longer, their additional skills will not be utilized in the labour market, while the labour market position of less educated workers will worsen.

This overeducation argument challenges the policy of many developed countries to promote further investments in education in order to improve the competitiveness of their economies. In contrast to this negative picture of the role of education in recent decades, there is a clear tendency in both the political and the academic debate to stress more and more the importance of knowledge in our society. Starting perhaps with Leontief (1953), who suggested that it was not the physical capital endowment of the USA, but rather its endowments in terms of skills, which explains the paradoxical trade patterns of the United States. The European Commission (1996) claimed that education and training should get priority with regard to European competitiveness. The Commission therefore suggested that one should 'treat material investment and investment in training on an equal basis'. In line with this, the OECD (1996) stated that 'OECD governments are strongly committed to improving the skills of their citizens as one of the principal means for dealing with current economic uncertainty'. In a similar way to technological progress, productivity growth may be obtained by an input of more skills in the production process i.e. an *upgrading* of the skill level of the labour force (Romer, 1990). Human capital will become the decisive factor in international competitiveness (Porter, 1990).

The question whether the overeducation or upgrading argument holds, is related to the literature on the development of the skilled-to-unskilled wage gap (e.g. Davis and Reeve, 1997; Johnson, 1997; Topel, 1997). Upgrading of the required skills is often mentioned as a major cause of the increase in the earnings differential between high-skilled and low-skilled workers (e.g. Bound and Johnson, 1992; Katz and Murphy, 1992). In a perfect market, this link between the need for educated labour and wages of course holds but, in the case of market failure, an overeducated workforce does not necessarily lead to a narrowing of the earnings differential between high-skilled and low-skilled workers, as low wages for high-skilled workers who are overeducated for their jobs may go together with high wages for those who are occupied at their own level of education. Furthermore, formal qualifications may not represent a constant mix and level of skills over time. The screening theory (Lang, 1994 and Borghans, 1998) suggests that increased enrolment may lower the average abilities of school-leavers, while Grogger and Eide (1995) explain part of the rise in the college premium by increased skills among graduates. Nicaise's analyses in Chapter 8, support these theoretical arguments for labour market failures.

Both the explanation of overeducation and of upgrading are consistent with the stylized fact that higher educated people tend to obtain jobs that used to be held by lower skilled people. From the overeducation perspective, this illustrates excess supply of high-skilled workers and suggests the underutilization of these skills, while from the upgrading perspective, this illustrates that occupations today require more skills. Moreover, although very different in their policy implications, both views share a pessimistic perspective for low-skilled workers. From the bumping-down point of view, low-skilled workers will be pushed into the least favoured jobs, or will even be crowded out from the working population, irrespective of their real abilities or potential productivity, whereas the upgrading view predicts that the role of low-skilled workers will become more and more marginalized, because their skill level no longer meets the minimum requirements in the labour market. For a policy that aims at improving the position of people at the lower end of the labour market and tries to combat unemployment of low-skilled workers, understanding of the relevant economic mechanisms underlying the observed shifts in allocation is therefore essential.

Knowledge of the allocation of workers over occupations will therefore not immediately provide an answer to the questions on the role of skills in the labour market. Grasping the significance of education and training for both economic development and the position of the weakest groups – the low-skilled workers – in the labour market, requires a better understanding of the skills people have and the way they utilize these skills in their work. Unfortunately, much less is known about how workers' productivity is related to the way in which people use their skills, than about the allocation of the workers in the labour market. Due to the difficulty of measuring skills, the available evidence remains limited to detailed case studies on the one hand, and rough and limited indicators about skills which are representative for the labour market as a whole. Since the limited direct evidence we have about skills utilization is largely based on case studies, it is difficult to relate these findings to information about market forces. In Chapter 4, of this book, however, Green and his colleagues provide a promising attempt to collect data about skills by direct measurement for the entire British labour force.

To get a better understanding of the consequences of a policy that stimulates education among the low-skilled and low paid, insight is required into the reasons why employment in various occupational groups moves towards the higher skilled.

In everyday language, it is common to state that a certain occupation requires a certain level of education. In such a simple picture of the relationship between education and work, it is implicitly assumed that jobs of a certain level cannot be performed by a worker with lower qualifications: the productivity of the latter is zero. On the other hand, people with higher qualifications than required for the jobs they have, are considered to waste their excess qualifications completely: their productivity in a job below their educational level equals the productivity of workers with an adequate educational background for this kind of job.

Many empirical studies, however, have questioned this rigid interpretation and suggest a more gradual relationship between productivity and educational background. Hartog and Jonker (1998) provide an overview of a large number of empirical studies which show a gradual, but non-linear relationship between the education of workers and their productivity. All empirical results that demonstrate this gradual non-linear relationship between education and productivity, are based on the assumption that wages reflect productivity. The neo-classical law that productivity equals wages, however, assumes an optimal allocation of workers across jobs. Since these analyses try to catch the consequences for productivity when allocation is changed, and therefore compare people with the same qualifications in jobs at different levels, this assumption is violated. Although very illustrative for the idea that productivity depends on allocation, the estimates are in fact based on an inconsistency. Neo-classical theory would state that either workers with the same educational background are indifferent between jobs at different levels, e.g. because the wages are equal in each job, or that there must be differences in skills between these people with a formally equal qualification. More insight is therefore needed into the way in which skills differences influence allocation and productivity.

2   OCCUPATIONAL PRODUCTIVITY PROFILES AND THE EDUCATION–WAGE PROFILE

In the so-called assignment or matching theory introduced by Roy (1950, 1951) and Tinbergen (1956, 1975), both productivity and wages are assumed to depend on the level of skills. Therefore, the relationship between productivity and skill level – *the occupational productivity profile* – will vary between different jobs. By contrast, in a perfect labour market the relationship between wage and skill level – *the education-wage profile* – is equal for the whole labour market, and may vary with labour market developments.

Figure 1.1 illustrates these relationships for a specific occupation. Such occupational productivity profiles were introduced by Knight (1979). In this example, wages increase gradually with the level of education, while productivity rises sharply around 15–18 years of schooling. For lower qualification levels, productivity remains low and does not catch up with the wage increase, while for higher qualifications, the additional productivity of one extra year of schooling will not compensate for the increase in wage costs. The ratio between productivity and wage costs shows that for employers, workers with 19 years of schooling provide the optimal combination of productivity and wages. This implies that even the 19th year of schooling, which increases productivity only to a limited extent, still contributes more to productivity than it costs.

Figure 1.1 also shows that, although the productivity–wage–ratio reaches its maximum at 19 years of schooling, the ratio has only modestly lower values in the 18–20 years of schooling interval. This may imply that employers are approximately indifferent between people with educational backgrounds within this interval. This is illustrated by the *Occupational Outlook Handbook* of the US Bureau of Labor Statistics (1984), in which educational requirements for a particular occupation are frequently expressed in terms of 'at least this level, but some/many employers prefer'.

Figure 1.1   An occupational productivity profile and a wage curve, together determining the optimal skill level for a specific occupation

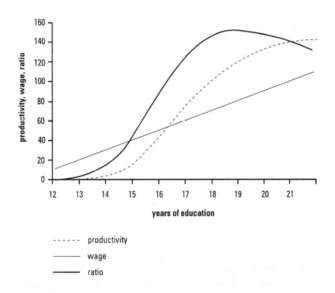

The allocation theory provides an explanation for what is meant by the statement that for a certain occupation a specific educational level is required. This refers to the match which is optimal given production possibilities and given the supply of labour. There are however, many reasons why in practice the match between the educational backgrounds of the workers and the jobs in which they are employed might differ from this optimum. However, within this theoretical framework, the required level is not fixed, but might change. Such changes can result also from shifts in the wage curve. These shifts can be the results of changes in the demand for certain occupations (in units of production) or the supply of labour at certain educational levels. On the other hand changes in the optimal level of education in a occupation can result from changes in the occupational production profile due to technological or organizational developments.

Figure 1.2   A shift in the optimal skill level of an occupation due to a shift in the education–wage profile, caused by changes in demand or supply

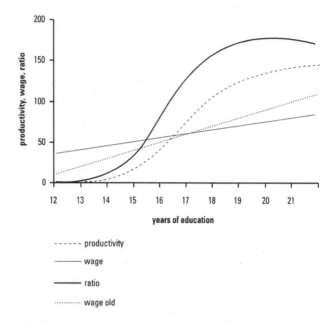

The changes in the optimal skill level in a certain occupation due to, for example, to a change in the supply of educated labour, which results in lower wages for higher educated workers is illustrated in Figure 1.2. Compared to Figure 1.1 the optimal level of education increases from 19 towards 20 years of education. Figure 1.3 shows the effect of a change in the occupational productivity profile on the optimal skill level. Compared to Figure 1.1 the optimal level of education in this occupation again increases from 19 towards 20 years of education.

Both in Figures 1.2 and 1.3 the people who are employed in this occupation have an educational background which is higher than it used to be. Such a shift might easily be associated with overeducation or underutilization. However, only in Figure 1.2 – by flattening the education–wage profile – does an excess supply of higher skilled people increase the optimal level of education in the occupation concerned. The figure therefore illustrates the *overeducation* view. Yet, although high-skilled workers are underutilized in this occupation their productivity is higher than the productivity of the workers in this occupation with less years of education. Furthermore – given labour market conditions – it is for these high-skilled workers not possible to reach a higher level of productivity.

Figure 1.3   A shift in the optimal skill level of an occupation due to a change in the occupational productivity profile, caused by the introduction of new technology

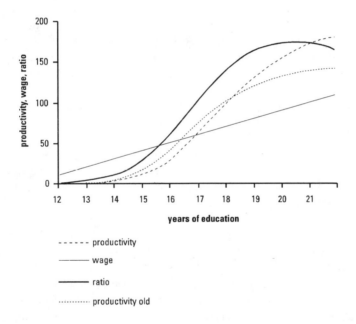

Figure 1.3, however, illustrates the *upgrading* view. Here the change in the production process due to such factors as technological or organizational developments, increases the demand for higher educated workers. This means that higher educated people will be employed in this occupation, which used to be the domain of people with lower levels of qualifications. The productivity

of these higher educated individuals will, however, not be lower than the productivity they have – and used to have – in their traditional occupational domain. New technologies have in fact opened up possibilities of utilizing the skills these people have productively in these new jobs too. Therefore there is no underutilization of their level of qualification.

Thus, the allocation theory is able to explain the tendency for higher educated people to occupy jobs that used to be held by lower educated individuals both from a supply and a demand side perspective. Within this neo-classical framework, skills are always utilized optimally, given the actual labour market conditions. Three grades of underutilization of skills can be distinguished:

- First, someone may be employed in a job in which people with the same educational background used to have lower productivity than in their original domain, but in which productivity is now at least equal to the productivity in the original domain. This is the case in an upgrading process, where actually one can only speak of *alleged underutilization* of skills.
- Second, someone may be employed in a job in which he/she has lower productivity than people with the same educational background used to have, but which equals the productivity that such people have today. This is the case in a situation of excess supply on a perfect labour market and may be called *intertemporal underutilization* of skills.

However, overeducation is generally associated with underutilization of skills in a labour market which is far from perfect and where part of the workforce with a certain skill level is occupied in jobs where they are less productive than others; therefore:

- Third, workers may be employed in a job in which they have lower productivity than some other people with the same educational background currently have. This may be called *genuine underutilization* of skills. This genuine underutilization is not explained by the allocation theory. In Chapter 4, Green et al. introduce the distinction between 'credentialism' and 'quali-fications used' that comes close to our distinction between genuine underutilization and other forms of underutilization. Credentialism means that some qualifications are required in the recruitment process but are never actually used.

3 JOB COMPETITION VERSUS WAGE COMPETITION

The analysis in previous section, based on education–wage profiles, typically represent so-called wage competition models. The basic assumption of these models is that the wage always represents productivity and therefore markets will always clear. In the literature about underutilization of skills and bumping down, wage competition is often opposed to job competition models. Job competition models are based on the assumption that wages for a certain occupation do not react to shifts in supply and demand. For that reason an increased supply of high-skilled workers does not lead to an adjustment of the wages. High-skilled workers will have to compete for a limited number of well-paid jobs and some of them will lose. They will be forced to accept a job with lower skill requirements and lower pay.

In Borghans and De Grip (2000), we developed a typology of economic theories on the possible causes and consequences of the observed changes in the allocation of skilled labour and the related policy implications with respect to the (macro) efficiency of training policies for low-skilled people. It is argued that for the policy question of whether or not the shifts in the employment in various occupational groups towards the higher skilled make additional investments in schooling worthwhile, the opposite positions of the wage competition model and the job competition model are not crucial. The crucial point is whether increased employment of higher educated individuals in jobs at lower levels, suggests the occurrence of a bumping-down process initiated by excess supply of the higher educated or that it points to a process of upgrading. Bumping down – which can be the outcome both in the job competition model and the neo-classical matching model – suggests that additional investments in education are not very effective. Underutilization versus upgrading, on the other hand, seeks increased educational investments. Upgrading therefore seems to be the most fundamental opposition with respect to the macroefficiency of training policies for low-skilled and low paid workers. For this reason, *underutilization or upgrading*? is the leading question for Part One of this book.

Two differences between the job competition and the wage competition model remain important, however. First, from the point of view of the wage competition model, bumping down is only an extreme case. The model does not exclude the possibility that additional demand absorbs part of the extra supply at a certain level of education, which results from training policies. The effects of training, therefore, need not to be totally cancelled out by a bumping down process, but may also lead to new employment opportunities at higher wages, depending on the elasticity of demand at the higher job levels. In the job competition model, however, elasticity of demand equals zero, since wages will not react to changes in supply and demand.

Muysken and Ter Weel (in Chapter 5) and Zwick (in Chapter 6), however, provide different arguments that may explain underutilization of skills based on search externalities and monoponistic power. Battu and Sloane (in Chapter 7) add to this the possibility of heterogeneity within a group of a certain skill level as an explanation for differences in pay and employment.

Second, although both in a world of job competition and in a world of wage competition, upgrading may occur in the sense that jobs become more complex, the labour market will provide no signals for this in the job competition case. In the case of wage competition, it may be very difficult to distinguish upgrading from bumping down, since both processes will lead to a shift in the employment structure of higher educated people to jobs that used to be occupied by the lower educated. Upgrading does, however, manifest itself in a changing employment structure. In the case of job competition neither the allocation of workers, nor their wages, will change as a result of upgrading. The increased productivity of the higher educated, which might make greater educational investments fruitful, will therefore remain unnoticed.

Lastly, it is interesting to note that not every form of training will be a useful instrument to cope with upgrading. It has been shown that upgrading in a specific group of occupations at a certain level of education may induce bumping down at lower levels of education. Training is therefore only fruitful if it increases the supply at a level of education for which the upgrading process has created a new demand. Training that increases peoples' educational level below the level where these upgrading tendencies occur, only further stimulates the process of bumping down. Gautier (Chapter 10) and Groot and Hoek (Chapter 11), however, strongly disagree on the levels of education where these spillover effects occur.

4   THE MEASUREMENT OF UNDERUTILIZATION

The problem of distinguishing between upgrading and underutilization is enlarged by the fact that – despite the large number of empirical studies on this field – the measurement of underutilization of skills is far from straightforward. The problem is not helped by the fact that various terms are used to describe essentially similar situations (Shockey 1989). Thus, skill underutilization, overeducation, overqualification, underemployment, overtraining, and occupational mismatch, are often used interchangeably.

Underutilization is most simply defined as a level of educational attainment greater than the educational requirement of an occupation. However, direct measurement of the way in which people organize their work and thereby utilize their skills is rare. An interesting example of such research is provided by Stasz (1998). On the basis of very extensive observations of people at work, she draws conclusions about the role of such competences as problem solving, communications, and team work at the workplace. Lam (1996) and Mason et al. (1996) also provide interesting detailed studies about the utilization of skills. Studies such as these require large resources, however, and therefore can never provide a complete picture of the developments in skill utilization on the labour market. To obtain such a more general view on the developments in skill utilization, indirect methods are needed.

There are three main alternatives in the measurement of underutilization. First there is the so-called *objective measure,* which depends on systematic evaluation by professional job analysts who attempt to specify the required level and type of education in particular occupations. In this book, this method is represented by Wolff (Chapter 2). The best-known data set used in a number of overeducation studies is the *Dictionary of Occupational Titles* (DOT), compiled by the US Employment Service. In this approach, the same job is first analysed in two different establishments in one State and then in two different establish- ments in another State. Six components of worker traits are assessed – training time, aptitudes, interests, temperaments, physical demands, and working con- ditions (see Rumberger, 1981). The Department of Labor's *Handbook for Analysing Jobs*, 1972, shows that the training time requirements are derived from two questions. The first asks what level of general educational develop- ment is necessary for a worker to obtain the required background knowledge to perform the work in question. The second asks how long – in terms of specific vocational preparation – it takes for a worker with a specified level of educational development to become a fully qualified worker on the job, compared to a trainee. European equivalents to DOT are few and far between. One exception is the ARBI code, which contains a classification into seven levels of job complexity, developed by the Dutch Department of Social Affairs (see Hartog and Oosterbeek, 1988). The classification takes into account both the job content and the employee's ability and knowledge in attaining the required level of proficiency. The scale ranges from very simple work with a training time of a few days (level one) to scientific work at level seven.

The second approach is based on worker self-assessment and can therefore be referred to as a *subjective assessment*. In the present book, this method is represented by Green et al. (Chapter 4). Examples include the Michigan Panel Study of Income Dynamics question, which asks 'how much formal education is required to get a job like yours?', or the British Social Change and Economic Life Initiative data set question, which asks 'if they were applying today, what qualifications, if any, would someone need to get the type of job you have now?' Related to these two different questions, Green et al. distinguish between credentialism and underutilization of skills. Credentialism means that an employer requires a certain skills level although these skills are not utilized. Workers with appropriate qualifications are just not recruited. A slightly different variant is the Spanish Living and Working Conditions Survey of 1985 (ECVT), which has been analysed by Alba-Ramirez (1993). This includes two separate questions. The first asks 'considering the job you do, how long would it take someone with the required education who begins the job, to do it correctly?' Such periods of time may be interpreted as on-the-job, training requirements, but may be influenced not only by the complexity of the job, but also by the ability of the individual. The second question in the ECVT survey asks 'what kind of education does a person need in order to perform the job?' This recognizes the possibility that there may be a distinction between the actual requirements of the job and the customary hiring requirements. This is consistent with the screening hypothesis, which suggests that the labour market is characterized by imperfect information and education is used as a signal to identify to employers the more able, ambitious, or productive workers. Lastly, some data sets may allow for the fact that there is no unique educational requirement. Thus, the 1980 UK National Survey of Graduates and Diplomates asks 'what was the *minimum* formal qualification required for (entering) this job?'. As Hartog (1997) notes, the above definitions are clearly different from one another, but they may not necessarily be perceived as such by the respondents.

The third approach focuses on the distribution of educational qualifications in a given occupation. Most commonly, underutilization is defined as a level of education more than one standard deviation above the mean, and under-education as a level of education more than one standard deviation below the mean (see, for instance, Verdugo and Verdugo 1989). In the present book, this approach is represented by Asplund and Lilja (Chapter 3) and by Battu and Sloane (Chapter 7). This so-called *empirical method* clearly differs from the above-mentioned measures in defining underutilization as being substantially underutilized. It also implies symmetry and will clearly give biased estimates where the tendency to underutilization or overutilization is skewed. The latter is generally the case, as in almost all studies of the US and British labour markets the percentage of workers whose skill level is underutilized exceeds the percentage of workers who are overutilized. However, the reverse seems to hold in the Netherlands and Spain. Therefore it seems more appropriate to consider the underutilization of skills in relation to the mode rather than the mean, as Kiker et al. (1997) do for Portugal and Alpin et al. (1997) do for Britain. De

Grip et al. (1998) formulate criteria that make it possible to identify a range of skill levels as appropriate on an empirical basis.

It is clear that the above approaches to the measurement of underutilization of skills can lead to divergent estimates. All three approaches have been criticized on various grounds. As Hartog (1997) notes, conceptually the job analysis approach has the advantage of being objective, having clear definitions and a detailed measurement methodology. Yet, there are a number of sources of potential bias. First, estimates of mean years of required schooling in an occupation are constructed by aggregating various jobs within that occupation, ignoring the fact that there is likely to be a distribution of required education across those jobs. Some workers may, therefore, be misclassified as over-educated as a result of within-occupation variation in job-specific schooling requirements (Halaby, 1994). Second, required schooling levels may vary for each occupation according to the abilities of job incumbents. As Rumberger (1987) and others have pointed out, workers with higher levels of ability may require fewer educational qualifications to perform tasks effectively and vice versa. Education and ability are substitutes. Third, converting job scores into years of schooling, as in the DOT approach in the USA, is far from un-contentious, although in European studies that use educational dummies this sort of problem may be avoided. Fourth, levels of education ignore the type of education received and some workers who are mismatched may be misclassified. As Halaby (1994) puts it, 'if plumbing requires a high school diploma then plumbers who work in any occupation requiring a high school diploma would be classified as matched even if plumbing skills are not used in the work'.

Most important however is that, fifth, such studies assume that the educational requirements of occupations do not increase over time, while in practice both tasks and the required level of knowledge do alter over time (Smith, 1986). Since the objective method is very expensive and time-consuming, occupational classifications become available long after they have been measured, while furthermore, these classifications are typically used for a very long time period, assuming no changes in the required level. However, as has been explained in Section 2, the optimal level of skills for a certain occupation depends on market forces. Moreover, technological and organizational developments may change the requirements. Measurement of developments of underutilization based on the objective method, therefore includes both shifts in the optimal level, both due to changes in the relative scarcity and technological and organizational developments. It is therefore not surprising that the objective method tends to provide high levels of underutilization of skills and also strong increases in these levels.

Worker self-assessment has been criticized because it is subjective and it is claimed that workers may not always have a clear insight into the actual level of education required. For example, workers may be inclined to overstate the requirements of their job in order to enhance the perceived status of their position. Stasz (1998), however, found that employees report the actual skill requirements much more accurately than employers. In contrast with the job analysis method, workers will be able to identify their own job rather than the occupation in general. Furthermore, workers may report changes in job requirements as soon as they show up. The method may therefore have clear advantages for measuring pure developments in underutilization, without incorporating influences from changes in the optimal levels of skills within an occupation. Employees may, however, simply state current hiring standards. Therefore tendencies of credentialism may be underestimated by the subjective method.

The empirical method has the advantage that it takes the theoretical foundation of the allocation theory as the point of departure. When the labour market functions well to some extent, it may be expected that the majority of workers within a certain occupation has an appropriate educational background. Moreover, this approach will be very sensitive to labour market conditions and technological development, picking up changes in skill requirements very quickly. Measurement based on the labour force as a whole may be hampered by the stickiness of existing working contracts to be adjusted. Based on information about school-leavers or other new matches on the labour market, the information may be very responsive, however. Another advantage of this method is that it incorporates the possibility that a range of educational levels is appropriate for a given occupation. The empirical method will therefore do a good job in identifying the appropriate level and changes in this level. The demarcation line between adequate levels and levels for which underutilization occurs, however, will be arbitrary to a large extent, since the method is based on criteria of frequency. If underutilization occurs more than only incidentally, the method may therefore fail, while it will not provide very precise measures of underutilization.

It can be concluded that, although it seems to be clear that occupations that used to be occupied by the lower-skilled tend to be occupied by people with higher levels of education, there is no indisputable way to determine to what degree this really indicates underutilization of the acquired skill level.

5 MAIN QUESTIONS OF THE BOOK

To improve the insight in the role of education in society, it is important to investigate carefully the arguments sketched above and to put the question: to what extent are these arguments of overeducation and upgrading valid? The main questions in this respect are:

1. Are people who work in jobs that used to be occupied by less-skilled people really underutilized, or have there been changes in the character of the job that justify this shift?
2. How can economic theory explain the underutilization of workers?
3a. What happens to the people who are employed in jobs below their skill level? Is their labour market position worse compared to others who have found an appropriate job, and is their abundance of skills really wasted?
3b. What happens to lower educated people who are confronted with higher educated workers in their labour market segments? Does their labour market position worsen, and does this have consequences for their wages and the unemployment rate among this group?

The aim of this book is to bring together contributions to the investigation of the above questions from different perspectives in order to obtain a complete picture of the debate in economics about underutilization of skills and bumping down. The book starts with three contributions to the first question about *under-utilization or upgrading?* Each chapter represents one of the three methodological approaches to the measuring of underutilization: the objective method, the subjective method and the empirical method. Edward Wolff analyses the factors responsible for the change in skills in the USA in the post-war period. These include intersectoral shifts in employment, technological change, institutional and organizational dimensions of production, and the degree of trade openness.

Using skill indices derived from the *Dictionary of Occupational Titles*, linked to employment matrices for census years 1950 to 1990, Wolff finds in Chapter 2, that both cognitive and interactive skills showed positive growth over this period in the USA, while manual skills experienced an absolute decline. Growth in all three workplace skill indices peaked in the 1960s. The growth of cognitive skills fell between the 1960s and 1970s, and again between the 1970s and 1980s. Investigation into the factors that affect the demand for skills indicates that growth in total factor productivity is generally deskilling. Other dimensions of technological activity – particularly, capital-labour growth, R&D intensity, and computerization – have a positive relation to the change in substantive complexity and interactive skills.

In Chapter 3, Rita Asplund and Reija Lilja investigate the effects on labour market allocation of the increased supply of higher educated labour. The aim of their paper is to explore whether the Finnish labour market can be argued to have been characterized by a bumping-down tendency over the period 1975 to 1995. Asplund and Lilja investigate the extent of shifts over time in the educational structure within different occupations. In addition, they ask the following questions: is there a clear tendency of more skilled workers bumping down less-skilled workers? If so, is this bumping-down phenomenon concentrated in certain occupations and time periods? Are also the earnings, age and gender structures of these occupations affected, and do these changes possibly differ from the general trends observable in the labour market in these years? The panel character of the data set allows Asplund and Lilja to investigate what has happened to the low-skilled workers that have been 'bumped down' by their more skilled colleagues. Especially in times of high unemployment, it can be expected that they are likely to be crowded out into unemployment or (early) retirement. There is, however, also the possibility that they have started studying in order to upgrade their skills or change to another occupation. A crucial question then is whether they later return into employment and, if so, in what type of occupation and pay level.

In Chapter 4, Francis Green, David Ashton, Brendan Burchell, Bryn Davies and Alan Felstead describe the shifts in skills demand in Britain. They present the preliminary results of their 'Skills Survey' in which developments in required skills are measured directly. Deploying several measures of skills, Green et al. find at both ends of the occupational spectrum, a rising demand for skills in Britain. Moreover, in the eyes of the job holders, there is no substantial rise in the extent to which employers are demanding qualifications just to ration jobs. Green et al. also indicate the types of skill change. They find an increased usage of problem-solving skills, of communication and social skills, and of computing skills, and a reduction in the manual skills used.

To understand the mechanisms that cause underutilization and bumping down, Part Two investigates some theoretical explanations of underutilization. In Chapter 5, Joan Muysken and Bas ter Weel investigate on the basis of a matching model, why people choose to invest in education that will not be utilized in the labour market. In this model, the search-theoretical analysis of Pissarides is applied to the demand for skilled labour and is extended to allow for job competition. It is combined with the human capital theory to explain the level of education. They argue that it is not an increased supply of higher educated workers that caused an increase in underutilization of skills, but rather a shift in some structural characteristics of the labour market. Increased bargaining power for employees, higher search costs, and structural imbalances can explain the changes on the Dutch labour market.

In Chapter 6, Thomas Zwick inverts this question and searches for the answer to the question of why some students decide not to acquire skills and consequently restrict themselves to the low-wage unskilled labour market. Zwick provides two answers to this question. First, high education costs may prevent workers from investing in additional schooling. Second, the risk of being overeducated after completing schooling reduces the attractiveness of human capital investments. This risk arises as a result of the sunk nature of human capital investments, i.e. it is not clear at the moment of schooling if an adequate job will be found afterwards. Using a simple model, Zwick shows the effects of the increased wage gap between skilled and unskilled workers and of the increased unemployment incidence of unskilled workers on skilled labour supply, and analyses the impact on social welfare. This model assumes monopolistic competition on the skilled labour market with a large number of different skills and unskilled workers needed in the production process. The more than compensating monopolistic skilled wage mark-up induces therefore Pareto-inefficiency, unemployment and overeducation. Two policy measures to combat overqualification in the presence of more than compensating wage mark-ups are proposed. Lastly, a policy measure is proposed that leads to the efficient labour market outcome with full employment and zero overqualification, but has an impact on rent distribution.

In Chapter 7, Harminder Battu and Peter Sloane investigate underutilization in Britain and focus on the role of heterogeneity as an explanation. The aim of this chapter is to establish whether the degree of overeducation in Britain has altered over time and whether the increase in the proportion of graduates and workers with other qualifications over the decade has led to a significant downward movement in the types of jobs undertaken by these workers. An important conclusion is, however, that according to Battu and Sloane, personal characteristics such as gender, age and job tenure seem to be more important determinants than labour market characteristics. This puts forward heterogeneity of workers with the same qualifications as an explanation for alleged underutilization. A change in the quality of school leavers may, in time, also explain changes in their labour market position.

In Chapter 8, Ides Nicaise tests two different hypotheses: do low-skilled workers leave the labour market because their wages do not exceed their reservation wage or are these people excluded from the labour market because high-skilled workers occupy their jobs? These empirical investigations support the view that labour market imperfections are a main cause of bumping down. People with lower skills, tend to be crowded out. Wage adjustments therefore seem not to clear the market completely. Nicaise finds no support for the opposite explanation that men with a low productivity leave the labour market because their wages do not provide enough incentives to work. For women, evidence for both explanations is found.

Part Three focuses on the consequences of underutilization and bumping down. In Chapter 9, Lex Borghans, Allard Bruinshoofd and Andries de Grip investigate the consequences for the wages of groups that are confronted with underutilization. On the basis of simulations in a model of the Dutch labour market, it is possible to assign the actual occurrence of low wages to three skill-related causes. First, people may have a low wage because their educational background does not meet the standard educational background introduced above. Second, even if the educational background is sufficient, underutilization of these skills may lead to a low paid job. Third, even if people find a job at their own (sufficient) educational level, excess supply may worsen the labour market conditions and therefore cause low wages. The results of the analyses of Borghans et al. indicate that having an inadequate skill level and labour market imbalances are the main causes for low wages among Dutch school-leavers. Achieving an educational career with at least a diploma at the level of Intermediate Vocational Education would have a considerable impact on the incidence of low wages, although labour market imbalances are also an important cause of low wages. The latter means that underutilization seems to affect not only the wages of people who are actually working below their educational level, but also – due to increased competition – of those who still find a job at their own educational level.

In Chapter 10, Pieter Gautier investigates in a job matching framework, the consequences of increased supply for the competition between different skill groups. He shows the consequences for the employment rates of both low-skilled and high-skilled people when unemployed high-skilled workers search for both simple and complex jobs and continue searching for complex jobs when they happen to come across a simple vacancy first. He also investigates whether more high-skilled workers occupy simple jobs during bad times, as the crowding out theories predict. The results of Gautier's analysis suggest that there is only weak evidence for crowding out of intermediate skilled workers by high-skilled workers in the beginning of the 1990s, but no evidence for the crowding out of low-skilled workers. Some evidence is given that supports the hypothesis that the high unemployment rates among low-skilled workers are caused by the fact that firing costs for simple jobs (where relatively many low-skilled workers are employed) are lower than for complex jobs.

In Chapter 11, Loek Groot and Albert Hoek investigate the same problem from a different theoretic perspective. First, they illustrate the working of a fictitious labour market under the assumption of the human capital theory and the job competition theory, respectively. This exercise enables them to demonstrate the differences in assumptions and predictions between the two theories. Groot and Hoek show that a sudden exogenous increase in the average level of education gives rise to different outcomes. According to the human capital theory, the average wages of the lower educated will increase, while those of the higher educated will decrease, but income inequality among educational categories increases. Second, Groot and Hoek test three hypotheses in line with the job competition theory: (i) an increase in the average level of education of the labour force causes a rise in income inequality between the higher and lower educated, (ii) schooling programmes for the lower educated cannot reduce unemployment among lower educated, and (iii) job competition will increase if unemployment among the higher educated increases. The last hypothesis is tested using the same data as Van Ours and Ridder (1995). Contrary to the findings of the latter authors, Groot and Hoek find that job competition mainly occurs at the intermediate level for medical, chemical, and social and cultural occupations.

REFERENCES

Alba-Ramirez, A. (1993), 'Mismatch in the Spanish Labor Market: Overeducation?', *Journal of Human Resources* **27** (2), 259–78.

Alpin, C., Shackleton, J.R. and Walsh, S. (1997), *Over and Undereducation in the UK Graduate Labour market*, Unpublished mimeo.

Borghans, L. (1998), *Human capital and screening with heterogenous learning activities*, Paper presented at the EALE-Conference, Blankenberge.

Borghans, L. and A. de Grip (2000), 'Skills and Low Pay: Upgrading or Overeducation?', in M. Gregory, W. Salverda and S. Bazen (eds), *Low-Wage Employment: A European Perspective*, Oxford University Press (forthcoming).

Bound, J. and G. Johnson (1992), 'Changes in the Structure of Wages in the 1980s: An Evaluation of Alternative Explanations', *American Economic Review* **82**, 371–92.

Davis, D.R. and T.A. Reeve (1997), *Human Capital, Unemployment, and Relative wages in a Global Economy*, NBER Working Paper Series 6133, Cambridge (Mass.).

De Grip, A., L. Borghans and W. Smits (1998), 'Future Developments in the Job Level and Domain of High-skilled Workers', in H. Heijke and L. Borghans (eds), *Towards a Transparent Labour Market for Educational Decisions*, Aldershot: Ashgate, pp. 21–56.

European Commission (1996), *Teaching and Learning. Towards the Learning Society*. White Paper, Brussels.

Freeman, R.B. (1976), *The Overeducated American*, New York: Academic Press.

Grogger and Eide (1995), 'Changes in College Skills and the Rise in the College Wage Premium', *Journal of Human Resources* **30**, 280–310.

Halaby, C. (1994), 'Overeducation and Skill Mismatch', *Sociology of Education* **67**, 47–59.

Hartog, J. (1997), *On Returns to Education: Wandering Along the Hills of Our Land*, Paper presented at Applied Econometrics Association, Maastricht.

Hartog, J. and N. Jonker (1998), 'A Job to Match your Education: Does it Matter?' in
Hartog, J. and H. Oosterbeek (1988), 'Education, Allocation and Earnings in the Netherlands: Overschooling?' *Economics of Education Review* 7 (2) 185–94.
Heijke, H. and L. Borghans (eds), *Towards a Transparent Labour Market for Educational Decisions,* Ashgate: Aldershot, 99–118.
Johnson, G. (1997), 'Changes in Earnings Inequality: The Role of Demand Shifts', *Journal of Economic Perspectives* 11, 41–54.
Katz, L. and K. Murphy (1992), 'Changes in Relative Wages 1963–1987: Supply and Demand Factors', *Quarterly Journal of Economics* 107, 35–78.
Kiker, B.F., M.C. Santos, M. de Oliveira, M. Mendes (1997), 'Overeducation and Undereducation: Evidence for Portugal', *Economics of Education Review* 16 (2), 111–25
Knight, J.B. (1979), 'Job Competition, Occupational Production Functions, and Filtering Down', *Oxford Economic Papers* 31, 187–204.
Lam, A. (1996), 'Work Organisation, Skills Development and Utilization of Engineers, A British–Japanese Comparison', in R. Crompton, D. Gallie and K. Purcell (eds), *Changing Forms of Employment,* London and New York: Routledge, 182–203.
Lang, K. (1994), 'Does the Human-Capital/Educational-Sorting Debate Matter for Development Policy?', *American Economic Review* 71, 475–82.
Leontief, W. (1953), *Domestic production and Foreign Trade: The American Position Re-examined,* Proceedings of the American Philosophical Society.
Mason, G. (1996), 'Graduate Utilization in British Industry: The Initial Impact of Mass Higher Education', *National Institute Economic Review*, May, 93–111.
Mason, G., B. van Ark and K. Wagner (1996), 'Productivity, Product Quality and Workforce Skills', in A. Booth and D.J. Snower (eds), *Acquiring Skills: Market Failures, their Symptoms and Policy Responses,* Cambridge: Cambridge University Press, 177–97.
OECD (1996), *Measuring what People Know,* Paris: OECD.
Porter, M. (1990), *The Competitive Advantage of Nations,* London: Macmillan.
Romer, P.M. (1990), 'Endogenous Technological Change', *Journal of Political Economy* 98, S71–S102.
Roy, A.D. (1950), 'The Distribution of Earnings and of Individual Output', *Economic Journal* 60, 489–501.
Roy, A.D. (1951), 'Some Thoughts on the Distribution of Earnings', *Oxford Economic Papers* 3, 135–46.
Rumberger, R.W. (1981), *Overeducation in the US Labor Market,* New York: Praeger.
Rumberger, R.W. (1987), 'The Impact of Surplus Schooling on Productivity and Earnings', *Journal of Human Resources* 22 (1), 24–50.
Shockey, J.W. (1989), 'Overeducation an Earnings: A Structural Approach to Differential Attainment in the US Labor Force (1970–82)', *American Sociological Review* 54, 856–864.
Smith, H. (1986), 'Overeducation and Underemployment: An Agnostic Review', *Sociology of Education* 59, 85–99.
Stasz, C. (1998), 'Generic Skills at Work: Implications for Occupationally-Oriented Education', in W.J. Nijhof and J.N. Streumer (eds), *Key Qualifications in Work and*

Education, Dordrecht, Boston, London: Kluwer Academic Publishers, 187–206.

Tinbergen, J. (1956), 'On the Theory of Income Distribution', *Weltwirtschaftliches Archiv* **77**, 156–73.

Topel, R. (1997), 'Factor Proportions and Relative Wages: The Supply-Side Determinants of Wage Inequality', *Journal of Economic Perspectives* **11**, 55–74.

US Bureau of Labor Statistics (1984), *Occupational Outlook Handbook. 1984–85 edition*, Washington, DC: US Department of Labor.

US Department of Labor (1972), *Handbook for Analysing Jobs*, Washington, DC: Department of Labor.

Van Ours, J.C. and G. Ridder (1995), 'Job Matching and Job Competition: Are Lower Educated Workers at the Back of Job Queues?', *European Economic Review* **39**, 1117–31.

Verdugo, R.R. and N.T. Verdugo (1989), 'The Impact of Surplus Schooling on Earnings', *The Journal of Human Resources* **24** (4), 629–643.

ACKNOWLEDGEMENTS

The authors would like to thank Peter Sloane who provided an extensive overview of studies on underutilization, and Harminder Battu for his comments on this chapter.

PART ONE

Underutilization or Upgrading?

2. Technology and the Demand for Skills

Edward Wolff

1 INTRODUCTION

The US economy has undergone major structural changes since 1950. First, there has been a gradual shift of employment from goods-producing industries to service-providing industries. Second, since the 1970s at least, the availability of new information-based technologies has made possible substantial adjustments in operations and organizational restructuring of firms. This has been accelerated, in part, by sharply increasing competition from imports. Evidence from industry-level case studies indicate that this restructuring is likely to have important consequences for the level and composition of skills required in the US workplace (see Adler, 1986, and Zuboff, 1988).

The direction and extent of changes in skill levels over the longer run has, however, been more uncertain, with case studies often finding a deskilling of the content of production jobs and aggregate studies finding little change or at most a gradual upgrading in overall occupation mix (see Spenner, 1988, for a survey of this literature). These trends have considerable policy significance since they help determine education and training needs. One important conclusion of this chapter, for example, is that a growing mismatch has been occurring between skill requirements of the workplace and educational attainment of the workforce, with the latter increasing much more rapidly than the former.

This chapter has two main aims. The first is to document trends in US skill levels in the postwar period. The second is to analyse the factors responsible for the change in skills. These include intersectoral shifts in employment, technological change, institutional and organizational dimensions of production, and the degree of trade openness.

The role of technological change in explaining the changing demand for skills warrants some comment. The notion that technological change may stimulate the demand for more skilled or better educated labour emanates from the work of Arrow (1962) and Nelson and Phelps (1966). Arrow introduced the notion of learning-by-doing, which implies that experience in the application of a given technology or new technology in the production process leads to increased efficiencies over time. One implication of this is that an educated labour force should 'learn faster' than a less educated group. Industries with more rapid rates of technological progress may thus favour workers with greater potential for learning.

In the Nelson-Phelps model, it is argued that a more educated workforce may make it easier for a firm to adopt and implement new technologies. Firms value workers with education because they are more able to evaluate and adapt innovations and to learn new functions and routines than less educated ones. In this model, too, technological change may stimulate the demand for skilled workers.

Several studies provide evidence (both direct and indirect) of a positive relation between the pace of technological activity and the demand for educated labour. Welch (1970) analysed the returns to education in US farming in 1959 and concluded that a portion of the returns to schooling results from the greater ability of more educated workers to adapt to new production technologies. Bartel and Lichtenberg (1987), using industry-level data for 61 US manufacturing industries over the 1960–1980 period, found that the relative demand for educated workers was greater in sectors with newer vintages of capital. They inferred from this that highly educated workers have a comparative advantage with regard to the implementation of new technologies.

A related finding is reported by Mincer and Higuchi (1988), using US and Japanese employment data, that returns to education are higher in sectors undergoing more rapid technical change. Another is from Gill (1989), who calculated on the basis of US Current Population Survey data for 1969–1984 that returns to education for highly schooled employees are greater in industries with higher rates of technological change.

The chapter is organized as follows: The first section documents changes in aggregate skill levels of the workplace over the period 1950 to 1995. I rely mainly on the *Dictionary of Occupational Titles* (DOT), which offers direct measures of the skill requirements of detailed jobs (see Rumberger, 1981, for example). Cognitive, interactive and motor skill indices from the fourth edition of the DOT (see US Department of Labor, 1977) are linked to consistent employment matrices for census years 1950, 1960, 1970, 1980, and 1990 (267 occupations by 64 industries) and to occupational data for 1995.[1] I also use standard measures of workforce skills based on educational attainment.

Comparisons in the trends of the two types of measures are highlighted in this section.

The second part of the chapter investigates skill trends at the sectoral level. Here it will become clear that some industries have been more dynamic than others in both upgrading and downgrading skill requirements. Differences in skill change between goods and service industries receive special attention. Changes in aggregate skill levels result from both changes in skill requirements at the industry level and structural shifts in employment patterns across industries. The former is normally interpreted as deriving from changes in technology and the latter from shifting patterns of demand. The last part of Section 2 provides a decomposition of changes in aggregate skill levels into these two components.

Section 3 of the chapter analyses the role of technological change in explaining the changing demand for skills. Regression analysis is employed to relate the change in skill indices to various measures of technological activity, including traditional measures of total factor productivity growth, as well as computer intensity, research and development intensity, and capital vintage. The regressions are performed at the industry level, for the period from 1970 to 1990.[2]

2   AGGREGATE SKILL TRENDS, 1950–1995

2.1 Measures of Labour Skills

Labour skills appear in a wide variety of dimensions. Jobs are defined by a set of tasks requiring some combination of motor skills (physical strength, manual dexterity, motor coordination), perceptive and interpersonal skills, organizational and managerial skills, autonomy and responsibility, verbal and language skills, diagnostic skills (synthetic reasoning abilities) and analytical skills (mathematical and logical reasoning abilities). Perhaps, the best source of detailed economy-wide measures of skill requirements for the period since 1960 is the fourth (1977) edition of the DOT. For some 12,000 job titles, it provides a variety of alternative measures of job-skill requirements based upon data collected between 1966 and 1974.[3] On the basis of this source, four measures of *workplace skills* are developed for each *occupation*, as follows:

1. *General Educational Development (GED)*. On a scale of one to six, GED measures mathematical, language and reasoning skills and is taken directly from the DOT.

2. *Substantive Complexity (SC)*. SC is a composite measure of skills derived from a factor analytic test of DOT variables by Roos and Treiman (Miller et. al., 1980: Appendix F). The results provided strong support for the existence of such a factor: it was highly correlated with General Educational Development, Specific Vocational Preparation (training time requirements), Data (synthesizing, coordinating, analysing), and three worker aptitudes – Intelligence (general learning and reasoning ability), Verbal and Numerical. Both GED and SC measure cognitive skills and are highly correlated across industries.

3. *Interactive Skills (IS)*. IS can be measured, at least roughly, by the DOT 'People' variable, which, on a scale of 0–8, identifies whether the job requires mentoring (0), negotiating (1), instructing (2), supervising (3), diverting (4), persuading (5), speaking-signalling (6), serving (7) or taking instructions (8). For comparability with the other measures, we have rescaled this variable so that its values range from 0 to 10 and reversed the scoring so that mentoring, the highest form of interactive skill, is now scored 10 and taking instructions is scored 0.

4. *Motor Skills (MS)*. MS is measured by another factor-based variable from the Miller study (1980, p. 339). Also scaled from 0 to 10, this measure reflects occupational scores on motor coordination, manual dexterity and 'things' – job requirements that range from setting up machines and precision working to feeding machines and handling materials. These traditional shop-floor skills have been the focus of much of the deskilling debate.

Another measure of workplace skills is derived from the 1970 Census of Population data:

5. *Median Years of Schooling-1970 (EDUC-1970)*. Median years of schooling is computed for each occupation in 1970 on the basis of actual schooling attainment reported by respondents in the 1970 Census of Population. In a sense, this measure gives us a 'constant educational requirements' measure by occupation, in contrast to the actual educational attainment of workers in each occupation on a year-by-year or 'current' basis. This is analogous to constant dollar versus current dollar output series. If the actual skill requirements of each occupation remain constant over time, then EDUC-1970 serves as an indicator of the changes in the educational *requirements* of the workplace. We shall return to this point below.

Average industry skill scores are computed as a weighted average of the skill scores of each occupation, with the occupational employment mix of the industry as weights. Computations are performed for 1950, 1960, 1970, 1980, and 1990 on the basis of occupation by industry employment matrices for each of these years constructed from decennial census data. There are 267 occupations and 64 industries. Since occupation and industry classifications have changed substantially with each census, we used Commerce Department compatibility tables for 1950–60, 1960–70 and 1970–80 to produce consistent matrices for 1950, 1960, 1970, and 1980. Fortunately, there were only very minor changes in classification between 1980 and 1990.

It should be emphasized at the outset that computing (weighted) averages of these skill score measures is somewhat problematic, since, with the exception of Substantive Complexity, the scoring system is based on discrete values rather than continuous ones. However, insofar as the values of these indices provide a natural ranking from lowest to highest, changes in their mean values roughly indicate general trends in skill upgrading or degrading over time. Still, caution should be exercised in interpreting the actual mean values (and their associated rates of growth) for these skill measures.

It should also be noted that no attempt is made to account for changes in the skill content of specific occupations. Such a project would require a comparison of skill levels over successive editions of the DOT. Moreover, the last edition was published in 1977. There is some evidence that the skill content of some jobs do change over time. Hirschhorn (1986) notes the increasing importance of diagnostic skills and synthetic reasoning abilities with the use of programmable automation. Similarly, Zuboff (1988, pp. 75–76) writes that operators increasingly require a new kind of thinking, which '. . . combines abstraction, explicit inference, and procedural reasoning.' However, the evidence from studies that have looked across all occupations suggests that there are changes in skill content in both directions, and the net effect is small (see Horowitz and Hernstadt, 1966, and Spenner, 1983, pp. 830–831).

Another point worth noting is that if the skill requirements of a job change substantially, then the US Bureau of the census classifies this as a new occupation. The number of occupations contained in the census data has grown considerably over time – particularly between 1960 and 1980, when the number increased from 277 to 505. It is probably not unreasonable, therefore, to assume that, *on average*, the skill levels of occupations have remained largely unchanged over the 1950–90 period.

Educational attainment has also been employed to measure the skills supplied in the workplace. The usefulness of schooling measures is limited by such problems as variations in the quality of schooling both over time and among areas, the use of credentials as a screening mechanism, and inflationary trends in credential and certification requirements. Indeed, there is some empirical evidence that years of schooling may not closely correspond to the technical skill requirements of the jobs (see Rumberger, 1981, for example).

For comparison purposes, I have also constructed three measures of the actual educational attainment of the adult population or workforce in each of the census years: (i) percentage of the adult population aged 25 and over with a high school degree; (ii) percentage of the adult population aged 25 and over with a college (BA) degree; and (iii) mean schooling of the workforce (see footnotes to Table 2.2 for sources and methods). These measures are based on economy-wide data (mainly household surveys) for the population but are not available on the industry level. Moreover, unlike EDUC-1970, these measures are based on current educational data for each of the census year and may thus be interpreted as an indicator of *workforce skills*.

2.2 Broad Occupational Trends

I begin with general trends in the occupational composition of employment over the period 1950 to 1995. As shown in Table 2.1, some of the changes have been quite dramatic. Professional and technical workers doubled as a share of employment, from 8.6 per cent in 1950 to 17.6 per cent in 1993. Managers and administrators also increased substantially as a proportion of the workforce, from 8.7 to 13.8 per cent. Clerical workers grew as a share over the same period, from 12.3 to 14.7 per cent. A much higher proportion of the labour force were also engaged as sales workers by 1993, with most of the increase apparently occurring during the 1980s.[4] The other major increase occurred for service workers (excluding private household workers), whose share rose from 7.8 to 12.9 per cent.

The other occupational categories all declined as a share of employment. The proportion of the labour force employed as craftsmen fell from 14.2 to 10.8 per cent and as operatives (that is, machine and transportation operators) from 20.4 to 10.5 per cent. Nonfarm labourers (that is, unskilled workmen except those employed on the farm) declined from 6.6 per cent of employment to 4.1 per cent. Domestic servants and other household workers declined as a proportion of the employed labour force from 2.6 to 0.7 per cent. Finally, farmers, farm managers, and farm labourers together fell from 11.8 per cent of total employment to only 2.8 per cent. In sum, the postwar period witnessed a sizeable relative reduction in blue-collar work and a corresponding increase in white-collar jobs, particularly professional and technical positions.

Table 2.1   The distribution of employment by occupational group, 1950–1995

Occupational group	1950 %	1960 %	1970 %	1977 %	1988 %	1995 %
Professional, technical, and kindred	8.6	10.8	13.8	14.6	16.1	17.6
Administrators and managers except farm	8.7	10.2	10.2	10.3	12.4	13.8
Clerical	12.3	14.5	17.4	17.7	15.9	14.7
Sales	7.0	6.5	6.1	6.2	12.0	12.1
Craft and kindred	14.2	12.9	12.8	13.1	11.9	10.8
Operatives	20.4	18.6	18.2	15.7	11.3	10.5
Labourers, nonfarm	6.6	6.0	5.0	5.3	4.2	4.1
Private household	2.6	3.3	2.0	1.3	0.8	0.7
Service except private household	7.8	9.3	10.5	12.5	12.6	12.9
Farmers and farm managers	7.4	4.0	2.1	1.5	3.0	2.8
Farm labourers	4.4	3.9	1.8	1.5		
Total	100.0	100.0	100.0	100.0	100.0	100.0

Sources: US Bureau of the Census, *Historical Statistics of the US: Colonial Times to 1970*, Bicentennial Edition, Part 2, Washington, DC, 1978; US Bureau of Labor Statistics, *Handbook of Labor Statistics 1978*, 1979; US Bureau of Labor Statistics, *Handbook of Labor Statistics 1989*, 1990; and US Bureau of the Census, *Statistical Abstract of the United States, 1997*.

2.3 Trends in Aggregate Skill Levels

The results portrayed in Figure 2.1 show that, with the exception of motor skills, changing employment patterns have had the effect of raising the skill requirements of jobs between 1950 and 1995. Of the five indicators of workplace skills, the average Substantive Complexity level in the economy as a whole had the highest growth, 19 per cent over the four and a half decades. General Educational Development and EDUC-1970 grew slower, at 11 and 8 per cent, respectively, while Interactive Skills increased by 9 per cent. Motor Skills, on the other hand, showed a 4 per cent decline over the 45 years.

Figure 2.1   Mean skill score by type and year, 1950–1995

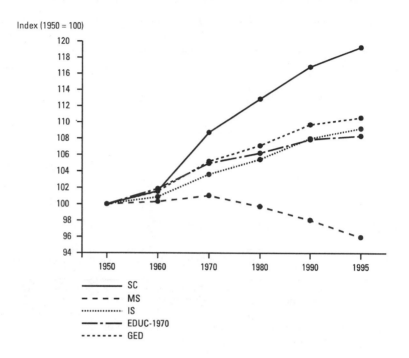

Index (1950 = 100)

Growth in workplace skills was dwarfed by increases in the educational attainment of the workforce and adult population, particularly as evidenced in the rescaled Figure 2.2. The fraction of the adult population (25 years of age and over) with a high school diploma or better, more than doubled between 1950 and 1995, from 34 to 82 per cent, while the proportion of adults who had completed at least four years of college almost quadrupled, from 6.2 to 23.0 per cent. The mean schooling level of employed workers grew slower than these first two indicators, at 45 per cent over the forty-five years. These figures compare to a 19 per cent rise in the average Substantive Complexity score and to a mere 8 per cent increase in EDUC-1970 (where it is assumed that educational requirements by occupations remain fixed over time). Thus, the educational attainment of the population increased considerably faster than the educational requirements of the workplace in the postwar period.

Figure 2.2   *Actual educational attainment and skills, 1950–1995*

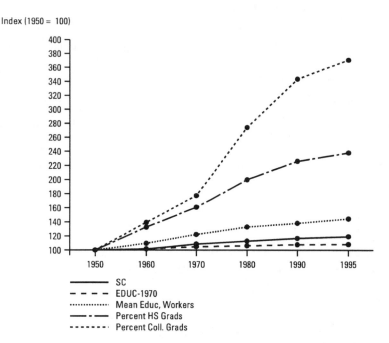

Index (1950 = 100)

Legend:
——— SC
– – – EDUC-1970
·········· Mean Educ, Workers
—·— Percent HS Grads
------· Percent Coll. Grads

Another striking result is the pronounced slowdown in the rate of growth for all 5 measures of workplace skills, with the exception of Interactive Skills, between the 1960s and the 1990s, after a rapid acceleration between the 1950s and 1960s (see Table 2.2 and Figure 2.3). Skill growth was quite low during the 1950s. Between the 1950s and 1960s, it increased more than fourfold for Substantive Complexity, tripled for Interactive Skills, more than doubled for both General Educational Development and Motor Skills, and rose by more than half for EDUC-1970. Skill growth peaked in the 1960s. Between the 1960s and 1990s, it fell off by about a third for Substantive Complexity, by about half for General Educational Development, and by about two-thirds for EDUC-1970. The growth in Motor Skills, which was positive in the 1950s and 1960s turned negative in the 1970s, 1980s, and 1990s. The annual growth in Interactive Skills fell from 0.27 per cent in the 1960s to 0.18 per cent in the 1970s but then rebounded to 0.23 per cent in the 1990s, though still somewhat below its pace in the 1960s.

Table 2.2   Annual rate of change of workplace and workforce skills, total
economy, 1950–1995

Skill Dimension	'50–'60 %	'60–'70 %	'70–'80 %	'80–'90 %	'90–'95 %	'50–'95 %
A. Workplace Skills						
Substantive Complexity (SC)	0.16	0.68	0.38	0.35	0.42	0.39
General Educational Development (GED)	0.15	0.35	0.18	0.24	0.16	0.22
Interactive Skills (IS)	0.09	0.27	0.18	0.24	0.23	0.20
Motor Skills (MS)	0.03	0.07	-0.13	-0.17	-0.43	-0.09
Median Year of Schooling, 1970 (EDUC-1970)	0.19	0.30	0.12	0.16	0.08	0.18
B. Workforce Skills						
Per cent of adults with 4 years of high school or more[a]	2.81	1.95	2.17	1.23	1.03	1.93
Per cent of adults with 4 years of college or more[a]	3.30	2.43	4.35	2.25	1.54	2.91
Mean years of schooling employed workers[b]	0.91	1.10	0.83	0.39	0.88	0.82

a. *Source:* US Bureau of the Census, *Current Population Reports*, available on the Internet. Adults refer to persons 25 years of age and over.
b. *Source:* US Bureau of Labor Statistics (1993). Figures are for the private business sector. Mean schooling is calculated by weighting educational attainment of workers by hours of work.

Patterns of skill growth generally correlate with changes in the broad occupational composition of the labour force. The growth in Substantive Complexity, General Educational Development, Interactive Skills, and EDUC-1970 over the four and a half decades reflects the increasing share of professionals and managers in the workforce, while the decreasing share of craft workers and operatives in employment appears responsible for the postwar decline in motor skills. The decade-by-decade correspondence is a bit rougher. The peak growth in cognitive skills during the 1960s seems to be due to the particularly rapid increase in the share of professionals in the labour force over that period (3 percentage points). The decline in motor skills after 1970 seems to be attributable to the very sharp reduction in the fraction of operatives in the workforce dating from that year. The rebound in Interactive Skills growth in the 1980s correlates with the large jump in the share of managers and administrators employed in the economy (about 2 percentage points).[5]

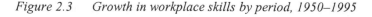

Figure 2.3   Growth in workplace skills by period, 1950–1995

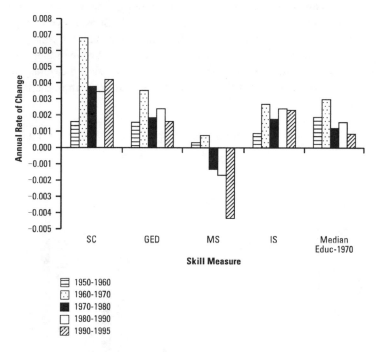

Figure 2.4 contrasts the growth in workplace skills with trends in the educational attainment of the population and the workforce. As noted above, the growth in educational attainment has been considerably greater than that of workplace skills. Here, we focus on the time pattern over the four and a half decades. As discussed above, the annual growth rate of Substantive Complexity increased sharply between the 1950s and 1960s, fell off in the 1970s and 1980s, and then picked up a bit in the 1990s. The growth in the mean education of the workforce had a similar time pattern, increasing slightly between the 1950s and 1960s, declining in the 1970s and again in the 1980s before accelerating once again in the 1990s. However, with the exception of the 1980s, its growth rate was about twice as great as that of Substantive Complexity, and over the whole 1950–95 period, it averaged slightly more than twice the growth rate of Substantive Complexity.

The time patterns are different for the percentage of adults with both a high school and a college education. In both cases, the growth rate fell off between the 1950s and 1960s, picked up in the 1970s, fell sharply in the 1980s and again in the 1990s. Over the 45-year period, the percentage of adults with a high school education grew at the rate of 1.9 per cent per year and the percentage with a college degree at 2.9 per cent per year, while Substantive Complexity increased at 0.4 per cent per year and EDUC-1970 at 0.2 per cent per year. These results again highlight the lack of correspondence between the growth in the demand for cognitive skills (as reflected in the direct skill measures) and the supply of such skills, as reflected in the educational attainment of the population.

Figure 2.4   Growth in workplace and workforce skills by period, 1950–1995

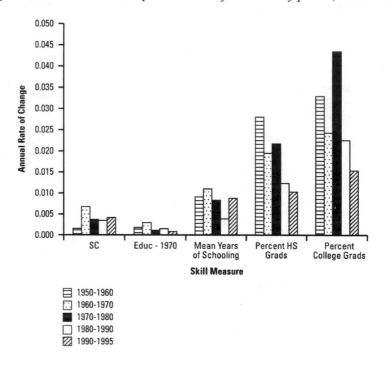

3   SKILL CHANGES AT THE INDUSTRY LEVEL

There are striking differences in skill requirements among industries in the US economy. These are shown in Table 2.3 for 9 major industrial groupings in 1970. Mean Substantive Complexity scores range from a low of 11 per cent below average in agriculture to a high of 25 per cent above average in finance,

Table 2.3 Mean skill scores by major industry in 1970 and change over 1950–1990 (Skill scores normalized so that overall skill score = 100 in 1970)

| | Mean Skill Score, 1970 | | | | Change, 1950–90 | | | |
	SC	IS	MS	Educ-1970	SC %	IS %	MS %	Educ-1970 %
Agriculture	89	76	98	84	0.5	0.7	-0.9	6.1
Mining	96	69	105	95	32.4	9.7	-1.7	9.8
Construction	101	64	116	93	23.5	6.4	-0.3	6.1
Manufacturing	88	61	108	96	20.8	5.7	-1.6	5.4
Transportation, communications and public utilities	91	85	105	98	13.5	3.2	-1.8	3.3
Wholesale and retail trade	94	97	90	98	1.3	0.4	4.8	0.9
Finance, insurance, and real estate	125	128	93	106	20.8	11.3	-4.9	6.3
Other services	114	149	97	108	12.2	6.6	-2.0	7.0
Government	107	110	99	104	10.3	4.7	-1.0	2.8
Goods Industries[a]	90	67	107	95	16.0	4.3	-0.1	7.2
Service Industries[b]	107	125	94	104	10.6	5.5	0.9	5.0
Total	100	100	100	100	16.9	8.3	-1.9	7.9
Addendum[c]								
Production Workers	74	48	111	90				
	(38)	(56)	(23)	(7)				
Non-Production Workers	116	133	93	106				
	(50)	(91)	(35)	(15)				

Notes:
a. Goods-producing industries are defined as: (1) agriculture; (2) mining; (3) construction; (4) manufacturing; and (5) transportation, communications and public utilities.
b. Service industries are defined as: (1) wholesale and retail trade; (2) finance, insurance, and real estate; (3) other services; and (4) government services.
c. Production workers include craft workers, operatives, and labourers. Non-production workers include all others. The standard deviation is shown in parentheses.

insurance, and real estate. Substantive Complexity levels are about a fifth higher in services than goods-producing industries. Median education levels are about 10 per cent higher in the service industries than the goods sectors. The highest median years of schooling is found in the other services sector, which includes a wide range of business and personal services, at 108 (i.e. 13.2 years), followed by finance, insurance, and real estate and the government sector. The lowest is recorded in agriculture at 84 (i.e. 10.3 years).

Interactive Skills are almost twice as great in services as in goods-producing industries. The top three sectors in terms of interactive skills are the same as for median education: the other services sector (49 per cent greater than the overall mean), finance, insurance, and real estate (28 per cent above average), and the government sector (10 per cent above average). Manufacturing has the lowest Interactive Skills level. In contrast, Motor Skill levels are 14 per cent higher in goods industries than in service industries. Not surprisingly, construction has the highest level of motor skills (16 per cent above average), followed by manufacturing (8 per cent above average), mining (5 per cent above average), and transportation, communications and public utilities (5 per cent above average) Wholesale and retail trade has the lowest level of motor skills.

Some industries have also been more dynamic than others in upgrading skill requirements. Interestingly, Substantive Complexity scores have grown much faster in goods industries than service industries over the years from 1950 to 1990 – 16 versus 10 per cent. Mining led the way with a 32 per cent increase, followed by construction (23 per cent) and then manufacturing and finance, insurance, and real estate (both at 21 per cent). In manufacturing, in particular, the results accord with anecdotal evidence about the 'white-collarization' of jobs in this sector (from 24 per cent of total manufacturing jobs in 1950 to 36 per cent in 1990 by my calculations). Agriculture and the trade sector experienced almost no change in Substantive Complexity levels.

A similar pattern holds for the skill measure EDUC-1970 (where jobs are rated according to their 1970 educational requirements). EDUC-1970 grew by 7.2 per cent in goods industries and 5.0 per cent in services. Mining, again, was at the top of the list (9.8 per cent increase), followed by finance, insurance, and real estate (6.3 per cent), and then agriculture and construction (both at 6.1 per cent). Growth in educational requirements was lowest in the trade sector. The upgrading of Substantive Complexity and educational requirements in the goods industries reflects the more rapid growth in white-collar jobs than blue-collar ones, particularly from the industrial restructuring of the 1980s.

Interactive skills grew slightly more in services than goods industries. Growth was strongest in finance, insurance, and real estate, at 11.3 per cent, followed surprisingly, by mining (9.7 per cent) and then by other services (6.6 per cent). Growth was weakest in agriculture, 0.7 per cent.

Unlike the other measures in this table, motor skills requirements declined after 1950. This was true of every major industry except trade. While case studies have suggested that deskilling has occurred via the decline in the skill content of many blue-collar jobs, these industry results indicate that changes in occupation employment patterns within industry also contributed to a reduction in the demand for manual skills.

Substantive complexity, interactive skills, and motor skills represent three relatively independent dimensions of job skills. From Table 2.3 it is clear that industries that are strong in one dimension of skill need not be strong in the other dimensions as well. For example, while the finance, insurance, and real estate category ranked highest in Substantive Complexity in 1970 and second in Interactive Skills, it ranked last in Motor Skills. Moreover, industries that grew rapidly in one skill direction did not necessarily grow in others. Finance, insurance, and real estate, for example again, had the highest growth in Interactive Skills, ranked third highest in Substantive Complexity growth but recorded the lowest growth in Motor Skills. This stresses the importance of considering multiple dimensions of skills rather than a single one, such as educational attainment, that is used in most studies on this subject.

The addendum to Table 2.3 provides another bifurcation of jobs – in this case, into production and non-production workers on the basis of the US Bureau of Labor Statistics definition for the manufacturing sector. Production workers are blue-collar workers with the exception of service workers, while non-production workers include white-collar and service jobs. This division has been used in many recent productivity and earnings studies, such as Berman et al. (1994), to distinguish between skilled and unskilled workers.

The results show that production workers score much lower than non-production workers in substantive complexity and interactive skills but, as expected, production workers have substantially higher motor skills. As a result, the difference in the composite skill index between the two groups is less pronounced than the one based on Substantive Complexity. The difference in schooling attainment between them in 1970 is only two years, also less marked in per centage terms than the gap in Substantive Complexity.

Another notable result is that the variation in skill levels within each of the two groups is quite high. Indeed, because of the high variance, none of the difference in mean skill values is statistically significant. The standard deviation of skill scores is also considerably higher among non-production than production workers, indicating that the former are a more heterogeneous group. These results suggest that it is rather precarious to use production versus non-production workers as a demarcation between skilled and unskilled jobs.

3.1 Changes in Industry Employment

Changes in aggregate skill levels result from both changes in skill requirements at the industry level and structural shifts in employment patterns across industries. The former is normally interpreted as deriving from changes in technology and the latter from shifting patterns of demand. Before presenting a formal decomposition, it is helpful to look at the broad changes in employment composition by industry over the postwar period (see Table 2.4). One of the most dramatic changes has been in agriculture, which accounted for 14 per cent of employment in 1950 and only 3 per cent in 1995. This relative decline has been going on for at least the last 100 years. In 1929, for example, the fraction of total employment accounted for by agriculture was 22 per cent. The proportion fell to 14 per cent in 1947, 8 per cent in 1960, and 4 per cent in 1978. The major decline in employment in the agricultural sector was from the exodus of owners of small farms and their families.

Table 2.4   Distribution of employment by major industry, 1950, 1970, and 1995

	1950 %	1970 %	1995 %
Agriculture	13.7	4.7	2.9
Mining	1.7	0.8	0.5
Construction	4.5	4.8	4.3
Manufacturing	29.1	26.1	15.3
Transportation, communications and public utilities	7.7	6.1	5.1
Wholesale and retail trade	17.9	20.2	22.9
Finance, insurance, and real estate	3.6	4.9	5.7
Other services	10.2	15.5	27.4
Government	11.5	16.9	16.0
Total	100.0	100.0	100.0

Source: Council of Economic Advisers, *Economic Report of the President, 1997.*

Another major change occurred in manufacturing, whose share of total employment fell by almost half, from 29 per cent in 1950 to 15 per cent in 1995. In absolute terms, employment in manufacturing peaked in 1980 at 20.3 million workers and has since fallen to 18.5 million in 1995. Much discussion has recently ensued over this development, which has been labelled by some as the 'deindustrialization' of America. However, it should be noted that much of the decline in employment in manufacturing is due to the high (labour) productivity growth of this sector. In fact, manufacturing accounted for almost the same share of total output in the mid-1990s as it did in the early 1950s.[6]

The share of employment in mining also declined rather precipitously between 1950 and 1995, from 1.7 to 0.5 per cent. The share of employment in transport and public utilities also fell over this period, from 7.7 to 5.1 per cent, while the proportion of workers in construction remained roughly constant, about 4 per cent.

If the share of employment fell in agriculture, mining, manufacturing, and transport and utilities, where did it increase? The answer is the service sectors, which absorbed most of the growth of employment in the postwar period. The proportion of total employment in wholesale and retail trade increased from 18 to 23 per cent, the per cent in finance, insurance, and real estate from 3.6 to 5.7, the per cent on government payrolls from 11.5 to 16.0, and the share in other services (personal and business) from 10 to 27 per cent. In sum, two major developments characterized the postwar period. The first was the shrinking share of workers employed in agriculture and manufacturing, and the second was the shift of the workforce out of goods-producing sectors into services.

3.2 Industry Effects on Aggregate Skill Growth

Changes in overall skill levels are a result of changes in the skill levels of individual industries (through changes in occupational mix) and employment shifts among industries. We can formally decompose the change in overall job skill requirements into an industry and occupation effect, as follows. Let

M = the occupation-by-industry employment matrix, where m_{ij} shows employment of occupation i in industry j;

e = vector with unit entries;

L = eM = (row) vector showing total employment by industry;

p = (row) vector showing the distribution of employment among industries, where

p_j = L_j/Σ_j;

s = (column) vector showing the average skill level of each industry j;

σ = ps = the overall or economy-wide average skill level of employed workers.

Then, for instantaneous changes,

$$d\sigma = pds + (dp)s$$

Table 2.5   Decomposition of the change in overall skill levels into an occupational composition and an industry employment shift effect, 1950–1990

Period	Actual change in overall skill level	Decomposition[a] 1st effect: change in occup. com- posit. within industry	2nd effect: shifts in employment among industries	Percentage decomposition Total change %	1st effect: change in occup. composit. within industry %	2nd effect shifts in employ- ment among industries %
A. Substantive Complexity (SC)						
1950–60	0.060	0.068	−0.008	100.0	113.9	−13.9
1960–70	0.267	0.150	0.118	100.0	56.1	43.9
1970–80	0.156	0.068	0.088	100.0	43.4	56.6
1980–90	0.149	0.043	0.106	100.0	28.6	71.4
1950–90	0.632	0.328	0,304	100.0	52.0	48.0
B. Interactive Skills (IS)						
1950–60	0.019	0.027	−0.007	100.0	136.6	−36.6
1960–70	0.060	0.053	0.007	100.0	87.9	12.1
1970–80	0.040	0.024	0.016	100.0	59.8	40.2
1980–90	0.056	0.016	0.040	100.0	27.8	72.2
1950–90	0.176	0.119	0.057	100.0	67.7	32.3
C. Motor Skills (MS)						
1950–60	0.016	−0.018	0.034	100.0	−114.0	214.0
1960–70	0.038	−0.017	0.056	100.0	−45.1	145.1
1970–80	−0.068	−0.019	−0.049	100.0	28.5	71.5
1980–90	−0.085	−0.009	−0.077	100.0	10.2	89.8
1950–90	−0.099	−0.064	−0.035	100.0	64.2	35.8
D. Median Education, 1970 (EDUC-1970)						
1950–60	0.220	0.206	0.014	100.0	93.6	6.4
1960–70	0.362	0.242	0.120	100.0	66.9	33.1
1970–80	0.148	0.081	0.067	100.0	54.5	45.5
1980–90	0.195	0.125	0.070	100.0	64.1	35.9
1950–90	0.925	0.654	0.271	100.0	70.7	29.3

Note: [a] See Equation 1.

Since our data are for discrete time periods, we use the discrete form,

$$\Delta\sigma = p\Delta s + (\Delta p)s \qquad (1)$$

where $\Delta s = s^2 - s^1$, $\Delta p = p^2 - p^1$, and superscripts refer to time period. The results are based on average period weights, providing an exact decomposition.

The results are shown in Table 2.5. During the 1950s, all the growth in Substantive Complexity was due to changes in the occupational composition of the workforce within industry (by our interpretation, technological change). In fact, employment shifted slightly in favour of industries with below average Substantive Complexity levels. During the 1960s, the period of greatest overall growth in Substantive Complexity, both the occupational mix effect and the industry shift effect were positive and strong. If the industry shares of employment had remained unchanged, economy-wide mean cognitive skill levels would have grown by 0.15, over twice the increase of the 1950s. However, higher-skilled industries experienced greater than average employment growth (the industry shift effect), which accounted for an additional 0.12 increase in mean cognitive skills. During the 1960s, a little over half of the growth in average Substantive Complexity was attributable to changes in occupational mix.

The contribution of the occupational mix effect fell off sharply between the 1960s and 1970s, from 0.150 to 0.068, and again between the 1970s and 1980s, from 0.068 to 0.043, while the industry shift effect fell off slightly and then picked up in the 1980s. As a result, overall Substantive Complexity growth declined in the 1970s and then stabilized in the 1980s. Moreover, the industry shift effect, which accounted for 44 per cent of overall Substantive Complexity growth in the 1960s, explained 57 per cent in the 1970s and over 70 per cent in the 1980s.

Similar patterns are evident for skill measure EDUC-1970, where it is assumed that occupational educational requirements are fixed over time. In this case, almost all the growth in the average skill level during the 1950s is again attributable to changes in occupational composition within industry. Between the 1950s and 1960s, the occupational composition effect climbed in importance and then underwent a sharp reduction between the 1960s and the 1970s but grew in the 1980s. The industry employment shift effect fell off between the 1960s and 1970s and but rose slightly between the 1970s and 1980s, so that the growth in overall EDUC-1970 likewise fell sharply between the 1960s and 1970s but recovered somewhat in the 1980s.

In the case of Interactive Skills, all the growth in the overall skill level during the 1950s is again attributable to changes in occupational composition within industry. Between the 1950s and 1960s, the occupational composition effect increased, and then declined between the 1960s and the 1970s and again in the 1980s. However, in this case, the industry employment shift effect rose steadily over time, from the 1950s to the 1980s, so that the growth in the overall Interactive Skills level rose sharply between the 1950s and 1960s, decreased in the 1970s but gained in the 1980s.

Changes in Motor Skills show a very different pattern from the other three skill measures. The occupational composition effect was negative and of very similar magnitude in each of the four decades, reflecting the shift of employment within industry from blue-collar to white-collar jobs. The industry shift effect was positive and relatively strong in both the 1960s and 1970s, favouring industries with above-average motor skills and accounting for the positive increase in motor skills over these two decades. However, the industry effect turned negative in the 1970s and even more negative in the 1980s, reflecting the dramatic shift of employment toward service industries and accounting for the decline in overall Motor Skills growth in those two periods.

In sum, over the entire 1950–90 period, changes in overall Substantive Complexity levels are about equally attributable to technological change (52 per cent) and to shifting demand patterns (48 per cent), with the former falling in importance and the latter growing in importance over time. The former primarily reflects the increasing share of white-collar workers, particularly professionals and managers, within industries, while the latter reflects the continuing shift of employment out of low-skill goods industries toward the higher skilled services, particularly finance, insurance, and business and professional services.

Over the four decades, about two thirds of the upgrading in Interactive Skills levels and over 70 per cent of the increase in the EDUC-1970 skill index are accounted for by the changes in occupational composition within industry. In the case of Interactive Skills, the occupational composition effect became less important over time while the employment shift effect increased in importance and became the dominant factor in the 1980s. In the case of EDUC-1970, the occupational composition effect remained the dominant factor over the four decades.

4   TECHNOLOGY AND SKILL GROWTH

The literature cited in the introduction above suggests that there may be a strong correlation between skill growth and the pace of technological change. The analysis begins with some descriptive statistics, illustrated in Figure 2.5. I use two standard measures of productivity growth – GDP per Full-Time Equivalent Employee (FTEE) and total factor productivity growth, measured using GDP for output and FTEE and gross capital stock for inputs.[7] Also shown on the diagram are the growth in Substantive Complexity, Motor Skills, and the mean education of the employed workforce.

Labour and TFP growth show a very similar time pattern. Both were strongest in the 1950s (1.7 and 1.1 per cent per year, respectively), fell slightly in the 1960s, and then precipitously in the 1970s (to 0.6 and 0.2 per cent per year, respectively), and then show a partial recovery in the 1980s (to 1.2 and 0.7 per cent per year, respectively). In contrast, the growth in both Substantive Complexity and mean years of schooling of the workforce increased between the 1950s and 1960s and then declined in the 1970s and again in the 1980s. Motor Skills growth also increased between the 1950s and 1960s and fell off in the 1970s and 1980s, but in this case Motor Skills growth is negative in the latter two periods. On the basis of these decadal averages, there does not appear to be any clear correspondence between the growth in skill demand (or educational attainment) and the growth in productivity.

Figure 2.5   Growth in skills, education and productivity by decade, 1950–1990

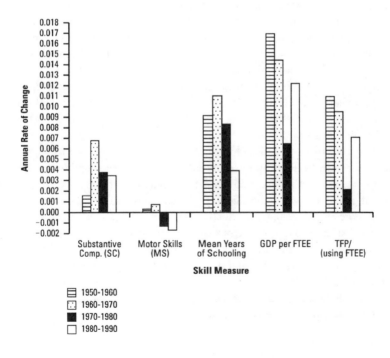

I next turn to regression analysis to analyse formally the relation between skill change and technological advance. Because of differences in industry classification schemes in the underlying data sources, I use 43 industries in the regression analysis. Moreover, because of data limitations, the period of analysis is limited to 1970–1990. The primary sample consists of pooled cross-section time-series data, with observations on each of the 43 industries in 1970–80 and 1980–90, for a total of 86 observations. A second sample, limited to the 30 goods-producing industries for a sample size of 60, is also used. The error terms are assumed to be independently distributed but may not be identically distributed and I use the White procedure for a heteroscedasticity-consistent covariance matrix in the estimation (see White, 1980).

The dependent variable in the regressions is the change in skill level over the ten-year period. I use five measures of technological activity: (1) average annual rate of total factor productivity growth (TFP growth), (2) investment in office, computer and accounting machinery over the previous 7 years per FTEE (OCA/FTEE); (3) ratio of expenditures on research and development to industry sales (R&D/Sales); (4) the ratio of computer programmers, computer systems analysts, computer specialists, n.e.c., and engineers to FTEE (CSE/FTEE); and (5) the average annual growth rate of the ratio of gross capital stock to FTEE (K/L Growth), which may be interpreted as an indicator of the rate at which new vintages of capital are introduced into the industry.

Other control variables are introduced as well. Relative factor prices between capital and unskilled labour are used to control for the possibility of capital–skill complementarity. Capital intensity, measured as the ratio of capital to output, is also used. High capital intensity may reflect the continued use of old technologies and methods of production that rely upon large–scale operations and high shares of semiskilled workers with specialized mechanical skills. A dummy variable distinguishing the 1970–80 from the 1980–90 period (DUM8090) is also introduced.

A number of structural and organizational dimensions of production may have independent effects on the demand for skills. These include: (i) the share of employees in an industry covered by union contracts (%UNION); (ii) the share of employees working in large establishments (defined here as those with 500 or more employees); (iii) industry employment growth; and (iv) a dummy variable distinguishing goods from service industries.

International competitiveness, as measured by the ratio of imports to industry gross output (IMP/GDO) and the ratio of exports to industry gross output (EXP/GDO), may also affect the rate of skill change. Industries competing against imports and those competing in international product markets may be forced to upgrade skills faster in order to remain competitive.

Table 2.6   Regressions of skill change on technology and other variables[a]

	Dependent Variable					
	Change in Substantive Complexity (SC)		Change in Interactive Skills (IS)		Change in Motor Skills (MS)	
Independent Variables	All Industries	Goods Only	All Industries	Goods Only	All Industries	Goods Only
Constant	0.047* (1.71)	0.074*** (2.87)	0.074** (2.28)	0.150*** (5.07)	−0.013 (0.48)	−0.030 (0.86)
TFP Growth	−0.929 (1.50)	−1.019* (1.74)	−0.613 (1.57)	−1.020*** (3.32)	−0.287 (0.96)	−0.304 (1.29)
Ln (OCA/FTEE)	0.012 (1.22)	0.032** (2.53)	0.017* (1.83)	0.019** (1.92)		
R&D/Sales	0.011* (1.71)	0.004 (0.59)	0.010** (2.58)	0.0077** (2.03)		
Ln(CSE/FTEE)					−0.040*** (4.66)	−0.027*** (2.78)
K/L Growth	1.963*** (3.34)	1.909*** (3.11)	1.209*** (2.78)	1.126** (2.26)	0.291 (0.57)	0.262 (0.80)
%UNION			−0.061 (1.11)	−0.159*** (2.97)	0.166** (2.30)	0.073 (1.11)
IMP/GDO				−0.078 (1.15)		
EXP/GDO				0.490* (1.70)	0.528* (1.68)	0.402 (1.41)
DUM8090			0.0018** (1.91)	0.0042*** (2.97)	−0.0016* (1.69)	−0.0014* (1.69)
R^2	0.24	0.38	0.39	0.67	0.31	0.33
Adjusted R^2	0.20	0.33	0.34	0.61	0.26	0.26
Std. error	0.14	0.11	0.088	0.059	0.097	0.063
Sample Size	86	60	86	60	86	60

Notes:

[a]   The 'all industries' sample consists of pooled cross-section time-series data, with observations on each of the 43 industries in 1970–80 and 1980–90, for a total of 86

observations. The 'goods only' sample is limited to the 30 goods-producing industries for a sample size of 60. The coefficients are estimated using use the White procedure for a heteroscedasticity-consistent covariance matrix. The absolute value of the t-statistic is shown in parentheses below the coefficient estimate. Key:

1) TFP Growth: average annual rate of total factor productivity growth, using full-time equivalent employees (FTEE) and gross capital stock (source: National Income and Product Accounts or NIPA on diskette).
2) Ln(OCA/FTEE): natural logarithm of the sum of constant dollar purchases of office, computer and accounting machinery over previous 7 years per FTEE (source for OCA: BIE computer tape; source for FTEE: NIPA on diskette)
3) R&D/Sales: ratio of expenditures on research and development to industry sales (source: National Science Foundation, *Research and Development in Industry*, various years)
4) Ln(CSE/FTEE): natural logarithm of the ratio of computer programmers, computer systems analysts, computer specialists, n.e.c., and engineers to FTEE (source for computer specialists and engineers: decennial Census data).
5) K/L Growth: average annual growth rate of the ratio of gross capital stock to FTEE (source: NIPA on diskette).
6) %UNION: share of employees covered by union contracts (*1970*: Freeman and Medoff, 1979; *1980*: Kokkelenberg and Sokell, 1985).
7) IMP/GDO: ratio of industry imports to industry gross output (source: U.S. input-output tables).
8) EXP/GDO: ratio of industry exports to industry gross output (source: U.S. input-output tables).
9) DUM8090: dummy variable which equals one for the 1980–90 period and zero otherwise.
* Significant at the 10% level (two-tailed test)
** Significant at the 5% level (two-tailed test)
*** Significant at the 1% level (two-tailed test)

Results are shown in Table 2.6 for the change in three skill dimensions, Substantive Complexity, Interactive Skills, and Motor Skills. I have selected the regression form with the highest adjusted R^2-statistic (or, correspondingly, the lowest standard error of the regression). Of the five technology variables, the strongest effects come from the growth in capital–labour intensity. The growth in both cognitive and interactive skills is strongly and positively linked to the rate of new investment, though the change in motor skills is not.

Both the rate of computerization (OCA/FTEE) and R&D intensity (R&D/Sales) have a significant positive effect on the change in interactive skills. Computerization also has a positive and significant relation to the growth in Substantive Complexity among goods industries only but not among all industries, whereas the coefficient of R&D intensity is positive and significant at the 10 per cent level for the change in Substantive Complexity among all industries but insignificant among goods industries only. Neither variable has much measured effect on the change in motor skills but the ratio of computer specialists and engineers to employment (CSE/FTEE) bears a very significant negative relation to Motor Skills change.

TFP growth generally has a negative effect on skill growth, though the variable is significant in only two of the six specifications. This result suggests that technological change by itself tends to simplify tasks and thus reduce reliance on skilled workers in all dimensions. This result is consistent with product life cycle models. As originally argued by Vernon (1966, 1979), the creation of a new industry or product line usually entails high startup costs, the development of specialized processes, the training of labour for new skills, and so on. However, once this technology is in place, there is constant pressure to routinize the technology so that it becomes cheaper to use. If it becomes routinized, then it may not have to rely on expensive, highly trained labour nor on special production processes to supply its inputs.

Relative factor prices between capital and labour (as well as their change over time) fail to appear as significant determinants of skill change. Of the organizational variables, only the percentage of employees in unions (%UNION) has any significant effect on skills. It has a negative and significant effect on the change in Interactive Skills among goods industries – presumably, by retarding the substitution of higher skilled (managerial and administrative) workers for lower skilled (operative) workers – and has a positive and significant effect on the growth in motor skills among all industries – probably, by supporting craft workers and operative jobs.

Import competition does not appear to affect skill change. However, industries that export a high percentage of their output have a higher than average growth in Interactive Skills (at least among goods industries) and a faster growth in Motor Skills (among all industries). The former result may reflect the need for additional administrative layers to compete successfully in international markets, whereas the latter may reflect the need to upgrade craft and operative jobs in order to produce higher quality output for the international market place.

5 CONCLUSION

Between 1950 and 1990, all three indices of cognitive skills – substantive complexity, general educational development, and median years of schooling measured in 1970, showed positive growth, as did interactive skills. Motor skills, on the other hand, experienced an absolute decline. Growth in all five workplace skill indices peaked in the 1960s. In the case of cognitive skills, this was due to both strong occupation and industry effects; for interactive skills, this was attributable to a very strong occupation effect; while in the case of motor skills, this was accounted for by a very strong industry effect.

Skill growth was lower in the 1950s, 1970s, and 1980s in all five dimensions. The growth of cognitive skills fell between the 1960s and 1970s and again between the 1970s and 1980s, due mainly to declining occupation effects. This suggests that the bias in technological change toward workers with cognitive skills was strongest in the 1960s but fell rather sharply in the 1970s and again in the 1980s. Despite stories of radical industrial restructuring of the 1980s, occupation effects were at their lowest level in this period for cognitive skills. This result casts doubt on recent analyses which posit a particularly strong technological bias in favour of educated workers during the 1980s.

The growth in interactive skills fell sharply between the 1960s and 1970s but then recovered in the 1980s, due to a strong industry effect. The growth in motor skills turned negative in the 1960s and became even more negative in the 1980s, due mainly to the sharp shift in employment toward service industries.

Overall, there is no evidence of deskilling in the 1980s, except for motor skills. However, the rate of increase of cognitive skill levels slowed down in the 1970s and 1980s, though the rate of growth of interactive skills in the 1980s was almost the same as in the 1960s.

Changes in the educational attainment of both the population and the workforce outstripped changes in workplace skills. These results emphasize the lack of correspondence between the growth in the demand for cognitive skills (as reflected in the direct skill measures) and the supply of such skills, as reflected in the educational attainment of the population. Indeed, they suggest that in both the 1970s and 1980s, the educational system in the US was producing far more educated workers than the workplace could absorb.

The results of the analysis contained herein depend on the assumption that educational requirements remain fixed over time *within* occupations (as, for example, reflected in the EDUC-1970 index). As noted in Section 1 above, the case studies that have examined this issue suggest that changes in skill content within occupation do occur over time but they move in both directions and the net effect is small. Moreover, if the skill requirements of a job do change substantially, the U.S. Census Bureau will usually classify this job as a new occupation.

Investigation into the factors that affect the demand for skills indicates that technological change, as measured by the growth in total factor productivity, seems to be deskilling, though the results are relatively weak (the coefficients are generally not statistically significant). This result is consistent with product life cycle models, which emphasize the constant pressure to routinize new technology so that it becomes less reliant on skilled labour. However, the result appears to conflict with those of Mincer and Higuchi (1988) and Gill (1989), who found higher returns to schooling in industries undergoing more rapid technical change.

I do find that other dimensions of technological activity – particularly, the pace of new investment as reflected in the growth in the capital–labour ratio, R&D intensity, and the rate of computerization – has a positive relation to the change in substantive complexity and interactive skills. Bartel and Lichtenberg (1987) also found that new vintages of capital stimulate the demand for more educated workers. On the other hand, the ratio of computer specialists and engineers to total employment within an industry has a very significant negative effect on the growth in motor skills, suggesting that their efforts are aimed at reducing the skill requirements of production-line workers.

Unionization generally has a negative effect on interactive skills and a positive effect on motor skills, a result that may be due to the retardant effect of unions on the substitution of higher skilled (management) workers for lower skilled (operative) workers. While import penetration does not seem to affect skill change, export-oriented industries appear to upgrade both interactive and motor skills more rapidly than domestically-oriented industries.

NOTES

1. This part extends the analysis contained in Howell and Wolff (1991), which was based on actual census employment matrices for 1960, 1970, and 1980 and a statistically imputed matrix for 1985.
2. This section updates previous econometric analysis (Howell and Wolff, 1992), which was conducted on skill change from 1970 to 1985.
3. For a discussion of some of the limitations of these data, see Miller et. al. (1980) and Spenner (1983).
4. The data show an increase in the share of sales workers from 6 per cent in 1977 to 12 per cent in 1988. However, these numbers should be interpreted with some caution, because the Census Bureau changed its classification of sales jobs during the 1980s.
5. Apparent anomalies are that interactive skills grew faster in the 1960s than the 1950s, whereas the share of managers in total employment grew faster in the earlier decade; and that motor skills had positive growth in the 1950s while the share of both craft workers and operatives in the labour force declined.
6. If a sector's output share remains constant and its labour productivity growth is greater than average, then its share of total employment must, of consequence, fall. This mechanism is often referred to as the 'unbalanced growth' effect. See Baumol et al. (1989), Chapter 6, for more discussion.
7. The data source is the U.S. National Income and Product Accounts, supplied on diskette by the U.S. Bureau of Economic Analysis.

REFERENCES

Adler, Paul (1986), 'New Technologies, New Skills', *California Management Review* **29** (1), Fall, 9–28.

Arrow, Kenneth (1962), 'The Economic Implications of Learning by Doing', *Review of Economic Studies* **29** (2), 155–73.

Bartel, Ann P. and Frank R. Lichtenberg (1987), 'The Comparative Advantage of Educated Workers in Implementing New Technology', *Review of Economics and Statistics* **69**, February, 1–11.

Baumol, William J., Sue Anne Batey Blackman and Edward N. Wolff (1989), *Productivity and American Leadership: The Long View,* Cambridge, MA: MIT Press.

Berman, Eli, John Bound and Zvi Griliches (1994), 'Changes in the Demand for Skilled Labor Within U.S. Manufacturing: Evidence from the Annual Survey of Manufactures', *Quarterly Journal of Economics* **109**, 367–398.

Council of Economic Advisers (1994), *Economic Report of the President, 1994,* Washington, DC: Government Printing Office.

Freeman, Richard B. and James L. Medoff (1979), 'New Estimates of Private Sector Unionism in the United States', *Industrial and Labor Relations Review* **32**, 143–74.

Gill, Indermit S. (1989), *Technological Change, Education, and Obsolescence of Human Capital: Some Evidence for the U.S.,* Mimeo, November.

Hirschhorn, Larry (1986), *Beyond Mechanization,* Cambridge, MA: MIT Press.

Horowitz, M., and I. Hernstadt (1966), 'Changes in Skill Requirements of Occupations in Selected Industries', in National Commission on Technology, Automation, and Economic Progress, *The Employment Impact of Technological Change,* Appendix, Volume 2 to *Technology and American Economy,* Washington DC: Government Printing Office, pp. 223–287.

Howell, David and Edward N. Wolff (1991), 'Trends in the Growth and Distribution of Skills in the U.S. Workplace, 1960–85', *Industrial and Labor Relations Review* **44** (3), April, 486–502.

Howell, David R. and Edward N. Wolff (1992), 'Technical Change and the Demand for Skills by US Industries', *Cambridge Journal of Economics* **16** 127–46.

Kokkelenberg, Edward C. and Donna R. Sockell (1985), 'Union Membership in the United States, 1973–81', *Industrial and Labor Relations Review* **38** (4), July, 497–543.

Kominski, Robert and Andrea Adams (1994), *Educational Attainment in the United States: March 1993 and 1992,* US Bureau of the Census, Current Population Reports P20–476, Washington, DC: Government Printing Office.

Miller, Ann R., Donald J. Treiman, Pamela S. Cain and Patricia A. Roos (1980), *Work, Jobs and Occupations: A Critical Review of the Dictionary of Occupational Titles,* Washington, DC: National Academy Press.

Mincer, Jacob and Yoshio Higuchi (1988), 'Wage Structures and Labor Turnover in the United States and Japan', *Journal of the Japanese and International Economics* **2**, 97–113.

National Science Foundation, *Research and Development in Industry*, Washington, D.C.: Government Printing Office, various years.

Nelson, Richard R. and Edmund S. Phelps (1966), 'Investment in Humans, Technological Diffusion and Economic Growth', *American Economic Review* **61** (2), 69–75.

Rumberger, Russell W. (1981), 'The Changing Skill Requirements of Jobs in the U.S. Economy', *Industrial and Labor Relations Review* **34** (4), July, 578–91.

Spenner, Kenneth I. (1983), 'Deciphering Prometheus: Temporal Changes in Work Content', *American Sociological Review* **48**, December, 824–37.

Spenner, Kenneth I. (1988), 'Technological Change, Skill Requirements, and Education: The Case for Uncertainty', in Richard M. Cyert and David C. Mowery (eds), *The Impact of Technological Change on Employment and Economic Growth*, Cambridge: Ballinger Publishing Co., pp. 131–184.

US Bureau of the Census (1971) *County Business Patterns, U.S. Summary CBP-70-1*, August, Washington, DC: Government Printing Office.

US Bureau of the Census (1978), *Historical Statistics of the U.S.: Colonial Times to 1970*, Bicentennial Edition, Part 2, Washington, DC: Government Printing Office.

US Bureau of the Census (1994), *Statistical Abstract of the United States, 1994* (114th Edition), Washington, DC: Government Printing Office.

US Bureau of Labor Statistics (1979), *Handbook of Labor Statistics 1978*, Bulletin 2000, Washington, DC: Government Printing Office.

US Bureau of Labor Statistics (1990), *Handbook of Labor Statistics 1989*, Bulletin 2340, Washington, DC: Government Printing Office.

US Bureau of Labor Statistics (1993), *Labor Composition and U.S. Productivity Growth, 1948–90*, Bulletin 2426, December, Washington, DC: Government Printing Office.

US Department of Labor (1977), *Dictionary of Occupational Titles*, 4th edition, Washington, DC: Government Printing Office.

US Department of Labor, Bureau of Labor Statistics (1986), *Employment and Earnings*, January, Washington DC: Government Printing Office.

Vernon, R. (1966), 'International Investment and International Trade in the Product Cycle', *Quarterly Journal of Economics* **80**.

Vernon, R. (1979), 'The Product-Cycle Hypothesis in a New International Environment', *Oxford Bulletin of Economics and Statistics* **41**, 255–67.

Welch, Finis R. (1970), 'Education in Production', *Journal of Political Economy* **78**, 35–59.

White, H. (1980), 'A Heteroskedasticity-Consistent Covariance Matrix Estimator and a Direct Test for Heteroskedasticity', *Econometrica* **48**, May, 817–38.

Zuboff, Shoshanna (1988), *In The Age of the Smart Machine: The Future of Work and Power*, New York: Basic Books.

ACKNOWLEDGEMENTS

Earlier versions of the chapter were presented at the OECD Expert Workshop on Technology, Productivity, and Employment, June, 1995; the NBER Summer Workshop, July 1996; and the University of Maastricht, May, 1997. I would also like to express appreciation to the C.V. Starr Center for Applied Economics at New York University, the Alfred P. Sloan Foundation, and the Jerome Levy Economics Institute of Bard College for financial support.

3. Has the Finnish Labour Market Bumped the Least Educated?

Rita Asplund and Reija Lilja

1 INTRODUCTION

There exists a huge body of international work on overeducation, but considerably less on undereducation.[1] This strong focus on overeducation and its implications no doubt reflects the assertion of overeducation being a more acute problem than undereducation. Obviously this stems primarily from the substantial investments in education that have been made in the industrialized countries over the past decades and the possibility that the economy has been unable to absorb the steady increase in the supply of well-educated labour market entrants. A major consequence would be that a non-negligible proportion of the labour force is actually overeducated.[2] Further support to the perception that not all workers are employed in jobs in which their educational attainment is a requirement, is provided by the declining trend in the rates of return to education that has been observed in many industrialized economies over the past decades.

The literature on overeducation is fairly rich in its attempts to test various predictions derived from a number of theoretical approaches offering explanations for the mismatch between individual educational attainment and job requirements. The theoretical approaches most frequently adopted in this context are: human capital theory, occupational mobility theory, matching theory, job competition models, job screening models and, most recently, assignment frameworks incorporating both the supply and demand sides of the labour market.[3] These theoretical approaches provide insight on three main issues on the overeducation agenda: What determines the existence of overeducation and to what extent does overeducation compensate for lower levels of experience, tenure and training? Is overeducation a short-term or a longer-term phenomenon at the individual level? What is the rate of return to overeducation?

In recent years, increasing attention has also been paid to another potential implication of overeducation, viz. the so-called 'bumping down' phenomenon. This term refers to a situation in the labour market where the overeducated, in accepting jobs below their educational attainment, take jobs away from those with a lower education (which would still be sufficient for matching the requirements of the job in question). As a consequence these lower-skilled workers are shifted (bumped) down the job requirement scale and, as a final outcome, may be forced into unemployment.[4]

Figure 3.1   Labour force and employment, 1975–1995

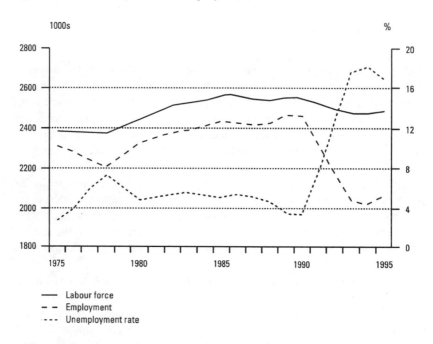

    —— Labour force
    – – Employment
    --- Unemployment rate

The present study focuses on the Finnish labour market and, particularly, on the labour market outcome of the least educated over a 20-year period (1975–1995). These years saw dramatic changes in the economic activity level with a longish economic upturn shifting into an economic boom in the late 1980s and then suddenly, in 1991, into the deepest recession since the economic crises in the 1930s (Figure 3.1). In three years (1990–1993), some half a million jobs were lost, resulting in an unemployment rate creeping close to 20 per cent (compared to one of the lowest in Europe – 3.5 per cent – in 1990). Weak signs of economic recovery were already discernible in 1993, mainly in the export sector. The unemployment rate remained largely unaffected, however.

The outstanding structural changes in the labour force that have occurred over this period, speeded up by the turbulent years in the early 1990s, can be expected to have hit the least educated part of the labour force especially hard. In view of the continuous growth in the demand for and supply of well-educated people, there is also the possibility that the labour market situation of the least educated has been further impaired by strengthening trends of occupational upgrading and overeducation also present in the Finnish labour market. Addressing these crucial aspects makes up the major part of this study.

The analysis is based on the *1970–95 Longitudinal Census Data Set* compiled by Statistics Finland. The data set has been constructed by merging register data covering the whole population. Information is available for every five years since 1970, with the most recent year being 1995.[5] From this whole-population data set a representative 10 per cent sample has been drawn, containing information on a total of 603,153 individuals for the whole period 1970–95.

The rest of the chapter is organized as follows. The next section displays trends in the educational structure of occupations over the 20-year period investigated. Section 3 describes changes in the labour market status of the least educated over the past 20 years, while Section 4 aims to explore whether these changes may, at least in part, reflect a growing overeducation problem in the Finnish labour market. In Section 5, an attempt is made to explain the observed transition patterns with the emphasis being on establishing whether or not the least educated in the Finnish labour market have faced a clear tendency of being crowded out of their 'traditional' jobs, possibly out of employment entirely. This econometric analysis is undertaken for two 10-year periods, 1975–85 and 1985–95, representing highly different levels of economic activity. Section 6 gives some concluding remarks.

2   TRENDS IN THE EDUCATIONAL STRUCTURE OF OCCUPATIONS

The subsequent descriptive analyses are restricted to 16–65 year-old full-year full-time[6] wage and salary earners with positive earnings.[7] Implementing various restrictions concerning the individuals' occupational status[8] produces a data set comprising some 100,000 employees for each year studied. These observations, distributed over close to 300 occupational categories, constitute the basis for the description of general trends in occupational upgrading over the period 1975 to 1995 given below.

Calculating the average schooling level for each occupational category reveals a remarkable increase in the educational level of workers in practically all occupations over the years 1975–95 (Figure 3.2).[9] This has occurred irrespective of the occupation's relative position on the educational scale.[10] Simultaneously the difference in average education across the occupations has increased, the standard deviation being 2.1 schooling years in 1995 compared to 1.7 in 1975. It is noteworthy, however, that the ranking of occupational categories according to average education has changed only marginally. The rank correlation coefficient of occupations between the two years is extremely high (= 0.944).

Figure 3.2   Comparison of average schooling years in 1975 and 1995, by occupational category

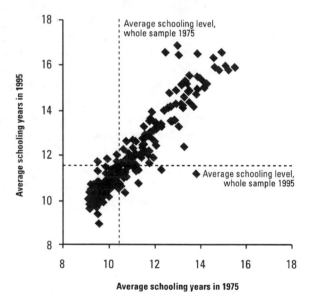

In 1975 the average educational level was rather low (below 10 years)[11] in a majority of occupations. Moreover, these occupations employed a considerable proportion of the labour force, some 52 per cent. By 1985 the share of occupations at the lowest end of the educational scale had declined to 25 per cent, and by 1995 to less than 9 per cent. The decline in employment in these occupations was equally dramatic: From over one half in 1975 to one fifth of the labour force in 1985 and to less than 2 per cent in 1995.

However, this dramatic drop from around 50 per cent in 1975 to below 9 per cent in 1995 in the share of the low-education occupations, does not mean that these occupations have disappeared altogether from the Finnish labour market. Instead, in 1995 one can find them higher up the educational scale, still employing a considerable proportion of the labour force (some 36 per cent in 1995).

This improvement in the skills level of workers, not least within occupations at the lowest end of the educational scale, raises the question: What has become of the least educated employees?

3   LABOUR MARKET TRANSITIONS OF THE LEAST EDUCATED

This section provides a brief description of transitions in the Finnish labour market in general and of the least educated in particular. The analysis is based on two samples of individuals, one for 1975 and one for 1985. In both cases, the mobility of the sample individuals is traced up to 1995.

Table 3.1   Transition probabilities of all employees, separately for the 1975 and 1985 samples

Transition category	Transitions for the 1975 sample				Transitions for the 1985 sample	
	1975–1980 %	1975–1985 %	1975–1990 %	1975–1995 %	1985–1990 %	1985–1995 %
Stayed in same occupation[a]	48.0	36.8	29.5	19.4	56.5	40.6
Change of occupation[b]	37.5	39.4	41.3	31.9	32.0	30.6
Unemployed	1.9	2.9	1.7	11.0	1.2	10.7
Student	1.0	0.3	0.5	0.9	1.1	1.8
Retired	4.5	11.1	18.6	25.8	5.1	11.1
Other	7.0	9.6	8.4	11.0	4.2	5.2
Total	100.0	100.0	100.0	100.0	100.0	100.0

Notes: [a] No change in the individual's 3-digit occupational code.
[b] The individual's 3-digit occupational code is different 5,10,15 or 20 years later.

As can be seen from Table 3.1 (row 1), the overall probability of staying in the same occupation declines rapidly with the years spent in working life. A comparison of the two samples points to a clear weakening in this tendency, though.[12] Correspondingly the probability of occupational mobility (row 2) has persistently been higher within the 1975 sample, except for the recession period in the early 1990s, when it dropped to much the same level as for the 1985 sample (i.e. some 31 per cent). The possibility of retirement does not seem to have been affected by the dramatic change in the economic activity level (the probability of being retired 10 years later is some 11 per cent for both samples). As is to be expected, the recession years differ from the boom years mainly in a much higher probability of becoming unemployed rather than of finding a new job.

Table 3.2   The relative risk of transition of the least educated as compared to the more educated (more than 9 years of schooling)

Transition category	1975 sample				1985 sample	
	1975–1980	1975–1985	1975–1990	1975–1995	1985–1990	1985–1995
Stayed in same occupation	0.90	0.77	0.68	0.54	0.91	0.72
Change of occupation	0.98	0.92	0.87	0.75	0.92	0.78
Unemployed	1.82	1.53	1.58	1.30	1.86	1.57
Student	0.73	0.83	0.79	0.66	0.53	0.57
Retired	2.65	2.61	2.24	1.79	3.96	3.24
Other	1.18	1.32	1.43	1.57	1.03	1.27

Table 3.2 answers the question whether the least educated, i.e. those with at most a basic education (9 years or less), have faced a higher risk of employment instability than their more educated colleagues.[13] The table shows that this is certainly the case. But the table also indicates that their smaller propensity to stay in the same occupation and to qualify for another occupation is largely compensated for by the much higher 'risk' of leaving for retirement. In other words, the negative consequences of the ongoing occupational upgrading in the Finnish labour market have been dealt with mainly through the retirement system and to a lesser extent by pushing the least educated into unemployment.

The propensities reported in Table 3.2 further indicate that the worsening of the labour market situation of the least educated has possibly been moderated also by the strong egalitarian feature of the Finnish education system providing all with a sound basic education. In that sense the least educated in Finland cannot be compared with the least educated in, for instance, the USA. In addition, the least educated also take an active part in personnel training, albeit not to the same extent as the more educated.[14]

4 IS THERE A TENDENCY TOWARDS OVEREDUCATION?

As indicated in the outline, the continuous growth of the well-educated share of the labour force may have resulted in a situation in the Finnish labour market in which an increasing number of employees are overeducated in their occupations. Such a tendency may have accelerated the deterioration of the labour market status of the least educated. A simple way of shedding some light on this question is to compare the shares of the overeducated in 1975 and 1995 for each occupational category. This is done in Figures 3.3 and 3.4, with the overeducated defined as those employees having an education exceeding the average educational level of the occupation plus one standard deviation.[15] Figure 3.3 compares occupational shares of overeducation using a changing definition, while Figure 3.4 provides a comparison based on a constant definition.[16]

Figure 3.3   *Share of the overeducated in 1975 and 1995, by occupational category, changing definition of overeducation*

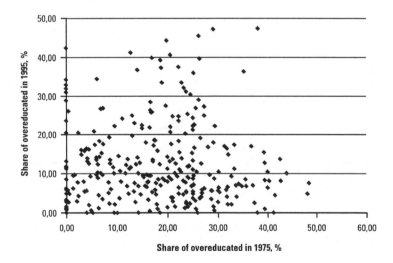

Between 1975 and 1995, the share of the overeducated declined in as much as 60 per cent of the investigated occupations if we use a changing definition of overeducation. In 1975 the share of the overeducated exceeded 30 per cent in 14 per cent of the occupations, against only 7 per cent 20 years later.[17] As is to be expected from the strong increase in the educational level of the Finnish workforce over the past decades, the extent of overeducation is much higher if we use a constant definition based on the 1975 situation; in the latter case, less than 10 per cent of the investigated occupations have seen a decline in the share of the overeducated over the past 20 years, and in almost two-thirds of the occupations the share of the overeducated exceeded 30 per cent in 1995.

It seems that the recession years in the early 1990s 'solved' the overeducation problem by forcing the least educated in particular into unemployment or retirement, thereby making the occupations educationally more homogeneous. Furthermore, the very low correlation (= 0.027) between the ranking of occupations according to their share of the overeducated in 1975 and 1995 using a changing definition of overeducation, suggests that the change in the share of the overeducated across occupations has not occurred in a systematic way. The corresponding correlation calculated using a constant definition of overeducation seems to lend further support to this conclusion: the correlation is rather high (0.692) but far from perfect.

Figure 3.4   Share of the overeducated in 1975 and 1995, by occupational category, constant definition of overeducation

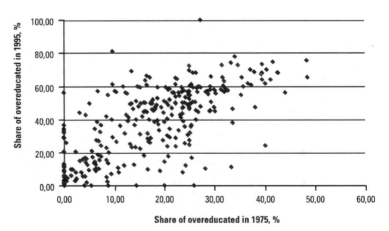

It may also be asked whether the share of the overeducated is related to the average educational level of the occupation or the unemployment rate among those belonging to the occupation. A strong negative correlation between the share of the overeducated and the average educational level across occupations as well as a strong positive correlation between occupational shares of the overeducated and occupation-specific unemployment rates could be interpreted as an indication of the least educated being crowded out in the Finnish labour market. Furthermore, in view of the large supply of highly educated youths and the fact that Finnish women are on average better educated than Finnish men, one could expect young people and women to be overrepresented among the overeducated. However, the correlation coefficients reported in Table 3.3 give weak support to these hypotheses; most of the correlation coefficients are small and of the expected sign, albeit statistically significant. It is noteworthy, though, that all four correlations are insignificant for 1995.

These overall patterns and trends of overeducation at the 3-digit occupational level may, however, even conceal substantial differences in the incidence and consequences of overeducation and non-overeducation at the individual level. As is evident from Table 3.4, the overeducated have a rather high tendency of remaining overeducated irrespective of whether a constant or a changing definition of overeducation is used. And compared to their non-overeducated colleagues, they seem to have experienced a considerably lower unemployment probability during the deep recession in the early 1990s. It is also of interest to note that the unemployed faced a clearly higher risk of turning up in a job below their qualifications in the high unemployment years of the early 1990s.

Table 3.3   Dependency between the occupations' share of overeducated and selected features

| Year | Correlation between the share of overeducated and | | | |
	Average educational level	Unemployment rate	Share of youths among overeducated	Share of women among overeducated
1975	-0.336^*	–	0.393^*	-0.046
1980	-0.351^*	0.146^*	0.380^*	0.093
1985	-0.288^*	-0.019	0.270^*	0.114
1990	-0.243^*	0.137^*	0.160^*	0.161^*
1995	-0.016	0.078	0.055	0.018

Note: * indicates significance at the 5% level.

Table 3.4   *Propensity to remain overeducated, based on a constant and a changing definition of overeducation*

| Status in 1975 | Status in 1985 | | | | | |
| | Constant definition of overeducated | | | Changing definition of overeducated | | |
	Over-educated %	Non-over-educated %	Unem-ployed %	Over-educated %	Non-over-educated %	Unem-ployed %
Overeducated	48.9	0.6	0.8	38.4	11.1	0.8
Non-overeducated	5.2	67.1	3.7	7.4	64.9	3.7
Unemployed	12.5	32.2	2.9	7.2	37.5	2.9

| Status in 1985 | Status in 1995 | | | | | |
| | Constant definition of overeducated | | | Changing definition of overeducated | | |
	Over-educated %	Non-over-educated %	Unem-ployed %	Over-educated %	Non-over-educated %	Unem-ployed %
Overeducated	48.8	1.1	3.3	36.5	13.3	3.3
Non-overeducated	4.1	64.2	12.2	5.9	62.3	12.2
Unemployed	40.1	0.0	33.5	9.1	31.0	33.5

5   EXPLAINING LABOUR MARKET TRANSITION PATTERNS

To explore how labour market transitions depend on individual background factors, we focus on the analysis of two samples, one collected in 1975 and the other in 1985.[18] The labour market performance of individuals is evaluated by looking at their labour market status after a period of ten years. The subsequent empirical analyses are restricted to four types of transitions; to those in which an individual stayed in the same occupation, changed occupation, became unemployed, or retired over the 10-year observation period. These transitions cover more than 90 per cent of all transitions (see Table 3.1).[19]

In modelling the transition probabilities, a multinomial logit model is used. The model is based on the assumption that the transitions are mutually exclusive. This assumption, which is in many ways restrictive, is in accordance with our decision to exclude the heterogeneous group of other transitions from our analyses.

Both demand- and supply-side factors influence the transition probabilities. Therefore, the estimated multinomial logit model can be regarded as a reduced-form model capturing the combined effect of both types of factors. A broad set of explanatory variables is used to detect pure 'bumping down' effects in the transition patterns observed among the least advantaged groups in the Finnish labour market. The included individual characteristics are: age, education, gender, marital status and region. The job-related characteristics are: relative wage position measured by wage quintiles, overeducation in one's own occupation, public versus private sector and socio-economic status.

Estimation results are presented in the Appendix for the period 1975–85 in Table 3A.1, and for the period 1985–95 in Table 3A.2. It appears from these tables that the chosen variables are statistically highly significant explanatory factors for the observed labour market transitions. The χ-squared tests show that the null hypotheses that the explanatory variables do not have any influence on the transition probabilities are strongly rejected in both samples. This is also reflected in the high values of t-statistics that most of the variables have received in the estimations. Next the most crucial results from the 'bumping down' perspective are discussed in more detail.

To get an overall picture of the general transition patterns in our data sets, average transition probabilities are calculated from the estimation results of the logit model and the mean values of explanatory variables (Table 3.5). These numbers thus represent transition probabilities of a person with an 'average background' in the two samples. Accordingly they differ from the crude probabilities presented in Table 3.1 above. These probabilities also differ from those in Table 3.1 in the sense that they are conditional on the fact that one of the four transitions specified above had occurred.

Table 3.5   Average transition probabilities

	Same occupation %	Change of occupation %	Unemployed %	Retired %
1975–85	44.0	49.4	3.1	3.5
1985–95	49.2	35.0	11.8	4.0

Table 3.5 shows that an average individual in 1975 had a 44 per cent probability of staying in the same occupation and an almost 50 per cent probability of changing occupation over the ten-year period to follow. Thus the steady economic growth during these years increased the possibility of making a career move.[20] There was only a 3 per cent chance for the average individual to become unemployed, and a relatively modest chance, about 3.5 per cent, to retire. It appears that for the average employee, the period 1975–85 represented quite a mobile labour market in Finland.

The situation changed markedly during the period 1985–95 when the Finnish economy experienced its deepest recession ever. The mobility among the employed dropped dramatically and labour market adjustment took place mainly through unemployment. The average individual in 1985 had an almost 50 per cent chance of remaining in the same occupation until 1995, but only a 35 per cent chance of changing occupations. The probability of becoming unemployed in ten years' time was 12 per cent, a four times higher figure than for the average employee ten years earlier. The propensity to retire increased slightly.

Table 3.6   Transition probabilities by education

	Same occupation %	Change of occupation %	Unemployed %	Retired %
Basic education				
1975–85	40.0	52.9	3.4	3.7
1985–95	44.8	36.0	14.7	4.5
Secondary education				
1975–85	48.0	45.8	2.8	3.4
1985–95	50.2	34.6	11.3	3.9
Graduate degree				
1975–85	52.5	41.5	2.8	3.2
1985–95	57.3	30.1	8.5	4.1
Post-graduate degree				
1975–85	54.8	41.7	1.3	2.2
1985–95	53.7	38.1	5.9	2.3

To study the potential presence of a 'bumping down' phenomenon in the Finnish labour market, we have calculated transition probabilities for different educational levels (Table 3.6). It should be noted that these figures reveal only how people who are already working may be bumped out from the labour market. They do not show another side of the 'bumping down' phenomenon related to educational level; crowding out of the least educated (re-)entering the labour market.

A higher level of education appears to bring along a more stable labour market career. Employees with a graduate or post-graduate degree had a more than 50 per cent chance of being in the same occupation ten years later, whereas among employees with a basic education this probability was around 40 per cent.

The steady economic growth during the period 1975–85 made it possible for the least educated employees to adjust to changes in the labour market through occupational change. These employees had a more than 50 per cent chance of shifting to another occupation during these years and only a 3 per cent chance of being hit by unemployment. However, the deep recession in the early 1990s changed the situation dramatically. Between 1985 and 1995, there was only a 36 per cent chance that employees with a basic education changed occupation, and an almost 15 per cent chance that they became unemployed (five times as high a number as in the former period). Among these employees the propensity to become unemployed was 2.5 times as high as in the group of employees with a post-graduate degree. Hence, the lower the level of education, the higher the risk of unemployment. The propensity to retire early is also highest among the least educated. These results are in accordance with the 'bumping down' hypothesis, which states that the unskilled are most likely to lose their jobs if labour markets are slack at the same time as skills are upgraded.[21]

When the economic situation worsened in the early 1990s, also the low-paid employees experienced high levels of employment insecurity. Their propensity to become unemployed rose even more than for the low-skilled, to 20 per cent. The unemployment risk was 2.7 times as high in the first quintile as it was in the fifth quintile. These results are in line with those reported for the different educational levels, since education and wages are highly correlated. Thus it seems that low-paid employees have been subjected to tough adjustments. Our results suggest that there have been factors at work in the labour market that have pushed unskilled employees at the low-end of the wage spectrum towards unemployment and out of the labour market.

A phenomenon that is closely related to skills upgrading and 'bumping down' is overeducation. To study the implications of overeducation on individual behaviour, transition probabilities for those who are overeducated in their occupations are reported in Table 3.7.[22]

If a person is overeducated in his/her occupation he/she turns out to be much more likely to change occupation than a person whose job is in line with his/her educational attainment level. The propensity to change occupation is 10 percentage points higher for the overeducated than for the others. For example, during the period 1975–85, when the economy grew steadily, the overeducated had a 58 per cent probability of shifting to another occupation. However, according to Table 3.4 this higher propensity to change occupation does not necessarily mean an improvement in the job match. Overeducation seems to be a highly individual-specific and time-dependent phenomenon.

Table 3.7   Transition probabilities by overeducation

	Same occupation %	Change of occupation %	Unemployed %	Retired %
Overeducated				
1975–85	35.7	57.9	3.2	3.3
1985–95	40.6	43.6	12.3	3.6
Non-Overeducated				
1975–85	45.9	47.5	3.0	3.6
1985–95	50.5	33.7	11.7	4.1

Contrary to the results in Table 3.4, it appears from Table 3.7 that when differences in individual characteristics are controlled for, overeducation does not, as such, provide protection against unemployment. The overeducated are found to be slightly more likely to become unemployed than the non-overeducated. All in all, overeducation does not bring any additional advantages with respect to overall labour market performance. Those who are better matched, perform at least as well as those who are overeducated.

6   CONCLUDING REMARKS

The Finnish labour market has seen a dramatic increase in occupational skills over the past few decades. The educational level has increased especially in occupations that were dominated by the least educated some 20 years ago. Nevertheless, the low-skilled workers seem to have managed to keep their jobs or to shift to another occupation, at least in times of steady economic growth. The fairly smooth adjustment of the least educated to the changing working environment has been made possible by the high standards of Finnish compulsory education and the training they have received during their working lives. For older employees a generous retirement system has opened an alternative way of adjustment.

The deep recession in the early 1990s, however, seems to have put an end to this favourable situation. The sudden loss of half a million jobs hit the least educated especially hard. Their probability of keeping their jobs as well as of changing occupations declined substantially. Instead, their fate was to an increasing extent to become unemployed or retired.

The declining employment among the least educated boosted the ongoing upgrading of occupational skills. Simultaneously those employees being overeducated in their occupation showed an increasing tendency of shifting to jobs that better matched their qualifications. These trends are, in turn, reflected in less overeducation within occupations in 1995 compared to the situation in 1975. In other words, occupations are today more homogeneous when it comes to educational attainment than some 20 years ago. A cautious conclusion would be that the radical change in the performance of the least educated in the Finnish labour market of the early 1990s, is the combined outcome of the economic crisis and a growing 'bumping down' problem.

APPENDIX

Table 3A.1 Multinomial logit estimation results for labour market transitions between 1975 and 1985

Variable	Change of occupation		Unemployed		Retired	
Constant	3.44	(0.35)	-0.27	(0.78)	-6.82	(1.01)
Age	-0.19	(0.03)	-0.05	(0.07)	0.33	(0.08)
Age squared	0.35	(0.10)	0.03	(0.22)	-1.02	(0.22)
Age to the third power	-0.02	(0.01)	0.01	(0.02)	0.14	(0.02)
Woman	-0.12	(0.02)	-0.64	(0.05)	-0.54	(0.05)
Married	-0.01	(0.02)	-0.28	(0.05)	-0.26	(0.04)
Secondary education	-0.33	(0.02)	-0.38	(0.06)	-0.29	(0.05)
Graduate degree	-0.52	(0.05)	-0.46	(0.18)	-0.44	(0.12)
Post-graduate degree	-0.55	(0.06)	-1.31	(0.34)	-0.86	(0.17)
Overeducated	0.45	(0.02)	0.29	(0.07)	0.17	(0.07)
Second wage quintile	-0.05	(0.03)	-0.42	(0.06)	-0.33	(0.06)
Third wage quintile	-0.15	(0.03)	-0.76	(0.07)	-0.53	(0.06)
Fourth wage quintile	-0.27	(0.03)	-1.14	(0.08)	-0.74	(0.06)
Fifth wage quintile	-0.41	(0.03)	-1.33	(0.09)	-0.85	(0.07)
Upper management	0.73	(0.06)	0.22	(0.19)	-0.52	(0.14)
Research & planning	0.59	(0.06)	0.03	(0.22)	-0.68	(0.16)
Education & training	-0.35	(0.07)	-0.87	(0.33)	-0.83	(0.16)
Other senior executives	0.03	(0.06)	-0.40	(0.23)	-0.28	(0.14)
Supervisors	0.18	(0.04)	-0.17	(0.12)	-0.16	(0.09)
Independent work	0.05	(0.03)	-0.11	(0.08)	-0.38	(0.07)
Routine work	-0.26	(0.04)	-0.41	(0.13)	-0.52	(0.10)
Other lower-level empl.	-0.20	(0.04)	-0.61	(0.14)	-0.13	(0.09)
Agriculture & related	-0.73	(0.08)	-0.17	(0.15)	-0.24	(0.15)
Distribution & services	-0.55	(0.03)	-0.37	(0.08)	-0.20	(0.06)
Manufacturing	-0.05	(0.03)	0.15	(0.07)	0.22	(0.06)
Public sector	-0.24	(0.02)	-1.00	(0.07)	-0.10	(0.04)
Southern Finland	0.24	(0.02)	-0.32	(0.05)	-0.14	(0.04)
Log-likelihood function	-71,555.56					
χ-squared test (d.f. 78)	40,714.45					

Note: Standard errors of coefficients are in parentheses.

Table 3A.2 Multinomial logit estimation results for labour market transitions between 1985 and 1995

Variable	Change of occupation		Unemployed		Retired	
Constant	3.43	(0.50)	2.68	(0.62)	-13.91	(1.39)
Age	-0.20	(0.05)	-0.20	(0.06)	0.97	(0.11)
Age squared	0.36	(0.14)	0.45	(0.17)	-2.97	(0.29)
Age to the third power	-0.02	(0.01)	-0.02	(0.02)	0.34	(0.03)
Woman	-0.13	(0.02)	-0.27	(0.03)	-0.40	(0.04)
Married	-0.05	(0.02)	-0.40	(0.02)	-0.25	(0.03)
Secondary educ.	-0.15	(0.02)	-0.38	(0.02)	-0.24	(0.04)
Graduate degree	-0.42	(0.04)	-0.80	(0.07)	-0.33	(0.10)
Post-graduate degree	-0.12	(0.05)	-1.09	(0.11)	-0.86	(0.13)
Overeducated	0.48	(0.02)	0.27	(0.04)	0.09	(0.06)
Second wage quintile	-0.15	(0.02)	-0.43	(0.03)	-0.34	(0.05)
Third wage quintile	-0.32	(0.02)	-0.78	(0.03)	-0.63	(0.05)
Fourth wage quintile	-0.50	(0.03)	-1.10	(0.04)	-0.67	(0.06)
Fifth wage quintile	-0.48	(0.03)	-1.36	(0.04)	-0.72	(0.06)
Upper management	0.65	(0.05)	-0.01	(0.09)	-0.24	(0.12)
Research & planning	0.24	(0.05)	-0.19	(0.09)	-0.93	(0.14)
Education & training	-1.24	(0.07)	-1.42	(0.17)	-0.93	(0.13)
Other senior executives	-0.19	(0.05)	-0.49	(0.08)	-0.46	(0.11)
Supervisors	0.22	(0.04)	-0.03	(0.05)	-0.33	(0.08)
Independent work	0.17	(0.03)	-0.08	(0.05)	-0.07	(0.08)
Routine work	0.25	(0.04)	-0.08	(0.05)	-0.07	(0.08)
Other lower-level empl.	-0.51	(0.03)	-0.69	(0.06)	-0.32	(0.07)
Agriculture & related	0.38	(0.07)	0.14	(0.09)	0.35	(0.14)
Distribution & services	-0.61	(0.03)	-0.44	(0.04)	-0.14	(0.06)
Manufacturing	0.03	(0.03)	0.17	(0.04)	0.13	(0.06)
Public sector	-0.23	(0.02)	-1.01	(0.03)	0.03	(0.04)
Southern Finland	0.30	(0.02)	0.25	(0.02)	0.07	(0.04)
Log-likelihood function	-105,674.60					
χ-squared test (d.f. 78)	62,893.12					

Note: Standard errors of coefficients are in parentheses.

NOTES

1. For a comprehensive review of the literature in this field, see Hartog (1997).
2. Estimates of overeducation among the US workforce range up to 40 per cent (Duncan and Hoffman 1981, Sicherman 1991, Cohn and Khan 1995 and Hersch 1995). The share of overeducated is estimated at 31 per cent in Britain (Sloane et al. 1995), 16 per cent in the Netherlands (Hartog and Oosterbeek 1988) and 17 per cent in Spain (Alba-Ramirez 1993).

3.   For a discussion of these theoretical approaches to the overeducation phenomenon, see for example, Hartog (1997) and Battu et al. (1997).
4.   See for example, Borghans et al. (1998) for an overview of the 'bumping down' process.
5.   More information about the structure of the data set can be found in Statistics Finland (1995).
6.   Full-timers and part-timers are not distinguished in the data for 1970, 1990 and 1995. This is the main reason for not using 1970 as the 'starting' year in the analysis.
7.   Hence, apart from wage and salary earners with zero earnings, employees with entrepreneurial income have also been excluded from the data used in the actual analysis. It may further be noted that replication of the analysis on a data set also including those employees who have worked less than 12 months during the year, did not change the results substantially.
8.   The occupational categories had to be known, had to comprise six or more observations and were not allowed to include a large share (20 per cent or more) of individuals recorded to have zero earnings. Excluding these 'outliers' leaves us with a total of 298 fairly homogeneous occupational categories.
9.   It is worthwhile mentioning that the dramatic increase in the average educational level of some occupations, as shown in Figure 3.2, is not primarily the result of a small number of observations. For example, the average educational level of the category of university teachers increased from 13.3 schooling years in 1975 (based on 198 observations) to no less than 16.8 schooling years in 1995 (based on 672 observations). This certainly reflects the reaction of the educational system to the rapid growth in the demand for high-quality university education in Finland over the past decades.
10. Of the occupational categories under study only some 4 per cent had experienced a slight decline in the average educational level over the 20-year period from 1975 to 1995.
11. To be compared with completed basic education representing 9 years.
12. In the 1975 sample, 48 per cent were in the same occupation five years later compared to 57 per cent in the 1985 sample.
13. Table 3.2 is constructed from tables similar to Table 3.1 above, one calculated for the least educated employees and one for employees with more than a basic education. Relating the percentage shares of the least educated to those of the better educated shows the risk to the least educated of being in a given labour market position relative to their more educated counterparts. An equally large share for both educational groups produces a value of one, indicating no difference in the relative risk. A value exceeding one points, in turn, to a higher relative risk of the least educated, and vice versa.
14. For more information on education, see the OECD publication *Education at a Glance*, and on personnel training, see statistics on in-service training reported annually by Statistics Finland.
15. The average educational level of the employees belonging to the occupation is, in other words, assumed to represent the skill requirements of that occupation. This method of defining overeducation dates back to Rumberger (1981a, 1981b) and Verdugo and Verdugo (1989). It is, however, by now a stylized fact that this measure produces lower estimates of overeducation than do more subjective measures derived from an explicit survey question on the educational attainment of individuals and the educational requirements to either obtain or perform their job.
16. Constant definition means that the threshold for being identified as overeducated is the same for 1995 as for 1975. Changing definition indicates, in turn, that the threshold for being overeducated differs for 1975 and 1995 due to changes over time in the mean and dispersion of the educational level of occupations.
17. The corresponding share was still close to 15 per cent in 1990.
18. As before, these samples are restricted to 16-65 year-old, full-year, full-time wage earners and salaried employees.

19. Individuals in other transition categories were excluded due to the fact that these categories were very heterogeneous, including students, housewives, permanently ill and people who died during the observation period. In our preliminary analyses, we did include these categories but it appeared that the background variables could not explain the probability of being selected into these groups. It seems, therefore, that these groups represent a fairly random sample in terms of observed characteristics in our data.
20. This result is in accordance with previous research in which labour turnover is found to be procyclical (see for example, Anderson and Meyer, 1994).
21. However, these results do not provide direct measures of the 'bumping down' effect and therefore indicate only indirectly the existence of this phenomenon in the Finnish labour market.
22. As before, a person is defined as being overeducated if his/her years of education are more than one standard deviation above the average years of education in his/her occupational group.

REFERENCES

Alba-Ramirez, A. (1993), 'Mismatch in the Spanish Labor Market: Overeducation?', *Journal of Human Resources* **27** (2), 259–278.

Anderson, B. and B.C. Meyer (1994), 'The Extent and Consequences of Job Turnover', *Brookings Papers: Microeconomics*, 177–248.

Battu, H., C.R. Belfield and P.J. Sloane (1997), *Overeducation Among Graduates: A Cohort View*, University of Birmingham and University of Aberdeen, mimeo.

Borghans, L., A. de Grip and P.J. Sloane (1998), 'Underutilisation of Skills, Bumping Down and Low Wages', in C. Lucifora, and W. Salverda (eds), *Policies for Low Wage Employment and Social Exclusion*, Milan: FrancoAngeli.

Cohn, E. and S. Kahn (1995), 'The Wage Effects of Overschooling Revisited', *Labour Economics* **2**, 67–76.

Duncan, G.J. and S.D. Hoffman (1981), 'The Incidence and Wage Effects of Overeducation', *Economics of Education Review* **1** (1), 57–86.

Groot, W. (1996), 'The Incidence of and Returns to Overeducation in the UK', *Applied Economics* **28**, 1345–1350.

Hartog, J. (1997), *On the Returns to Education: Wandering Along the Hills of ORU Land*, Keynote speech at the conference of the Applied Econometrics Association held in Maastricht, May 15–16, 1997.

Hartog, J. and H. Oosterbeek (1988), 'Education, Allocation and Earnings in the Netherlands: Overschooling?', *Economics of Education Review* **7** (2), 185–194.

Hersch, J. (1995), 'Optimal Mismatch and Promotions', *Economic Inquiry* **33**, 611–624.

Rumberger, R.W. (1981a), *Overeducation in the US Labor Market*, New York: Praeger.

Rumberger, R.W. (1981b), 'The Rising Incidence of Overeducation in the US Labor Market', *Economics of Education Review* **1** (3), 293–314.

Sicherman, N. (1991), 'Overeducation in the Labor Market', *Journal of Labor Economics* **9** (2), 101–122.

Sloane, P.J., H. Battu and P.T. Seaman (1995), *Overeducation, Undereducation and the British Labour Market*, University of Aberdeen and University of Dundee, mimeo.
Statistics Finland (1995), 'Economic Activity and Housing Conditions of the Population', *Population 1995* **6**, Helsinki.
Van der Velden, R.K.W. and M.S.M. van Smoorenburg (1997), *The Measurement of Overeducation and Undereducation: Self-report vs. Job Analyst Methods*. Paper presented at the Ninth Annual EALE Conference held in Aarhus, September 25–28, 1997.
Verdugo, R.R. and N.T. Verdugo (1989), 'The Impact of Surplus Schooling on Earnings: Some Additional Findings', *Journal of Human Resources* **24** (4), 629–643.

ACKNOWLEDGEMENTS

We want to thank Sinikka Littu and Eija Savaja for research assistance. Financial support from the Technology Development Centre (TEKES) is gratefully acknowledged.

4. Are British Workers Becoming More Skilled?

Francis Green, David Ashton, Brendan Burchell,
Bryn Davies and Alan Felstead

1 INTRODUCTION: THE IMPORTANCE OF SKILLS

Changing skills are at the heart of explanations and predictions of long-term economic growth in Britain, of conjectures about the reasons for increasing inequality and of discussion about the economic role of education and training. It is often claimed that technological changes, reinforced by changes in work organization, are in this present age biased towards raising the demand for high-skilled labour relative to low-skilled labour. Information technology, in particular, is pervasive through all industries, requiring masses of workers to acquire relevant skills or miss the economic boat. And, with the reported demise of assembly line 'Fordist' production methods in the advanced industrial world, it is commonly stated that greater proportions of workers are required to analyse and resolve problems and to exercise communication skills in their day-to-day work.

At the same time as, and partly driven by, the technological changes, the increasing global integration of the economy is also predicted to have an impact on skills. If firms based in the older industrialized countries – are to compete with firms drawing on cheap labour from areas not previously within the capitalist domain, notably China, then workers must become more skilled to keep their productivity advantage. Policies to raise educational standards, which in bygone days might have been desirable in themselves or for some social or political end, are now in effect economic policies (Reich, 1988; Marshall and Tucker, 1992).

These propositions should not, however, be taken as self-evidently true. It cannot simply be *assumed* that skills are on the increase in Britain, or that this is how British business has competed with some success over recent decades.

Indeed history tells us that, for many parts of the capitalist world, long stretches
of the 20th century have witnessed the decline of craft labour in the face of new
methods of 'scientific management', involving close control of detailed labour,
little discretion, and decreasing skill. Moreover, even global integration does not
necessarily call for an upskilling of the entire workforce. A possible scenario is
that Western firms maintain their advantage for substantial periods of time by
increasing their management efficiency, intensifying the effort but not necessarily the skill of the rank and file workers. Access to markets, political and
social stability, and automation can combine to mean that firms do not have to
raise continually the skills of their lower-ranked workers. Such a prospect would
indeed be worrying from the point of view of equality of opportunity. How then
can we come to understand the main skill trends in the modern era? The answer
lies in doing detailed theoretically-informed empirical studies. Because of the
centrality of skills to our knowledge of modern economies, it is important for
a detached scientific analysis to discover as much as possible about the levels
and types of skills used by British workers. Unfortunately, this is a field where
there is a great deal of conjecture but where the evidence hitherto is uncertain
and contested. This chapter presents first findings from a major new study of
skills in Britain, undertaken as part of a research programme entitled 'The
Learning Society', which is funded by the UK's Economic and Social Research
Council.

The chapter is unashamedly empirical, and concentrates on showing what
has been happening to skills demand in British workplaces since the mid-1980s.
In particular, it will examine:

- Has the usage of skills been increasing in Britain?
- If so, have some groups been increasing their work skills faster than others?
  Are there any identifiable groups whose work skills have been stagnating or
  even declining?
- How far are the qualifications which workers bring with them to the
  workplace actually being used at work?
- What types of work skills are changing?

2   WHAT DO WE ALREADY KNOW ABOUT SKILLS IN BRITAIN?

While it is not easy to define skills used at work, a common way of measuring
the skills of the workforce is by taking a look at their levels of educational
qualifications or, simply, the number of years of schooling. For example,

Britain's paucity of intermediate-level vocational qualifications has figured strongly in explanations of relatively low productivity (e.g. Mason and van Ark, 1993). Yet, taking educational attainment as the benchmark, it is easy to conclude that over the last decade or so, as also for much of the last century, the British workforce has been getting more skilled. Most remarkably, the propensity to stay on at school after legal compulsion has ended has risen substantially since the middle of the 1980s: the proportion of 16–18 year-olds in full-time education was only one in three in 1985/6, but by 1995/6 it had risen to 57 per cent. Correspondingly the proportion of 19–20 year-olds in higher education more than doubled from 12 per cent to 27 per cent. The proportion of the working age population that possesses some sort of qualification rose from 63 per cent to 80 per cent, while the proportion of degree holders went from 7 per cent to 12 per cent[1] – an expansion of the stock of qualifications in the workforce that is sure to continue as qualified cohorts replaced unqualified retirees. Some doubt may be raised as to whether the increase in participation is sufficient for economic purposes, if only because other countries too are raising both standards and participation, arguably faster (Green and Steedman, 1997).

It is also possible to be sceptical, and many are, about how far these new qualifications are always necessary or appropriate for the jobs that people later do. While it may be argued that graduates in 'non-graduate jobs' may nevertheless transform those jobs, this has yet to be proven on a wide scale. It has been strongly argued that at least part of the skills problem facing Britain has been a deficiency of demand for high-skilled labour, born of strategic decisions by many sections of British business to concentrate on comparatively low value-added processes and products with accompanying low-skill and low pay (Keep and Mayhew, 1996; Ashton and Green, 1996).

Indeed, Mannocorda and Robinson (1997) have argued persuasively that the rise in qualifications says nothing in itself about movements in job skills, suggesting that employers simply recruit more workers with qualifications if there are more such people available. Using data from the Labour Force Survey in 1984 and 1994, they argue that the increased qualifications are not concentrated in those occupations or sectors which might be expected to have rising skill requirements; rather the qualifications are spread broadly across the workforce. Moreover, after reviewing a small number of case studies, they could find little evidence of employers consciously raising the qualifications criteria for recruitment to jobs with increasing skill. One problem, however, with the use of case studies is that they covered only a small proportion of the workforce. Moreover, since a number of technological changes commonly discussed might be expected to pervade almost all areas – for example, information technology or changing work organization – one might expect to see new qualifications quite evenly spread if they were being used to match a rising skills demand. Finally, there are significant measurement problems with the LFS qualifications data on which the Mannacorda and Robinson study is obliged to rely (Bradley et al., 1997). For all these reasons, the issue remains open as to whether the general rise in qualifications reflects an upskilling of work in Britain.

A second way in which it is proposed that skills have risen is by looking at the changing proportions of employees in different occupations. Rising proportions of non-manual workers or alternatively of 'non-production' workers are typically interpreted as indicating increased skill levels. Indeed, it is widely observed that there are increasing proportions of managers in the workforce, and despite the fact that the declines in manual workers come mainly from the skilled groups (that is, craft workers) most advanced industrialized countries appear to experience an upward trend in the average occupational status. In a recent comparative analysis which impressively covers several countries and industries Machin and Van Reenen (1998) utilize *both* educational attainment *and* broad occupational classification as measures of skill. Their evidence is consistent with the hypothesis that technological and organizational changes are driving a widespread process of upskilling.

Nevertheless the occupational measure of skill trend has been contested by some social scientists, upon observation of the spread of scientific management techniques to non-manual workers. Changes in the nature of non-manual work have rendered many jobs as little more than routine, requiring low-skill levels, and resembling traditional manual work in all but the extent of physical strength required. While occupational titles may remain steady for decades the content of each occupation may be radically altered, leading to higher or even lower skills. What, for example, does being a 'manager' mean, and has not that meaning changed over the years? It is necessary not only to look at occupational titles but also at changes within each title.

One approach to this task has been to ask individual respondents to a survey whether they thought their work skills had increased or decreased or remained the same, compared to their jobs five years previously (Gallie, 1991). Such a question was asked in a survey, part of a research project entitled the 'Social Change and Economic Life Initiative' (SCELI), which was carried out in 1986. While 52 per cent reported an increase in skills, only 9 per cent reported a decrease. It appears that there was widespread upskilling within most occupational classes. One potential problem with this method is that it requires the individual to judge the change, and there may be a notable impetus from self-esteem to exaggerate increases and downplay any decreases. Moreover, individuals might interpret changes in the type of skills used at work as increases in skill, thereby masking possible skill losses. Though Gallie's evidence is suggestive of a genuine upskilling, it needs substantiation from methods less likely to be prone to upward subjective bias.

3 A NEW METHOD FOR EXAMINING SKILL TRENDS

In early 1997, a major new survey of employed people was conducted in Britain, which was designed to examine the skills actually used at work by all sections of the workforce. This survey – henceforth the 'Skills Survey' – had several purposes, one of which was to permit a new method to be used to examine skill trends. Occupation and educational attainment are of course included in the survey. In addition, however, some detailed questions about the skills people use at work enable a much more secure judgement to be made about work skill trends. The judgement is more secure because the measures refer to the skills actually used at work, and because there are a number of alternative measures that together can be used to build up a robust picture of the changes going on in the British economy.

For the examination of skill trends, two approaches were followed. In the first, and major, approach the idea was to ask identical questions on skills to those asked in the SCELI survey of 1986, referred to above. In the second approach the respondents to the Skills Survey were asked to state their use of particular skills both now and also five years ago. By comparing answers for the present with those for five years earlier a qualified judgement can be made about the trend in these particular skills between 1992 and 1997.

Consider first the method of comparing SCELI with the Skills Survey. Three types of question were included word for word identical in the two surveys (see Appendix). The first set were questions on qualifications, including what qualifications respondents *had*, what qualifications they would now require to *get* the same job and how necessary these qualifications are for *doing* the job competently. While qualifications held is a useful measure of the skills brought to the job by the individual, it is rather the level of qualification both required and necessary to do the job that is a closer measure of the actual skill involved in the job. A second type of question was to ask respondents how long a training was necessary for the type of work that they were doing. Third, respondents were asked how long it had taken (or would take) them to learn to do the job well. The presumption here was, simply, that high-skill jobs take a lot of learning, while jobs that can be picked up competently after a short time are not likely to be highly skilled. This measure of skill has a certain ambiguity, because it might be argued that a more highly educated person would be able to learn a job of given difficulty more quickly than a less educated person. Hence this skill measure has to be seen in conjunction with the other measures. Nevertheless it is an important measure if only because of the well-recognized role of job experience in inculcating work skills.

These questions lead to several measures of skill and skill trend (see next section) which can be used to build up a consistent picture, but they are far from perfect. In particular, they do not allow investigation of the types of skills used at work, nor of the competences of the individuals using them. The Skills Survey aimed to investigate many types of skills and competences, but the responses cannot be compared with SCELI which did not ask these questions. However, a subset of sixteen detailed questions was asked about the skills respondents exercised five years previously, assuming they were in employment at that time. This subset focused on the levels of usage of problem-solving skills, of communication and social skills, of manual skills and of computing skills. In each case respondents ranked on a 5-point scale how 'important' each detailed skill was in their work. This method, derived and adapted from standard job analysis procedures, seeks to obtain the workers' analyses of their own jobs quite separate from any judgement about how competent or effective they were at each skill. With each detailed skill, it is therefore possible to say if it has become more or less important in their jobs or remained at the same level. An aggregate picture can then be obtained of how each type of job skill has changed over five years. The picture is, however, incomplete, partly because it was not possible to ask about all kinds of skills and partly because a proportion (15.7 per cent) of respondents were not in work five years earlier.

An important issue concerns whether it is valid to deduce trends about Britain from a comparison of the two surveys. While the Skills Survey was designed to be representative of the whole of Britain, the larger SCELI sample was taken from six major urban areas. Nevertheless, the SCELI sample turns out to be broadly representative of Britain in several key respects, and it can be maintained that comparisons of the two surveys are therefore permissible. In the Appendix, more details are given about the ways that the two surveys were conducted.

4 THE FINDINGS

4.1 Skill Trends, Comparing 1997 with 1986

4.1.1 Qualifications held

The first trend to note is that many more of those in work in the Britain of 1997 hold some sort of qualification, compared to those in work eleven years earlier. Whereas in 1986 some 28 per cent of employed workers in the SCELI sample possessed no qualifications, by the time of the 1997 Skills Survey only 19 per cent had no qualifications. This trend parallels the trend in the qualifications of the population at large. Though important, the trend is entirely to be expected, given the increased educational participation of young people compared to that of workers from previous generations who have left the workforce in the intervening period.

4.1.2 Qualifications required

While qualifications held provides one useful measure of skills supplied by the workforce, it does not indicate, except indirectly and with possible inaccuracy, the skills demanded in the workplace. A better measure of the skill demanded is the qualification level that new recruits are required to have. On this measure, there has also been an increase in work skills (Table 4.1). Whereas 62 per cent of jobs required at least some qualifications in 1986, by 1997 this proportion had risen to 69 per cent. For 'High Level' qualifications (anything above A-level) the proportion rose from 20 per cent to 24 per cent. In fact, skill requirements rose at all levels of highest qualification except for NVQ3 where they dipped a bit.

4.1.3 Credentialism and qualifications 'used'

In this chapter we make a distinction between 'credentialism' and 'over-education'. Credentialism is where employers, for whatever reason, raise their qualifications requirements when recruiting even though the jobs to be done are unchanged. By contrast, where an individual acquires a qualification then gains a job that does not require that qualification for recruitment, the individual is defined as 'overeducated'.[2] Where credentialism occurs, there might be no rise in the prevalence of overeducation, even if the supply of qualifications rises while the usage of skills in jobs remains the same. While overeducation has been quite widely studied (e.g. Sloane et al., 1995), credentialism as defined above has so far received little attention. To investigate credentialism here, respondents were asked to respond on a 4-point scale as to how necessary were the qualifications, which were required of recruits, for doing the job. At each qualification level, a fall in the perceived necessity of the qualification would be indicative of credentialism at that level.

The trend differs according to position in the qualifications spectrum. For those jobs recruiting at level 2 – the equivalent of GCSE grades A to C – the extent to which that qualification is judged 'fairly necessary' or 'essential' has substantially increased, from 65 per cent to 72 per cent of job holders at that level (Table 4.1). At other levels, the perceived necessity for qualifications has slightly decreased. Thus, among those in 'high level' jobs the proportion who judged the qualification requirement to be 'fairly necessary' or 'essential' for actually doing the job fell from 81 per cent to 77 per cent.

Table 4.1   Qualifications required in Britain, 1986 and 1997

Qualification Level[a]	Highest qualification now required to get current job (% of all workers)		Required qualification is 'fairly necessary' or 'essential' to do the job (% of workers at each job Qualification Level)[b]	
	1986 %	1997 %	1986 %	1997 %
High Level	20.2	24.3	80.5	76.9
of which:				
degree	9.7	14.1	77.8	75.3
subdegree	10.5	10.2	82.8	79.2
Level 3	15.2	13.8	77.3	74.1
Level 2	18.5	21.2	64.7	71.7
Level 1	7.7	9.2	79.3	77.2
None	38.5	31.5	na	na

Notes:
[a]   Highest qualification level, ranked as National Vocational Qualification (NVQ) levels 1 to 5 equivalents. 'High Level' means everything above A-level; sub-degree means any of: Higher National Certificates or Higher National Diplomas (HNC/HND, or SHNC/SHND), or a nursing qualification, or a teaching or other professional qualification (e.g. law, medicine). Level 3 is roughly equivalent to A-level, Level 2 roughly equivalent to General Certificate of Secondary Education (GCSE) grades A-C, and Level 1 to GCSE grades D and below. All qualifications were precisely matched between surveys.
[b]   Where respondents indicated that qualifications were required of recruits to their current job, they assessed whether those qualifications were 'essential', 'fairly necessary', 'not really necessary' or 'totally unnecessary' to do the job competently.
In this and subsequent tables, the data have been weighted by a factor determined by the number of eligible respondents at each address visited and by a factor that takes account of the slight over-representation of females in the raw samples.

One good measure of skills 'used' in a job is the level of qualification which is *both* required of new recruits (now) *and* either 'essential' or 'fairly necessary' to do the job. On this score, there has also been a significant increase in skills: the proportions in jobs using (in the sense just described) degree level skills rose significantly from 7.5 per cent to 10.6 per cent (see Table 4.2, last row). This change suggests that the changes in the qualifications requirements are not just a case of pure credentialism by employers.

Table 4.2   The demand for qualifications in Britain, 1986 and 1997

Qualifications required	All		Males		Females	
	1986 %	1997 %	1986 %	1997 %	1986 %	1997 %
• Percentage of all workers in jobs where some qualifications are now required to get job	61.6	68.5	69.1	71.0	51.5	65.3
• Percentage of such workers for whom 'those'[a] qualifications are 'fairly necessary' or 'essential' to do job	74.8	74.8	75.4	73.7	73.8	76.2
• Percentage of all workers in jobs where degrees are required to get job now	9.7	14.1	12.8	15.2	5.5	12.8
• Percentage of such workers for whom a degree is 'fairly necessary' or 'essential' to do job[b]	77.8	75.3	77.4	73.7	86.8	81.8
• Percentage of all workers in jobs where degrees are *both* required *and* either 'fairly necessary' or 'essential' to do job[b]	7.5	10.6	9.8	11.1	4.4	10.0

Notes:
[a]   By 'those' is meant those qualifications named by each respondent as currently required of recruits.
[b]   See Table 4.1

4.1.4 Overeducation
Since 1986, an older cohort with fewer qualifications has been replaced by a more highly educated younger cohort. If the rise in qualifications held fails to keep up with qualifications demanded, there will result a period of skills

shortage. But if the supply of qualifications rises 'too fast', we are likely to observe more individuals in jobs for which they are overeducated.

The facts about overeducation are shown in Table 4.3. Row 1 shows the unsurprising finding that the proportion of workers with degrees has risen substantially. Row 2 shows, however, that there has been a reasonably good match between supply and demand. There has been only a small (statistically insignificant) rise in overeducation for degree holders. Nevertheless, with both surveys showing that about 3 out of 10 degree-holders are in jobs not requiring degrees, it might be suggested that the demand for degree-level skills remains chronically low. At the same time, however, many workers become 'undereducated' as skills demands rise, in that their formal qualifications would not now equip them to obtain the job they now hold and which they were appointed to in the distant past. The extent of this undereducation of employees in degree-requiring jobs (not shown in the table) fell from 47 per cent in 1986 to 39 per cent in 1997. Thus the overall impression is one of poor matching of qualifications supply and demand at the degree level.

Table 4.3   'Overeducation' of workers in Britain, 1986 and 1997

	1986 %	1997 %
• Per cent of all workers who have a degree	7.2	12.6
• Per cent of degree-holders in jobs where degrees are not required of recruits	30.2	31.6
• Per cent of all workers who have a sub-degree[a] but no degree	13.3	12.5
• Per cent of sub-degree holders in jobs where neither their qualification nor a degree is required of recruits	31.7	29.4
• Per cent of workers who have no qualifications	28.3	18.6
• Per cent of qualification-holding workers in jobs where no qualification is required	25.7	22.4

Note:
[a] See Table 4.1.

There is also interest in the further expansion of further education in Britain. Row 3 indicates that there has been no expansion in the proportions of workers holding highest qualifications just below degree level (but above A-level). Unsurprisingly, there has also not been a rise in the overeducation of this group (Row 4).

Finally, Row 5 shows that there has been an overall fall in the proportions of workers holding no qualifications at all. This fall broadly matches the fall in jobs demanding no qualifications recorded above (Table 4.1). The result is a small but statistically significant decrease in the overall extent of overeducation amongst those with any qualifications. In 1986, 25.7 per cent of those with a qualification were in jobs for which no qualification at all was demanded. By 1997 this proportion had fallen to 22.4 per cent.

It is necessary to add a minor health warning to these results concerning overeducation. The SCELI data on qualifications held were collected in a manner different both from that used by the Skills Survey, and from the methods used by the Labour Force Survey in 1986 and 1997. The figures are more reliable at either end of the skills spectrum; within the middle ranges, the levels of qualifications are sometimes fuzzy, and the grades and qualifications achieved are in most surveys of this nature, including the Labour Force Survey (LFS), less accurately reported. These matters are discussed in the Appendix. For this reason, Table 4.3 presents no figures concerning overeducation at intermediate levels.

4.1.5 Gender differentiation
The skills increases are much more pronounced for females than for males (Table 4.2). Although women remain behind men in terms of both qualifications required and degree qualifications 'used', they have caught up substantially. Whereas, for example, 71 per cent of men's jobs now require some qualification, up a little from 69 per cent in 1986, for women the proportions rose dramatically from 51 per cent to 65 per cent. That women's job skills appear to be converging on those of men is consistent with the long-term narrowing of the male/female wage differential, and is further evidence of increasing integration of women in the modern economy. Over 1985 to 1995 the male/female qualifications gap in the population of working age remained fairly steady (Murray and Steedman, 1998).

4.1.6 Training time and learning time measures
Let us consider now whether the upward trend in skill identified from the qualifications measures can be corroborated using other measures of skill. Table 4.4 shows that indeed they can. There has been a notable decrease from 66 per cent to 57 per cent in the proportion of workers whose type of work required only short (less than three months) training, and an increase from 22 per cent to 29 per cent in the proportion with long training requirements (over two years). Similarly there has been a fall from 27 per cent to 21 per cent in the proportion of jobs which respondents judge take only a short time (less than a month) to

'learn to do well'. The proportion taking more than two years did not significantly change overall, but for women there was a rise and for men a fall. In respect of all these measures, the skill levels of female workers have been catching up with those of male workers but still lag behind.

Table 4.4   Further measures of job skill trends

Qualifications required	All		Males		Females	
	1986 %	1997 %	1986 %	1997 %	1986 %	1997 %
Length of training for the type of work						
• less than 3 months	66.0	57.0	58.4	53.9	76.4	60.9
• more than 2 years	22.4	28.9	30.1	33.6	11.9	23.2
Time taken to learn to do job well (employees only)						
• less than 1 month	27.1	21.4	18.2	15.5	38.4	28.0
• more than 2 years	24.3	24.3	34.2	30.9	11.7	17.0

4.1.7 The young and the old

Hence, across almost all the measures of skill there is a consistent picture of aggregate upskilling, with job skills rising more for females than for males. The fact that different measures present a similar picture is reassuring, given the difficulties of precisely and uniquely defining what skill is.

An interesting question is whether the rapid expansion in the supply of well-educated young people joining the workforce in the last decade has been a very important driving factor in the upskilling of the workforce. If it were, one might expect to find upskilling concentrated mainly in the younger part of the workforce. Accordingly, Table 4.5 takes the six skill measures and splits the samples according to whether respondents are above or below 35 years of age.

They show that skills have increased as much or more in the older part of the workforce as in the young: for example, amongst older workers the proportions needing only a short time to learn their jobs fell from 29 per cent to 21 per cent, whereas for younger workers it fell from 25 per cent to 22 per cent. This finding is suggestive of the importance of demand-side changes being important, as these are likely to have had an impact on all age groups.

4.1.8 Occupations

As previously mentioned, a traditional way of measuring skill changes is through the changing proportions of higher-status (usually non-manual) occupations. The samples here show an increasing proportion of non-manual workers, especially managers and administrators who rose from 10.6 per cent to 14.4 per cent of the workforce (Table 4.6), consistent with the pattern of change shown in larger surveys such as the Labour Force Survey. Nevertheless a key question is whether skills have increased *within* each occupational group.

Table 4.5   Skill trends by age

	Under 35 years		35 years and older	
	1986 %	1997 %	1986 %	1997 %
Requiring some qualifications[a]	64.4	68.8	59.6	68.3
Using 'high level' qualifications[b]	14.7	15.8	16.5	20.1
With low prior training[c]	62.7	55.3	68.4	58.1
With high prior training[d]	24.3	28.4	21.0	29.2
With short time to learn job[e]	24.9	22.3	28.8	20.8
With long time to learn job[f]	21.7	19.2	26.3	27.8

Notes:
[a]   At least some qualifications required currently for new recruits to job.
[b]   'High level' qualifications (above A-level) both required and 'fairly necessary' or 'essential' to do job.
[c]   Type of work requires less than 3 months' prior training.
[d]   Type of work requires more than 2 years' prior training.
[e]   Job requires less than a month to learn to do it well; employees only.
[f]   Job requires more than 2 years to learn to do it well; employees only.

Table 4.7 presents the relevant data for all the six skill measures. Within every group the broad picture is for an increase in skills, although this does not apply for every measure and every occupation. Also, the sample size in several of the cells is quite small, and so for this table we also show results of tests of statistical significance for the differences between 1986 and 1997. Several of the differences do not establish statistically significant differences in the employed population. Nevertheless, there is a statistically significant rise in skill for every occupation according to at least one measure. Thus, for managers and administrators skills increase is signalled by longer learning times, while for plant and machine operators skills increase is signalled by lengthier prior training.

Table 4.6   Occupational structure in Britain, 1986 and 1997

	1986 %	1997 %
Managers & administrators	10.6	14.4
Professionals	9.9	10.3
Associate professionals & technicians	8.1	10.0
Clerical & secretarial occupations	16.9	16.8
Craft & related	17.8	13.0
Personal & protective service	10.5	10.5
Sales	6.8	7.2
Plant & machine operatives	10.5	11.0
Other occupations	8.2	6.8

4.1.9 Industries

The same cannot be said of every industrial sector. Table 4.8 examines the same skills measures according to industry, and finds that in most industries there is clear upskilling. There are, however, some notable exceptions. In the Wholesale industry there is a statistically significant fall in the proportions of workers in jobs that take over two years to learn. Other indicators for the Wholesale industry show only small and insignificant movements in skills. Another exception is the Health sector, where there is an increase in skill in that there are lower proportions requiring at most short training, but a decrease in skill in that there is a significant drop in the proportions of workers in jobs that take over two years to learn. Neither of these industries is directly exposed to the forces of global economic integration. If the latter is driving the skill increases in internationally exposed industries, it would be predicted that the less-exposed industries would have a smaller skills increase or even a decrease in skills as a result of displaced unskilled workers moving to those sectors. Nevertheless, other industries partly protected from trade also had skills increases – for example, Education. The stagnating or even falling skills in the Wholesale industry and the mixed picture in Health can only be fully explained by a more detailed industry analysis, taking into account, for example, the transformation of contractual arrangements in the National Health Service.

Table 4.7   Skill trends by occupation

Occupation	requiring any qualifi- cations	using degrees	with low prior training	with high prior training	with short time to learn job	with long time to learn job
	%	%	%	%	%	%
Managers						
& administrators				**	*	
1986	78.8	13.0	55.9	28.8	14.5	32.1
1997	78.5	17.0	51.8	32.4	5.8	39.5
Professionals			**	**		
1986	97.2	45.4	46.5	36.7	6.7	49.8
1997	98.2	49.9	32.2	54.1	5.7	51.5
Associate professionals						
& technicians		**	*		**	
1986	86.3	11.9	41.3	41.0	13.0	39.7
1997	89.6	20.4	34.4	43.9	5.7	36.7
Clerical & secretarial						
occupations		**	**	**		
1986	78.4	1.2	72.0	11.4	21.1	10.1
1997	81.4	3.0	65.2	17.1	19.6	9.4
Craft & related			**	**	**	
1986	68.1	1.5	54.1	36.2	15.2	39.7
1997	72.3	1.9	42.1	45.3	7.3	41.1
Personal & pro-						
tective service	**	*	**	**	**	
1986	33.2	0	77.0	14.0	48.1	16.4
1997	59.1	0.9	55.5	23.4	30.3	14.1
Sales occupations			**	*		*
1986	31.7	1.8	89.0	6.3	49.0	7.6
1997	37.6	1.4	81.7	11.9	44.5	3.5
Plant & machine						
operatives				*		
1986	41.9	0.4	80.7	10.1	36.1	16.8
1997	43.1	0	77.8	15.5	38.3	13.3
Other occupations						**
1986	16.1	0.9	92.8	4.2	63.4	2.0
1997	20.3	0	89.4	7.2	58.9	6.0

Notes: Significance levels for difference between 1986 and 1997: * =10%, **=5%.
Other notes: See Table 4.5.

Table 4.8   Skill trends by industry

Industry	requiring any qualifi- cations %	using degrees %	with low prior training %	with high prior training %	with short time to learn job %	with long time to learn job %
Manufacturing		**	**	**		
1986	60.7	5.3	66.1	23.0	23.5	24.4
1997	64.5	9.5	56.9	29.9	19.6	26.0
Construction	**			**		**
1986	67.8	3.6	52.9	39.8	25.1	44.6
1997	77.4	2.0	42.2	46.6	5.3	51.7
Wholesale						**
1986	46.1	2.3	80.3	13.9	34.0	16.1
1997	43.0	1.3	77.4	14.2	34.2	11.7
Hotels	**	*	**	**		
1986	27.2	0.7	86.3	4.0	53.6	9.5
1997	57.0	3.9	70.1	14.9	43.1	16.2
Transport		*		**	**	
1986	63.3	2.9	71.0	12.5	27.8	14.3
1997	67.3	6.5	68.1	21.2	18.6	20.6
Finance		**				
1986	82.1	4.0	53.5	29.9	11.9	20.2
1997	86.7	11.2	42.6	39.8	10.6	24.8
Real estate	**		**	**	**	
1986	66.4	12.7	64.9	24.0	31.3	24.1
1997	79.2	16.9	52.3	33.8	20.8	25.5
Public admini- stration	**		**			**
1986	74.2	6.2	59.9	24.6	17.6	36.5
1997	85.4	10.0	48.9	32.7	14.4	18.1
Education	**	**	**	**	**	**
1986	69.3	28.1	61.8	21.2	30.0	30.9
1997	86.4	40.5	51.9	31.2	16.1	40.0
Health			*			*
1986	68.2	7.1	53.4	32.1	22.0	28.2
1997	70.8	9.8	45.4	34.5	24.5	21.8
Other community	**	*	**	**	**	**
1986	49.8	4.2	71.4	19.7	53.0	9.2
1997	65.3	10.4	51.1	31.0	23.6	34.7

Notes: Industries with less than 100 valid observations have been excluded from this analysis. Significance levels for difference between 1986 and 1997: * =10%, **=5%.
Other notes: See Table 4.5.

4.1.10 Pockets of credentialism and of increasing overeducation

Earlier we showed that, in aggregate, the rise in required qualifications could not be dismissed simply as credentialism with no changes in skills used. Further confirmation of this conclusion derives from the finding that the other measures of skills also showed increases in aggregate and the same pattern according to gender. These other measures capture different aspects of skill which are nevertheless related to qualifications requirements. Thus, the Spearman rank correlation coefficient between required qualification level and learning time works out at 0.52 for 1986 and 0.46 for 1997. The correlation coefficients of qualifications level required with the training time requirement were 0.45 for 1986 and 0.43 for 1997. All these correlations were highly significant ($p = 0.00$). There was also a positive correlation observed at the industry level, between the change in average qualification requirement and either the change in learning time or the change in training time requirement. In other words, those industries which had a greater than average increase in qualifications required tended to have above average skills increases according to the other measures. Together, these findings lead us to reject the notion that all the qualifications rise in Britain has done is to feed a pure credentialism or generate more overeducation.

Nevertheless, this conclusion does not exclude there being some sectors in which credentialism is important. We analysed the data by sector and by occupation in search of patterns consistent with the case studies discussed by Manacorda and Robinson (1997) and for other possible areas of credentialism.

One area cited by Manacorda and Robinson is sales assistants, as an instance of rising qualifications but no skill increase. In respect of sales occupations in our data there is a tendency for qualifications held to outrun demand. As a result, amongst those in sales occupations holding any qualifications in 1986, 61 per cent were in jobs with some sort of qualification requirement; by 1997 this figure had fallen significantly to 52 per cent. Nevertheless, there was no significant change in the level of necessity with which these qualifications were regarded. Hence, for this group we conclude that there was an element of increasing overeducation, but there is no evidence of credentialism.

Another area to which Manacorda and Robinson draw attention is the deployment of clerical workers, especially in the financial sector. However, we could find no evidence of increasing overeducation or of credentialism for clerical workers. A slightly higher proportion of workers in clerical occupations with degrees were in jobs for which degrees were not required (46 per cent in 1997 compared with 40 per cent in 1986). However, the difference is not statistically significant owing to the small numbers in the cell. Therein lies a salient point: even if this difference were confirmed with a larger sample, the particular group of clerical workers with unnecessary degrees, though seen as an instance of under-use of skills, remains only a small fraction of the labour force. It is unsafe to make general conclusions from the experience of this group.

One sector where credentialism is apparent is in the Real Estate industry. There were significant falls in the extent to which required qualifications were deemed necessary or essential, at NVQ levels 1 and 3, and at degree level. The figures were: from 74 per cent to 39 per cent at NVQ1, from 85 per cent to 58 per cent at NVQ3 and from 83 per cent to 56 per cent at degree level. These declines do not mean that skills were falling in the Real Estate industry. As Table 4.8 shows, skills were increasing according to the other measures. Rather it suggests that there was a parallel process of formalization of qualification requirements by employers in this industry which exceeded those judged necessary by many job-holders.

While our data showed no other industries with significant declines in the necessity of qualifications requirements, it must be noted that, especially in the less numerically important industries, the relatively small numbers in each cell do not permit strong tests for significant differences between 1986 and 1997: there are some other cases where necessity levels fell, but insignificantly given the small numbers. No strong argument can be made in these instances.

4.2 Trends in Particular Job Skills, 1992-97

While this chapter has presented a consistent picture of upskilling according to all measures used, the broad character of those measures does not permit any understanding of the sorts of skills which are increasingly in demand. As stated above, it was possible with the Skills Survey to examine such trends over a shorter period of five years, for a selective range of skills. Four categories of skill were selected on the basis of widespread commentary on the changing nature of jobs. First, problem-solving skills and computing skills are both said to be increasingly required by incoming technology. Furthermore, if workers are being increasingly given more scope, being empowered, or required to take on multiple tasks, problem-solving again becomes more important. Similarly, with the delayering of management it is frequently argued that workers have to communicate more with other workers, or with clients or suppliers. In all these areas, it is hypothesized that increased skills are required. By contrast, in parallel with the decline in manual occupations, it is arguable that with increasing automation there is a decreasing need for manual skills.

The findings, shown in Table 4.9, are remarkably consistent with those suggested above. For all problem-solving skills, communication and social

Table 4.9   Type of work skill changes in Britain 1992 to 1997

Skill type	Increasing[a]	Decreasing[a]	Average change[b]	Average change[b] for low paid[c]
	%	%	%	%
Problem-Solving Skills				
Spotting problems or faults	34.6	20.4	0.25	0.12
Working out the causes of problems or faults	36.7	20.2	0.29	0.10
Thinking of solutions to problems or faults	34.1	19.9	0.25	0.06
Analysing complex problems in depth	39.3	18.6	0.37	0.04
Communication and Social Skills				
Dealing with people	34.7	12.6	0.34	0.26
Instructing, training or teaching people	46.7	17.3	0.62	0.47
Making speeches or presentations	31.9	12.4	0.27	0.20
Persuading or influencing others	36.4	21.8	0.25	−0.01
Selling a product or service	29.4	20.1	0.20	0.04
Counselling, advising or caring for customers or clients	36.9	24.6	0.45	0.57
Working with a team of people	34.9	27.8	0.27	0.15
Manual Skills				
Physical strength	20.7	27.3	−0.12	0.10
Physical stamina	20.2	31.0	−0.20	−0.24
Skill or accuracy in using hands or fingers	23.1	29.0	−0.10	−0.26
Computing Skills				
Using a computer, PC, or other types of computerized equipment	42.0	10.4	0.63	0.14
Level of computer usage[d]	29.2	6.1	0.27	−0.01

Notes:
[a]   Work skills were self-assessed by job-holders against the 5-point scale: 'Essential/ Very Important/ Fairly Important/ Not very important/ Not at all important or does not apply'. A skill increase (decrease) is defined as a move up (down) one or more points of this scale between 1992 and 1997.
[b]   Calculated as the average number of places moved up or down the skill response scale. A positive means a skill increase, while a negative means a skill decrease.
[c]   Bottom quintile of gross hourly pay.
[d]   Assessed on a scale: 'Straightforward/Moderate/Complex/Advanced', using examples.
The base is all those who were in employment both in 1997 at the date of interview and five years earlier.

skills, as also for computing skills, the proportions of respondents reporting a higher level in 1997 than they reported for their jobs five years previously substantially exceed those reporting lower levels. For example, 32 per cent reported increases in importance of making speeches or presentations, while just 12 per cent reported a decrease. For computing skills, not only is there a balance showing a higher level of importance of computer usage, there is also an increase in the reported level of sophistication of usage.

If each move up or down the skill scale is counted as one, the average change of position can also be calculated (see third column of Table 4.9). This too is positive for all these skills. By contrast, in the case of all three physical skills there is a significant decrease in their usage, both in terms of the balance of increasing versus decreasing importance and in terms of the average change.

It might be argued that such skill changes merely reflect ageing of the sample rather than a shift in the skills of the workforce as a whole. There is indeed some tendency for most skills to rise between the 20–24 age bracket and the 25–29 age bracket. However, beyond that all the skills showed no significant upward link with age, and some downward link beyond 55. To confirm that the upskilling results are not just a matter of ageing, the same exercise was carried out as shown in Table 4.9 except for those over 30, thereby excluding those under 25 in 1992. This exercise showed similar upskilling across problem-solving, communication and social skills and computing skills.

In further analyses not shown here we explored these changes a little further. First, an analysis by gender showed that on average both males and females in the sample had experienced rises in problem-solving skills, in communication and social skills and in computing skills, while manual skills were decreasing in importance. Second, it was found that some of the skill changes were more marked among those who had changed jobs in the course of the five years compared to those who had stayed with the same employer. Nevertheless, the opposite was true for other skills. There was no obvious pattern, and it was evident that skill change happens in general as much within jobs over time as for people moving jobs.

4.3 Who is Missing Out?

While the overall picture of skill change in Britain shows an upward movement, and while most groups have benefited in some way (with the exception of the two industries mentioned – Wholesale and Health), the movement of the average may conceal the possibility that a substantial minority of individuals are losing skills or missing out on the general improvement. Many people lost skills whether or not they were in a different job compared to five years earlier. That these people were in a minority ought not to lessen concern for the issue, in so far as it is a widespread declared policy objective to attempt to develop a 'learning society'. While a learning society has a range of dimensions, and while it has been variously defined, we take it here that a necessary condition for a learning society is that lifelong learning should be universally available and broadly experienced. In that light it will be of interest to see whether those who fail to increase their skills are concentrated in any particular sector of society.

Table 4.10 Exclusion from skill rises

	Proportions excluded from skill rises, 1992–1997[*] %
All	15.9
Male	15.0
Female	16.9
Full-Time to Part-Time	30.3
Part-time to Part-Time	20.6
Full-Time to Full-Time	14.3
Part-Time to Full-time	4.7
Self-Employed in 1997	21.9
Employed in 1997	15.1
Aged Under 50	13.4
Aged 50 and Over	25.0
Remained in lower occupation	22.3
Remained in other community industry	28.2
Remained in manufacturing industry	11.7

Note:
[*] To be excluded from a skill rise, an individual must have experienced neither a rise in the sum total of problem-solving skills, nor a rise in the sum total of communication and social skills, nor a rise in the importance of using a computer, PC, or other types of computerized equipment in his/her job. See Tables 4.9 to 4.11 for definitions of problem-solving, and of communication and social skills.

For this purpose we focus on problem-solving skills, communication and social skills and the use of computers (see Table 4.9), these being the key skills that have been found to be generally increasing. To obtain a simple picture of exclusion from skill change, we devised a straightforward indicator as follows. First, we sum the individual elements of changes in problem-solving skills and communication/social skills, to obtain two measures: the total change in problem-solving skills and the total change in communication/social skills. It is then assumed that an individual participating in a skills transformation must experience an increase in either of these types of skill, or in the importance of computer-usage in their jobs. If none of these skill rises is experienced, the individual is deemed to have been 'excluded from skill rises'. While this is a somewhat crude index of skill exclusion, it is nevertheless quite strong. Any individual caught by this definition is failing to progress on any of several fronts thought to be important in modern industry. Table 4.10 indicates that nearly 16 per cent of workers in 1997 were excluded according to this definition.[3]

Table 4.10 also allows us to identify those more likely to lose out. They are those in part-time jobs (especially those who switched from full-time to part-time), those self-employed in 1997, those over 50 years of age, those who remained between 1992 and 1997 in one of the lower status occupations and those who remained in the 'Other Community' industry. Those remaining in Manufacturing were less likely than the average to be excluded. However, the difference between males and females is small and insignificant.[4]

In future work with the Skills Survey, it is intended to identify the important determinants of skills. For the present, it is worth noting an important if unsurprising finding: those respondents who have missed out on lifelong learning to the extent that their skills are not rising are disproportionately concentrated in the lowest quintile group of hourly pay. Another way of seeing this connection focusing on the particular types of skills, is shown in the final column of Table 4.9. This column indicates that, for all but one of the various problem-solving, communication, social, and computing skills, the average rise in skill is lower for those in the bottom pay quintile than for the rest of the population. One can safely conclude that deprivation of skill increase is a correlate of low pay.

4.4 Low skills and low pay

Moreover, preliminary analysis confirms that pay and skills as defined in this chapter are related in the manner expected by economic theory. Two aspects of the trend in hourly pay bear out this correlation: the convergence of males' and females' pay, and the sharply increasing inequality of pay among females.

According to the SCELI and SS data, the average gross hourly pay of males was 1.55 that of females in 1986, but the gap narrowed to 1.42 by 1997. This trend is consistent with findings from other data sources. It is also consistent with our finding that, according to all measures common to SCELI and SS, women's work skills were catching up on men's skills but still lagged behind in 1997.

The second aspect of the hourly pay trend is increasing inequality within each gender. This finding also mirrors those of many others, based on larger data sets and over a range of periods within recent decades. As measured by the ratio of the 90th to 10th percentiles, inequality in our samples rose between 1986 and 1997 from 3.17 to 3.40 among males, and rose even more sharply from 2.67 to 3.30 among females.

A picture of changing inequality in skills is given in Table 4.11, which focuses on the experience of the lowest paid quintile compared to the rest of the population. It may be observed that, amongst men, the lowest paid quintile experienced skill rises of orders of magnitude comparable with those gained by the rest of the male population, according to all the measures used. Amongst women, however, the lowest quintile experienced comparatively smaller skill rises (as measured both by the proportions in jobs with no qualifications required and by the proportions in jobs with short learning times), than the whole population of females. This contrast between men and women is consistent with the observation (above) that inequality increased more for women than men. Nevertheless, this connection is no more than suggestive of a possible explanation for the changing inequality. The question remains as to how much, if any, of the changes in men's and women's pay inequality can be accounted for by changes in the distribution of human capital. This topic is the subject of future research.

Table 4.11 Changing skills of the lowest paid quintile, males and females

	1986 bottom quintile %	1986 all %	1997 bottom quintile %	1997 all %
Males				
In jobs requiring no qualifications	55.3	31.0	51.5	28.7
Holding no qualifications	40.3	25.5	29.2	17.7
With low prior training[a]	77.4	58.5	69.2	53.9
With short time to learn job[a]	34.7	18.2	36.8	15.5
Females				
In jobs requiring no qualifications	75.8	48.5	65.5	34.1
Holding no qualifications	48.8	32.0	43.6	19.8
With low prior training[a]	90.5	76.3	77.1	60.9
With short time to learn job[a]	61.9	38.4	55.9	28.0

Note: [a] See Table 4.5 for definitions.

5 CONCLUSIONS

Whether the usage of skills in British industry is increasing or not, and if so by how much and for what kinds of employees, is a matter of fundamental importance both for economic efficiency and for equality of opportunity. This chapter has presented some early findings from a study of skill trends, employing a new methodology designed to examine skills actually used at work rather than just the qualifications attained by the population. The findings show a consistent pattern of increasing skills used in Britain, deploying several different measures of skills. In the aggregate, jobs in 1997 compared to jobs in 1986 are more likely to require qualifications (including high level qualifications) for recruitment and broadly no less likely to need those qualifications to be used in the work. The 1997 jobs are also less likely to require very short periods of training and more likely to require very long periods of training, less likely to need only a short time to acquire proficiency and more likely to need a very long time to gain proficiency.

One consequence of the rising demand for skills is that there is no evidence of substantially rising 'overeducation'. While a greater proportion of the workforce now has a degree or better, so too a greater proportion of jobs are demanding degrees. Moreover, at least in the eyes of the job-holders (who might know best but might show bias) there is no substantial rise in the extent to which employers are demanding qualifications for the sake of it, perhaps just to ration jobs or to screen for other characteristics. Credentialism did, however, appear to be taking place in the Real Estate industry and we cannot rule out that there may be other pockets of credentialism elsewhere in the economy. We hardly need add that these findings are retrospective. Recent increases in educational participation are sure to feed through to further increases in the supply of qualifications, even if there is no further rise in participation; it remains to be seen whether the increased supply will continue to be used by employers.

Equally remarkable is the finding that women are catching up on men. Back in 1986 most measures of skill saw the average female worker lagging some way behind the average male worker. Since then, while males have increased their job skills by a small amount, females have raised theirs by substantially more and are converging on those of males.

We now also know something about the types of skill change that are taking place. Comparing 1997 with 1992, at least for the large majority of the workforce that have stayed in employment, there has been on balance an increased usage of problem-solving skills, of communication and social skills, and of computing skills, and at the same time a reduction in the use of manual skills.

While there are of course, many individuals whose job skills have not improved or have even deteriorated, are there any identifiable groups that have lost out? Perhaps surprisingly, there are no major occupational groups that have not experienced skill increases of some sort between 1986 and 1997. At both ends of the occupational spectrum there is evidence of rising skills. To this extent one cannot deduce that there has been a polarization of the workforce – a conclusion at odds with previous findings based on the analysis of the SCELI survey in 1986. Inclusive access to skills augmentation and the ability to use new skills at work is a necessary (though not sufficient) ingredient of what might be envisaged as a 'learning society'. The findings here are optimistic in this respect but they apply, it should be remembered, only to those in employment. Nothing has been said about skill acquisition for those out of employment. Moreover, the learning society embraces much more than just the world of work.

Other findings have cast a less optimistic light on changes in the system. There are the Wholesale and the Health industries, both among the industries relatively protected from international competition, which have shown virtual stagnation in skills since 1986.

Second, even among those individuals in employment both in 1992 and 1997, there remains a substantial minority who have not been able to benefit from skill rises. One's chances of exclusion are significantly raised for part-timers, the self-employed, those in their fifties, and those remaining in lower occupations.

Exclusion from increases in skills matters, if only because of the link with pay and other work rewards. Those in the lowest pay quintile have experienced the lowest skill rises and are more likely to have had skill falls. According to our main measures of skill, the link is strong. For example, those in jobs using qualifications beyond A-level currently receive on average some 63 per cent more pay than those in other jobs, while those in jobs where it takes more than two years to learn to do it well are getting 59 per cent more pay than those in jobs learnt more quickly. In terms of particular skills, jobs where computing skills are 'very important' or 'essential' carry a premium of 44 per cent, and for the skill of 'persuading and influencing people' the premium is 52 per cent. These various measures of skill are overlapping, and one line of future research will be to examine the pay impact of each skill when a number of measures are considered simultaneously, and controlling for other influences on pay. A further line of research will focus on the respective roles that education, training and work experience play in determining the levels of particular skills achieved by respondents to the Skills Survey.

APPENDIX

Table 4A.1 Comparison of SCELI with LFS 1986

	SCELI (1986) %	LFS (Spring 1986) %
Age		
20–29	28.0	28.5
30–39	31.1	27.2
40–49	23.6	24.3
50–60	17.2	19.9
Employment status		
Employee	90.6	88.2
Self-employed	9.4	11.8
Ethnicity		
White	97.9	96.6
Black	1.4	1.1
Asian	0.3	1.8
Other	0.3	0.5
Working Time		
Full-time	78.5	80.2
Part-time	21.5	19.8
Industry (SIC 80)		
Agriculture	1.3	2.0
Energy	3.5	2.8
Extraction	2.5	3.5
Metal goods	15.3	10.9
Other manufacturing	10.2	10.1
Construction	6.1	7.2
Distribution	18.1	18.5
Transport	5.7	6.3
Banking	8.3	9.9
Other services	28.9	28.8
Social Class		
Professional	4.8	5.4
Intermediate	26.4	26.3
Skilled Non-Manual	21.5	22.5
Skilled Manual	22.8	24.1
Partly Skilled	18.6	15.7
Unskilled	5.7	5.1
Armed Forces	–	0.9

Note: For comparison purposes, the LFS86 sample was restricted to 20–60-year-olds in employment, located in Great Britain.

Comparing results from one data set with those from another rests on the assumption that both sets are representative of the British population. It is important therefore to note the differences between SCELI and the Skills Survey. SCELI's aims were wider, consisting of several surveys only one of which was concerned with work. SCELI also had a wider focus than the Skills Survey in that it sampled the workforce as a whole rather than just those in employment. For the purposes of the comparisons made in this chapter, only those in employment between ages 20 and 60 were examined.

The geographical coverage of the two data sets also requires comment. SCELI was based on data from six labour markets – Aberdeen, Coventry, Kirkcaldy, Northampton, Rochdale and Swindon. All, apart from Aberdeen, represented a Travel-To-Work Area, a geographical area in which most of the population worked and lived. The six areas were selected to give a range of patterns of economic change, and were not necessarily designed to be representative of Britain in 1986. The Skills Survey, on the other hand, was indeed designed to be a nationally representative sample survey of the employed population in Britain in 1997. There were also other technical differences, concerning the procedures for selection of addresses for sampling, and the method of data collection. However, in both surveys the main method of data collection for the relevant questions on skills was through face-to-face interview.

Despite these differences, it can be maintained that SCELI does provide a broadly representative picture of Britain in 1986 (e.g. Marsh and Vogler, 1994) and that by design the Skills Survey is representative of Britain in 1997. We allowed in the SCELI/SS comparisons, by use of a weighting factor, for the fact that both samples slightly over-represented females. Using the same weights, Table 4A.1 compares SCELI with the Labour Force Survey in 1986, along several other key socio/economic dimensions. The table indicates that the SCELI sample is fairly close to the LFS sample according to age, ethnicity, employment status, full-time/part-time status and social class. There appears to be a small under-representation of those over 50 and of the self-employed in SCELI, and something of an over-representation of the partly-skilled (by just under three percentage points).

These differences are unlikely to be large enough to vitiate the trends discussed in the chapter, but need to be borne in mind. As regards industrial spread, SCELI has an over-representation of respondents working in the metal goods manufacturing industries. It is not surprising that some degree of unrepresentativeness arises in respect of industry, given the geographical concentration of the sample. Nevertheless, all other industries are represented in proportions quite close to those in the LFS.

With regard to the categorization of qualification levels, Skills Survey respondents were offered the same set of qualifications options in exactly the same order as had SCELI respondents eleven years before. However, the qualification options were amended to include National Vocational Qualifications (NVQs) and General National Vocational Qualifications (GNVQs) which were not available in the mid-1980s. Unfortunately it is not possible to map the responses given exactly onto today's NVQ hierarchy which ranges from Level I to Level V (see Felstead, 1997 for more detail). Instead, this chapter uses approximate NVQ levels when reporting qualifications required to get jobs, as described in the notes to Table 4.1.

It is necessary to record a potential problem concerning the measurement of qualifications held. In the Skills Survey, respondents were asked to name up to three qualifications, starting with the highest – essentially the method used in the Labour Force Survey. In SCELI, however, data on qualifications held was collected as part of the work history part of the survey. They were first asked whether they had gained any qualifications by age 14, and then asked about qualifications gained at subsequent dates. In principle, this should result in accurate information about the highest qualification received but it is possible that it would arrive at a slightly different answer in some cases, compared with the LFS-type procedure. A further complication is that, since the coding of qualification categories differs from that used by the LFS, it is problematic to use the LFS as a check on the accuracy of the SCELI qualifications data. The coding comparisons are simplest at either end of the skills spectrum: for those with degrees or sub-degree qualifications, and for those with no qualifications. For those with middle level qualifications, the classification of categories was difficult to compare.

A recent study has shown, however, that there are notable shortcomings in the qualifications data collected by the LFS (Bradley et al, 1997). The major problem concerns the prevalence of proxy interviewing: this is most prevalent among young people, and more common among males than females. Many parents were found to under-report their children's qualifications. Fortunately, the Skills Survey did not use proxy interviewing, and hence avoids the main problem. However, an additional problem was that even some of those interviewed in person tended to mis-report the grades achieved, especially for lower level qualifications. For these reasons, our study in the main text of over-education concentrated on those with higher-level qualifications, and on those with at least some qualifications (where there was no issue about their level).

As can be seen from Table 4A.2, compared with the LFS, SCELI under-represents people with degrees by 2.1 percentage points, and also under-represents those with no qualifications by 4.2 percentage points. For the above reasons this comparison does not imply that the SCELI data are inaccurate in this respect. It is possible that the SCELI method of collecting qualifications data is more accurate than the LFS data. In particular, Bradley et al. (1997) showed that the LFS does tend, because of the proxy interviewing problem, to overestimate the proportions of workers with no qualifications.

Finally, the relevant skills questions asked with identical wording, emphases and response categories in SCELI and in SS were:

- If they were applying today, what qualifications, if any, would someone need to *get* the type of job you have now?
- How necessary do you think it is to possess those qualifications to *do* your job competently?
- Since completing full-time education, have you ever had, or are you currently undertaking, training for the type of work that you currently do? If YES: How long, in total, did (or will) that training last?
- How long did it take for you after you first started doing this type of job to learn to do it well?

Table 4A.2 Comparison of data on qualifications held

Proportions with:	SCELI (1986) %	LFS (Spring 1986) %
Degrees	7.2	9.3
Sub-degrees	13.3	13.9
No Qualifications	28.3	32.5

Notes: see Table 4.1

NOTES

1. Department for Education and Employment, *Education Statistics 1996*, HMSO; and *Training Statistics 1996*, HMSO.
2. Some writers use the term 'credentialism' more generally to include an increase in over-education; we prefer to use the term in the above more precise sense.
3. But note again that those not in employment five years earlier are not counted in this calculation.
4. These conclusions have also been investigated in a multivariate analysis using a logit specification: all hold as independent effects.

REFERENCES

Ashton, D. and F. Green (1996), *Education, Training and the Global Economy*, Cheltenham: Edward Elgar.

Bradley, M., I. Knight and M. Kelly (1997), *Collecting Qualifications Data in Sample Surveys – A Review of the Methods Used in Government Surveys*, Research Paper RS10, Department for Education and Employment.

Felstead, A. (1997), 'Unequal Shares for Women? Qualification Gaps in the National Targets for Education and Training', in H. Metcalf (ed.), *Half Our Future: Women, Skill Development and Training,* London: Policy Studies Unit.

Gallie, D. (1991), 'Patterns of Skill Change: Upskilling, Deskilling or the Polarization of Skills?' *Work, Employment and Society* **5** (3), 319–51.

Green, A. and H. Steedman (1997), *Into the Twenty First Century: An Assessment of British Skill Profiles and Prospects,* London: LSE, Centre for Economic Performance.

Keep, E. and K. Mayhew (1996), 'Evaluating the Assumptions that Underlie Training Policy', in A. Booth and D. Snower (eds), *Acquiring Skills. Market Failures, their Symptoms and Policy Responses,* Cambridge: Cambridge University Press.

Machin, S. and J. Van Reenen (1998), 'Technology and Changes in Skill Structure: Evidence From Seven OECD Countries', *Quarterly Journal of Economics* **113** (4), 1215–44.

Manacorda, M. and P. Robinson (1997), *Underskilled or Overqualified? Qualifications, Occupations and Earnings in the British Labour Market*, paper presented to the LoWER Conference, Centre for Economic Performance, LSE, December 12–13.

Marsh, C. and C. Vogler (1994), 'Economic Convergence: a Tale of Six Cities', in D. Gallie, C. Marsh and C. Vogler (eds), *Social Change and the Experience of Unemployment*, Oxford: Oxford University Press.

Marshall, R. and M. Tucker (1992), *Thinking for a Living*, New York: Basic Books.

Mason, G. and B. Van Ark (1993), 'Productivity, Machinery and Skills in Engineering: an Anglo-Dutch Comparison', *National Institute of Economic and Social Research Discussion Paper* (New Series 36).

Murray, A. and H. Steedman (1998), *Growing Skills in Europe: the Changing Skills Profiles of France, Germany, the Netherlands, Portugal, Sweden and the UK*, London School of Economics, Centre for Economic Performance, Discussion Paper 399.

Reich, R.B. (1988), *Education and the Next Economy,* Washington, DC: National Education Association.

Sloane, P., H. Battu and P. Seaman (1995), *Overeducation, Undereducation and the British Labour Market*, Working Paper 95-09, University of Aberdeen.

PART TWO

Causes of Underutilization

5. Overeducation and Crowding Out of Low-skilled Workers

Joan Muysken and Bas ter Weel

1 INTRODUCTION

When Gottschalk (1997) discusses the increase in income inequality in the Nordic countries, the Netherlands, France and Japan in the late 1980s and early 1990s, he observes that 'the relatively small increase in inequality in the Netherlands reflects a decline in the college premium, which largely offsets the substantial increase in inequality between experience groups and the increase in inequality within groups.' And this decline is due to 'the large increase in the supply of college workers' while this 'supply shift' is not further explained (pp. 34–35). He observes a similar phenomenon for Sweden.

The Swedish situation is presented by Topel (1997), who shows a sharp decrease in the college premium from the late1960s onwards, and again a small increase after the mid-1980s. Male school enrolment also drops sharply in the early 1970s 'which shows that college enrolments do respond to declining returns to schooling' (p. 69). However, Topel does not comment on the much greater increase in school enrolment in the late eighties and early nineties, compared to the very modest increase in the college premium. With respect to the latter, he comments that 'the returns to education in Sweden remain extraordinary low' (p. 70). Thus we observe the stylized fact that returns of schooling have declined strongly over time and are only recovering gradually, whereas schooling attainment if it declined at all, did recover much more strongly.

This observation is consistent with another stylized fact: there is a fairly general level of overschooling, which means that many individuals are working in jobs that require less schooling than obtained. We illustrate this for the Netherlands in Table 5.1. The table shows that in particular in the lower segment of the labour market there is a great deal of overschooling.[1] One may wonder to what extent this is consistent with the crowding out of low-skilled workers by high-skilled workers,[2] but at least it indicates that high-skilled school-leavers find jobs more easily than low-skilled ones.

Table 5.1   Percentages of workers with excess education in the Netherlands

Educational level of vacancies:	CBA 1995 %	De Beer 1996 %	CBS 1990 %	CBS 1995 %
Basic	83	43	65	72
Lower (LGSE)	31	32		
Medium (IVE)	16	11	32	36

Source: CBA (1995), De Beer (1996), CBS (1995)

This is also observed in Gelderblom and De Koning (1994, pp. 40–41), who estimate age–activity profiles for men and women respectively, based on OSA panel data for the Netherlands 1990. Their results show that the participation is higher, the higher the type of education. In particular in the case of women, the difference is striking. The notion that high-skilled school-leavers find jobs more easily than low-skilled ones, is also corroborated by the observation that the unemployment spell for school-leavers decreases with educational level. And this is also reflected in the well-known fact that the rate of unemployment decreases with the educational level – cf. Table 5.2 This is the third stylized fact we would like to present.

Table 5.2   Education and unemployment in 1990

Level of education	Unemployment of educational group %
Basic	15
Low	7
Medium	4
High	4
Total unemployment	6

Source: CBS (1995)

Finally, Table 5.3 illustrates the widely observed phenomenon that the rate of return to overeducation (O) is lower than the rate of return to required education, but nevertheless positive.[3] This constitutes our fourth stylized fact.

Table 5.3 Returns to human capital in the Netherlands

Studies	Over-education	Required education	Under-education
Hartog and Oosterbeek (1988)	0.057	0.071	-0.025
Sicherman (1991)	0.039	0.048	-0.017
Van Smoorenburg and Van der Velden (1995)[a]	0.027	..	-0.022
Cohn and Khan (1995)	0.049	0.077	-0.038
Sloane et al. (1995)	0.028	0.178	-0.034
Oosterbeek and Webbink (1996) (males)	0.052	0.092	-0.033
Groot (1997)	0.028	0.061	-0.026

Note: [a] These authors used education required as a reference point.
Source: Van Eijs and Heijke (1996) and Hartog (1999)

Together these stylized facts suggest that today the decision on education is no longer primarily influenced by future wages, but by the possibility of getting a proper job.[4] The relevant characteristic of the job that determines schooling is therefore not primarily the level of education required and its corresponding wage level, but the probability of obtaining that job at all – although the corresponding wage level may be relatively low. This notion is consistent with the sorting hypothesis and the related labour queue theory.[5] For employers typically use education as a screening device for unobserved characteristics such as the ability to learn, and a low quit rate. Workers therefore use this as a device to signal their unobservable characteristics.

According to the human capital theory, productivity, and hence wages, are not influenced by job characteristics but by individual endowments; this implies that the wage rate is merely determined by the supply side. Estimating wage functions and explaining differences in these wages are important issues in the human capital theory. Ability, education and training are the determinants of the amount of human capital that an individual embodies and, as a result, of an individual's productivity on the job.[6] Embedded in a neo-classical framework, human capital theory implies that a higher ability and more education do not only result in a higher level of productivity but also lead to a higher wage rate. This wage rate varies with the absolute amount of human capital an individual embodies. This feature of the human capital theory is criticized in Thurow (1975). In his job competition model, productivity and wages are tied to jobs instead of individuals. Workers are ranked in a so-called labour queue based on their training cost. This means that high-skilled workers are ranked higher than low-skilled workers, because the former group is easier to train than the latter, i.e. the relative educational level determines the individual's employment chance.

While the human capital theory focuses on the supply side of the labour market and job competition models focus on the demand side, the matching theory concentrates on both. On the one hand, the demand side of the labour market is assumed to consist of jobs with different skill requirements. On the other hand, the supply side consists of individuals who have acquired skills by means of education.[7] Pissarides (1990), Layard et al. (1991), and Phelps (1994) build a model that deals with both sides of the labour market. However, the relation between job competition models, the human capital theory and the matching theory is never explicitly stated.

Starting from a matching function, we will build a model that captures all ingredients of both the human capital theory and the labour queue theory.[8] We will show that the adjustment mechanism in the economy is determined on the one hand by wages, and on the other hand by the number of jobs supplied by employers, given the level of skills. In addition, we will be able to show that the wage level is quite stable despite the major absolute increase in the level of education. Here the human capital theory would predict an enormous rise in wages, whereas the labour queue theory defines a stable wage level in accordance with a stable supply of the relative skill level.[9]

To be able to explain the four stylized facts, we will apply a more precise analysis of the interaction of schooling decision, duration of unemployment and wages. A framework for such an analysis is presented in this chapter. We will proceed in the following way. First, we will build a model on matching, ability and years of schooling which serves as our general framework for the remainder of the chapter. Then, we will extend this model in Section 3 to show the impact and implications of different levels of skills for our analysis. In Section 4 we will explain and show some evidence with respect to the stylized facts stated in the introduction. We will end with some concluding remarks.

2 MATCHING, ABILITY AND YEARS OF SCHOOLING

2.1 The General Structure

The labour market consists of two sectors. One sector requires skilled labour – which has a level of skills s of at least a given level $\hat{s}$ – whereas the other sector requires only unskilled labour. The supply of skilled labour can be increased by means of schooling. We assume the wage rate for unskilled labour to be fixed at the level w_u, which is above the unemployment benefit level. Moreover, employers will prefer skilled labour to unskilled labour to perform unskilled jobs at the wage rate w_u. Hence we assume unemployment, if any, to be concentrated in unskilled workers. Skilled workers working in the unskilled sector are called underemployed.

In the analysis, we will focus on the skilled sector. Since employers are looking for skilled labour, we first analyse the matching process resulting from the search for skilled workers. This shows how the duration of underemployment is related to labour market tightness. The latter is ultimately determined by the wage formation process for skilled labour. Therefore we elaborate how, given the level of skills required, $\hat{s}$, the wage w_s is determined in a bargaining process between workers and companies. Given both the duration of underemployment and the wage levels for skilled and unskilled work, we then analyse how many years of education a worker wants take in order to obtain that required skill $\hat{s}$. This ultimately defines the supply of skilled labour and underemployment in the skilled sector.

2.2 The Matching Process

Employers in the skilled sector require skilled labour and hence will search for that type of labour, whereas skilled workers prefer to work in the skilled sector since it will pay higher wages. To make this more explicit, we will introduce the matching process in the analysis.[10]

Using the concept of a matching function, the rate at which a vacant job becomes filled, m/v, is determined by

$$\frac{m}{v} = q(\theta) \qquad q_\theta, \ q_{\theta\theta} < 0 \tag{1}$$

where q represents the matching function and $\theta = v/u$ represents labour market tightness - m, v and u are the rate of matches, vacancies and unemployment, respectively.[11]

In this context, v represents vacancies for skilled workers, while u is the actual underemployment of skilled labour. That is, u refers to skilled workers working in the unskilled sector. They have invested in education, but are unable to obtain work in the skilled sector. The mean duration then refers to the time they are working in the unskilled sector at a wage w_u. To that end, we introduce a waiting period d between the end of schooling j and the start of working in a proper – *i.e.* skilled – job. During that period, which can be interpreted as the period of searching for a proper job, one can earn the unskilled wage w_u. By definition, the mean duration of underemployment, or search duration, equals

$$d(\theta) = \frac{1}{\theta q(\theta)} \qquad d_\theta < 0 \qquad (2)$$

A final observation is that the model can be used to determine equilibrium underemployment, u^*. In the steady state, this is equal to

$$u^* = \frac{x}{x + \dfrac{1}{d(\theta)}} \qquad u_\theta < 0 \qquad (3)$$

where x is defined as the flow into underemployment, relative to employment, resulting from such factors as structural shifts in the demand for labour. As one might expect, equilibrium underemployment will follow search duration d closely.

2.3 Wage Formation and Underemployment

Let production in the sector with skilled labour exhibit constant returns to scale in capital and labour. Labour is assumed to have a level of skills of at least $\hat{s}$, determined by the employers beforehand. Then the production structure is represented by the production function

$$y = f(k) \qquad f_k > 0, f_{kk} < 0 \qquad (4)$$

where y represents output per worker, k represents the capital stock per worker and s is defined as the skill level per worker. The production function is assumed to be well behaved and given the interest rate, r, the capital stock k, is determined by

$$f_k = r + \delta \qquad (5)$$

where δ is defined as the rate of depreciation. Thus, from equation (5) we observe that the marginal product of capital is equal to the marginal cost of capital, i.e. the interest rate plus the depreciation rate. Finally, if equation (5) is satisfied, the marginal product of labour $\hat{g}$ is given by:

$$\hat{g} = f(k) - (r + \delta)k \qquad (6)$$

When looking at the demand for skilled labour by the firm, we should also take the search process into account. Essential in the analysis of Pissarides is the notion that an open vacancy represents search and hiring cost to the firm of γ_0

per period of time. As a consequence, the expected capitalized value of the firm's hiring cost enters the demand function for labour, next to the marginal product of labour. That is, in the demand function for labour the usual marginal productivity condition is amended as follows:

$$\hat{w}_s = \hat{g} - \frac{(r+x)\gamma_0}{q(\theta)} \qquad (7)$$

In this equation, $\hat{g}$ is the marginal product of labour, while the last term of the right-hand side is the expected capitalized value of the firm's hiring cost. It varies positively with the interest rate and the rate of outflow of employment into unemployment, and negatively with the matching rate. Equation (7) shows a negative trade-off between labour market tightness and wages employers are willing to offer. The reason is that when labour market tightness increases, this will decrease the probability of finding a good match and hence increase the capitalized value of the firm's hiring cost. In order to compensate for these costs, the firm will then be willing to offer lower wages.

Wages are determined by a Nash-bargaining process, in which the bargaining power of workers and employers are represented by β and $1 - \beta$, respectively, with $0 < \beta < 1$. The resulting wage can be represented by

$$w_s^* = (1-\beta)w_u + \beta(\hat{g} + \theta\gamma_0) \qquad (8)$$

where w_u is the worker's fall-back position – *i.e.* working in the unskilled sector. Since $\theta\gamma_0$ is the average hiring cost for each new worker, it is intuitively clear that these are added to the marginal product of labour.[12] This also explains why the bargained wage is an increasing function of labour market tightness, θ – cf. the bargained real wage (BRW) curve in Figure 5.1.

The equilibrium wage w_e then is determined by $\hat{w}_s = w_s^*$. Hence we find the wage for skilled labour as a premium on the wage of unskilled labour:

$$w_e = w_u + \frac{\gamma_0 \cdot \beta}{1-\beta}\left(\theta_e + \frac{r+x}{q(\theta_e)}\right) \qquad (9)$$

where θ_e is the equilibrium level of labour market tightness. As one might expect, the premium increases when the bargaining power of workers and the search and hiring cost increase.

This equilibrium is illustrated in Figure 5.1. It is obvious that equation (8) – the BRW curve – is a straight line, increasing in labour market tightness θ with slope $\beta\gamma_0$. Equation (7) – the demand for labour – on the other hand, decreases in labour market tightness: the higher the elasticity of the matching function is with respect to θ in absolute terms, the stronger the function will be sloping downward. The intersection between the two lines defines θ_e and $w_{e \cdot 13}$ The lower half of Figure 5.1 shows the inverse relationship between duration and labour market tightness – cf. equation (2). Thus the equilibrium labour market tightness θ_e determines search duration d_e. And the equilibrium rate of underemployment is determined by substituting d_e in equation (3).

2.4 Supply of Skills and Schooling

With respect to the supply of labour, we assume an ability distribution over the labour force N. More specifically, we assume that abilities a are distributed uniformly across the range $[0, A]$. However, although abilities imply a certain amount of skills, the skills can be improved by schooling.[14]

Therefore, we define the level of skills s as a positive function of ability a and years of education j. A convenient expression is:

$$s = ae^{\alpha j} \qquad \alpha > 0 \tag{10}$$

Thus workers with an ability below the level of skills required in the skilled sector, $\hat{s}$, can try to obtain work in that sector by schooling themselves. The parameter α indicates the productivity of schooling – the higher α, the more productive is schooling.

Given the level of skills demanded, $\hat{s}$, one sees from equation (10) that the marginal ability $\hat{a}$ at which a worker qualifies for skilled labour, decreases with the number of years of schooling. Thus, the supply of skilled labour is determined by the years of schooling in the following way:

$$\frac{L^s}{N} = \int_{\hat{a}(j)}^{A} da = 1 - \frac{\hat{s}e^{-\alpha j}}{A} \tag{11}$$

It is obvious that the supply of skilled employment increases with years of schooling. The remaining part of the labour force, with an ability below $\hat{a}$, constitutes the supply of unskilled labour.

With respect to the determination of years of schooling, we follow the tradition of the human capital theory. We therefore assume that schooling is an investment decision, with regard to the years of education, which pays off in the form of higher wages. While unskilled work pays a wage w_u, it is expected that a higher educational level will earn a higher wage w_s. From the human capital theory, we know that the individual with a marginal ability will obtain education for j years such that

$$\int_0^\infty w_u e^{-rt} dt = -\int_0^j ce^{-rt} dt + \int_j^\infty w_s e^{-rt} dt \qquad (12)$$

holds. In this equation r represents the rate of interest and c corresponds to the real cost of schooling per year (minus any direct utility from schooling).

Figure 5.1   *Determining the relation between labour market tightness, wage and duration*

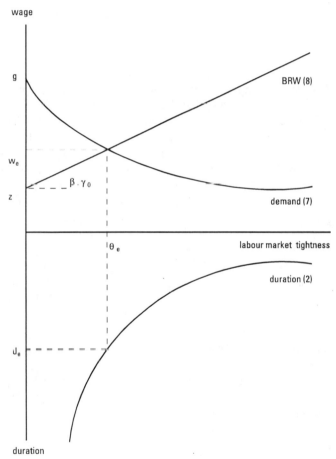

Note: z is equal to $(1-\beta)w_u + \beta g$.

However, due to the introduction of the search process, we have to adapt the above representation of the human capital theory to explain this phenomenon. Since skilled workers expect a search duration d_e as determined in Figure 5.1, they expect to earn w_u during d_e periods, before earning the skilled wage w_e. We assume that the expectations will always be realized. Therefore, we elaborate equation (12) in the following manner:

$$\int_0^\infty w_u e^{-rt}dt = -\int_0^{j_e} ce^{-rt}dt + \int_{j_e}^{j_e+d_e} w_u e^{-rt}dt + \int_{j_e+d_e}^\infty w_e e^{-rt}dt \qquad (13)$$

where w_e and d_e are defined by the analysis in Figure 5.1, and j_e represents the corresponding years of schooling. Solving equation (13), yields

$$w_e = e^{rd_e}(e^{rj}-1)\ (w_u+c)\ +\ w_u \qquad (14)$$

Equation (14) gives an implicit solution j_e of years of schooling of the individual with a marginal ability, such that the required skill level $\hat{s}$ is reached. Substituting j_e in equation (11) then determines the supply of skilled labour.

It should be emphasized that equation (14) refers to the individual with marginal ability. Others with a higher ability will obtain less schooling. Actually, individuals in the range $[\hat{a}, A]$ will take exactly the required number of years of schooling to obtain skill $\hat{s}$. This follows immediately from the insight that the right-hand side of equation (13), which represents the total returns to schooling, decreases with the number of years of schooling.

From equation (14), one sees that the marginal individual's decision to obtain education depends positively on the wages this person can earn after schooling, w_e, and negatively on forgone income w_u, search duration d_e, and the cost of education c. However, it is remarkable that in the analysis, the level of skills required has no impact on schooling whatsoever. We will return to this point below.

2.5 Equilibrium on the Skilled Labour Market

Thus far we have determined the wage rate w_e and supply of labour L^S, but demand for labour still has not been discussed. Actually it is implicit in the analysis, and to point that out enhances our understanding of the nature of the equilibrium of the labour market.

As is obvious from the above analysis, equilibrium is determined through the process of wage formation. Given the level of skills required, the equilibrium wage w_e is determined in a bargaining process. This implies that a certain labour market tightness θ_e and a corresponding search duration d_e are necessary to ensure that the bargained real wages – cf. equation (8) – equals the real wages employers are willing to offer – cf. equation (7). As a consequence the equilibrium rate of underemployment is determined by substituting d_e in equation (3). This implies that employers will demand labour consistent with that rate, given a certain supply of labour. Hence demand for labour L^D will equal:

$$L^D = \frac{1}{1 + xd_e} L^S \qquad (15)$$

where L^S follows from substituting j_e – cf. equation (14) – in equation (11).

3 THE IMPACT OF SKILLS

3.1 The Matching Process

In the above model, employers in the skilled sector search for skilled labour at a given level of skills. However, we have ignored the fact that schooling has a positive impact on the matching process since more job opportunities arrive when the level of education is higher.[15] As a higher educated person can perform a job at a lower level, but a lower educated person cannot perform a job at a higher level, an employer will prefer to hire a person with a higher level of education for a lower skilled job at the same wages he would pay a lower skilled worker for at least two reasons.[16] First, the worker may turn out to be more productive than a lower skilled worker – which will be compensated by a higher wage to an extent depending on the bargaining power of both parties. Second, the lower skilled job provides a good opportunity to observe and monitor the qualities of the worker, before he might be offered a higher skilled job. This argument is consistent with the screening hypothesis and the job queue theory mentioned in the introduction. The screening theory underscores information generated on individuals by education. The general idea is that higher educated and, therefore, highly skilled individuals are more productive than less educated/skilled individuals. Spence (1973) describes this process as follows. An applicant knows his productivity and skills when he applies for a job. However, the employer observes both exogenous indices such as race, age and gender and endogenous signals given by the applicant such as education and commitment to influence his choice. The employer uses both the exogenous and endogenous variables to estimate the applicant's productivity, i.e. he computes according to a kind of inference rule. Now, an equilibrium is obtained when the applicant's signals given to the inference rule and the inference rule itself are correct. Since information is imperfect, a potential employee's productivity cannot be recognized beforehand and hence employing a worker at first in a low-skilled job is a good opportunity for the employer to monitor his newly hired employee. The related labour queue theory assumes that specific skills are required which have to be acquired by on-the-job training. As we mentioned in the introduction, well-educated individuals are easier to train, hence they are in front of the labour queue. In Thurow's words: 'Education and training have to a great extent been based on a "wage competition" view of the labour market. They have not had the predicted impact since they have ignored "job competition" elements in the labour market.' (Thurow, 1979, pp. 17–18). Instead of competing against each other on the basis of wages, individuals compete for jobs on the basis of background characteristics.

When we integrate the notions of screening and labour queue theory in the matching function, we assume that the level of skills required by the employers is $\hat{s}$, i.e. their inference rule states that they have to employ workers with skills of at least $\hat{s}$. Then the rate, m/v, at which a vacant job of skill level $\hat{s}$ becomes filled by a person with skill s is determined by:

$$\frac{m}{v} = q(\theta, s/\hat{s}) \qquad q_s > 0, \; q_\theta, \; q_{\theta\theta} < 0, \; s \geq \hat{s} \tag{16}$$

From the discussion above it follows that the probability of finding a match increases with the level of skills s. This may provide an incentive to individuals to obtain a skill level which is higher than $\hat{s}$.

It is obvious that the search period is negatively related to the level of skills since the higher the skill, the easier it is to find a job. Thus we have:

$$d(\theta, s/\hat{s}) = \frac{1}{\theta q(\theta, s/\hat{s})} \qquad d_s, \; d_\theta < 0 \tag{17}$$

Finally, equilibrium underemployment is defined analogous to equation (3):

$$u(\theta, s/\hat{s}) = \frac{x}{x + \dfrac{1}{d(\theta, s/\hat{s})}} \tag{18}$$

Both equilibrium underemployment and average search duration will decrease in s, the level of skills obtained. We will now analyse how this level is determined. But first some brief comments on wage formation.

3.2 Wage Formation

With respect to wage formation, we essentially follow the analysis from the previous section. The skill required by employers is $\hat{s}$, which is determined primarily by technology. Moreover, employers evaluate their hiring costs at a search effort consistent with $q(\theta, 1)$, instead of consistent with the search duration of equation (17) with the skill level that is actually chosen. The reason is that skill competition does not necessitate the employers passing on the rents from lower hiring costs to skilled workers.

The outcome then is again as in the upper half of Figure 5.1: an equilibrium wage and labour market tightness, w_e and θ_e, respectively. From the above analysis it is obvious, however, that search duration and equilibrium underemployment are determined in a way different from the lower half of Figure 5.1. We will elaborate on this below.

3.3 Supply of Skills

With respect to the supply of skills, it can be shown that the total benefits of schooling increase with the level of skills obtained, provided that the impact of skills on search duration is sufficiently large. We assume this to be the case.[17] Hence, given the level of skills set by the entrepreneurs $\hat{s}$, there is always a potential for higher skills. This is also consistent with the notion mentioned above that skill competition does not necessitate the employers to pass on the rents from lower hiring costs to skilled workers.

For each ability, the optimal level of skills s^* can be obtained from maximizing the total benefits of schooling with respect to skills – cf. the right-hand side of equation (13) with endogenous duration d_e. This yields:

$$-\alpha s^* d_s\left(\theta_e, \frac{s^*}{\hat{s}}\right) = 1 + \frac{w_u + c}{(w_e - w_u)e^{-rd\left(\theta_e, \frac{s^*}{\hat{s}}\right)}} \tag{19}$$

The optimal level is such that the impact of skills on search duration exactly balances the cost of schooling. It is interesting to note that the optimal level of skills s^* is independent of the ability: any individual who adopts schooling will obtain the level s^*. As a consequence, the higher the ability of an individual is, the lower his or her optimal years of schooling are. And this implies that the total returns to schooling , i.e. life-time income, increase with ability. Therefore the rate of return to schooling increases with ability too.

Given s^*, the analysis of the previous section still holds for the marginal ability. Hence the years of schooling j^* are determined analogous to equation (11):

$$w_e = e^{rd\left(\theta_e, \frac{s^\cdot}{\hat{s}}\right)}(e^{rj^*} - 1)(w_u + c) + w_u \qquad (20)$$

Since $d[\theta_e, s^*/\hat{s}] < d[\theta_e, 1]$, the years of schooling j^* of the marginal individual exceed those found in the analysis of the previous section, j^e – compare equation (14). In order to enhance the possibility of finding a skilled job, the marginal individual will have more years of schooling.

The marginal ability a^* will be determined by:

$$a^* = s^* e^{-\alpha j^*} \qquad \alpha > 0 \qquad (21)$$

Since both $j^e < j^*$ and $\hat{s} < s^*$, the impact on the marginal ability has opposite effects. However, it can be shown that these effects neutralize each other such that the marginal ability a^* is exactly equal to the marginal ability $\hat{a}$ found in the previous section – cf. equation (11).This implies that the supply of labour is equal to that of the analysis in the previous section in terms of number of persons. However, the level of skills is higher.

3.4 Equilibrium and Overeducation

Since the level of skills is higher than required – i.e. $s^* > \hat{s}$ – the search duration is lower and therefore the equilibrium underemployment is also lower, as can be seen from equation (18). We then know from equation (15) that the demand for skilled labour will be higher. The reason for a higher demand for labour lies in the lower hiring costs than expected. Employers evaluate the expected hiring costs at a skill $\hat{s}$, whereas the skills turn out to be higher at a level s^*.[18] As a consequence the matching process is improved and hiring costs are lower.[19] At the same wages, more persons will be hired.

When we compare this situation with the situation in the previous section, where the impact of skills on the matching process is ignored, the following observations can be made. The level of skills demanded by employers and the wage rates for skilled labour have not changed. The same number of persons will offer skilled labour. However, the level of skills offered s^* is higher and lies above the level of skills $\hat{s}$ demanded. In that sense, overeducation is a general phenomenon for skilled labour. Since wages have not increased, this implies lower returns to schooling, while schooling attainment has increased. In addition, the rate of return to overschooling is positive for all persons with a skill higher than the marginal skill. This follows from the observation made above that the total returns to schooling increase with ability.

On the other hand, the rate of underemployment is lower. Hence less skilled persons will be working in the low-skilled sector. And therefore also less crowding out will take place.[20]

These observations show already that the model we have constructed here can be used to explain the stylized facts that we mentioned in the introduction of our chapter. However, for a proper discussion, we have to analyse the evolution of the labour market in the course of time. This is the subject of the next section.

4 THE STYLIZED FACTS EXPLAINED

It seems reasonable to argue that several of the variables that are exogenous to our analysis have changed in the course of time and therefore had an impact on overeducation and underemployment, as can be explained from the analysis in the previous section. The resulting picture then is consistent with the stylized facts as we shall show below.

4.1 Changes over Time in Exogenous Variables

We first look at the process of wage formation as depicted in the upper half of Figure 5.1. The slope of the wages offered by employers – cf. equation (7) – is equal to $-(r + x).\gamma_0.\epsilon(q, \theta)/q$, where $\epsilon(q, \theta)$ is the absolute value of the elasticity of matching with respect to labour market tightness. The slope of the bargained wages – cf. equation (8) – is equal to $\beta\gamma_0$. Hence the higher the hiring costs are and the stronger the bargaining power of workers is, the steeper equation (8) will be. Moreover, higher hiring costs also imply a larger slope of equation (7). The same holds for a higher of interest and a higher rate of turnover.

In the early 1970s most of these variables increased.[21] Moreover, the UV curve shifted outwards, indicating a deterioration of the matching process.[22] This also had an impact on the slope of equation (7).[23] The resulting shifts are shown in Figure 5.2, which shows how higher wages came about, together with an increasingly slack labour market – cf. the increase from w_1 to w_2 and the decrease from θ_1 to θ_2, respectively. The consequences of this process for un(der)employment can be derived from the lower half of Figure 5.2, through the impact on duration. While the increasingly slack labour market already implies an increase in duration of unemployment, the impact was worsened by the outward shift in the duration curve due to the worsening of the matching process.

Many of these tendencies have been reversed in the eighties and nineties. Although no hard figures are available, it seems highly plausible that the power of the unions β and the search and hiring costs γ_0 have declined, when compared to the early 1970s. For instance, in the Netherlands the percentage of union members among the working labour force fell from 38% in 1975 to 25% in 1996.[24] In addition, since the early 1980s wage moderation has been an important component of labour market policy.[25]

The decline in search and hiring costs can be explained by the increase in part-time work. The OECD (1998, pp. 160–166) argues that even when schedules in a firm are fixed within the working day, part-time employment may add to flexibility if it can be arranged to coincide with peaks in labour requirements. In establishment surveys in some European countries, the majority of managers said that the primary reason for the introduction of part-time work was to meet the needs of the firm. In such circumstances, managers favoured shorter hours (< 20 a week), and mainly saw a need for low-skilled part-time workers. Moreover, for the European Union, calculations from the European Union Labour Force Survey show that one third of all part-time workers are employed during evenings, nights and weekends. Particularly and most importantly, part-time workers are very unlikely to attract overtime premiums and may well be cheaper than the same hours worked by full-time workers. Finally, it should be noted that the extent of part-time employment is very large in the Netherlands. In 1996, part-time employment as a percentage of total employment was 36.5% whereas it was only 16.6% in 1979. By contrast, Austria, Belgium, Finland, France, Portugal and Spain do not even reach the Dutch 1979 level in 1996, while Sweden and Switzerland are numbers two and three with only 23.6% and 27.4% part-time workers – cf. OECD (1998).

These trends will lead to a reversion of the process in the 1970s as depicted in the upper half of Figure 5.2. Wages have a tendency to decrease from w_2 towards w_1 and labour market tightness will increase from θ_2 to θ_1.

From the point of view of our analysis, another important change occurred in the matching process. It seems plausible that the impact of schooling on matching has increased strongly. Such an effect has been underlined by, amongst others, Howell and Wolff (1991) for the USA and by Goux and Maurin (1996) for France. These authors argue that the increased demand for skilled labour could be stimulated by slacks in labour markets which induce longer stays in initial formal education to delay entry into the labour market and by individuals trying to improve their chances of finding employment. In their view the increased demand for education is therefore certainly part of the explanation for increasing average levels of education and the number of years of education attended as apparent in all OECD countries.

Figure 5.2   What happened in the 1970s?

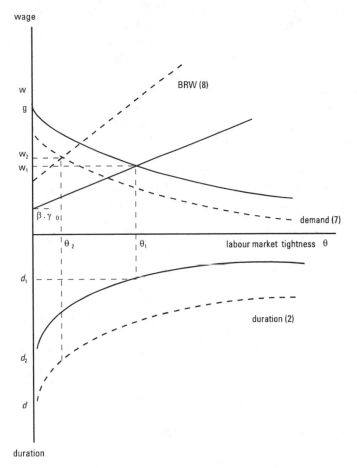

The observation that an increased demand for schooling may result from a slack labour market is consistent with our analysis, since a change in labour market tightness will affect the optimal level of skills and hence schooling. From equation (19), it can be derived that under plausible assumptions a slack labour market will correspond to a higher level of skills, i.e. $ds*/d\theta < 0$.[26] This is also intuitively clear since in a slack labour market, the matching probability is lower and hence there is a greater need for additional schooling.

However, it also seems plausible that the elasticity of matching with respect to schooling has increased. Employers are believed to be more focused on skills nowadays than they were in the early 1970s. One of the reasons is a ratchet effect: once a level of skills is provided above the level demanded by the employers, the employers will automatically adapt to that level and hence demand higher skills than they originally intended to do. Another reason is the wider availability of schooling opportunities in general. Amongst others these reasons imply an inward shift of the duration curve as represented in the lower half of Figure 5.2, because matching improves given labour market tightness. As a consequence, the tendencies in the late 1980s and 1990s which led to a tighter labour market, as we have indicated above, will not automatically lead to a lower optimal level of skills.

Also, an important reservation should be made with regard to the analysis above, for not all workers faced a decline in search duration during the 1980s and 1990s. If search duration had fallen to the levels of the 1960s and early 1970s, unemployment levels should have been down too. This is not what we observe in the contemporary Dutch labour market. Only high-skilled workers have faced a dramatic fall in search duration and unemployment in the second half of the 1990s, which was mainly due to an upturn in the economy in favour of high-skilled workers. This notion of skill-biased technical change has reduced the demand for low-skilled workers relative to high-skilled workers; particularly in the R&D-intensive and rapidly expanding sectors of the Dutch economy – cf. Bruinshoofd and Ter Weel (1998) for a recent empirical analysis.

In addition, hysteresis in unemployment – in particular in the low-skilled sector – should be taken into account. As explained in for example, Lindbeck and Snower (1986), it can be acknowledged that long-term unemployed workers are not included in the (Nash) bargaining process of wage determination. Thus wages are set so that involuntary unemployment remains (and becomes long-term), but the unemployed are nevertheless unable to improve their position through underbidding. These latter notions are not included in our present analysis. Nevertheless, our analysis highlights some aspects of skill formation and the matching process that enable us to explain the stylized facts mentioned above.

4.2 The Stylized Facts

In the introduction, we presented four related stylized facts, which we have elaborated on in our analysis. First, we have shown that the returns to schooling declined strongly over time, which is in line with our first observation. Our intuition was that people today invest in schooling not only to obtain higher wages but also to get a decent job. In our framework, we have shown that this statement can plausibly be modelled and explained by taking into account both supply-side and demand-side characteristics of the labour market.

Second, the general level of overeducation is explained. Not only are individuals who are unable to find employment in the skilled sector overeducated, workers in the skilled sector also turn out to be overeducated. This can be explained in accordance with our first findings, i.e. that the investment decision is not merely taken to maximize life-time income, as would be the outcome of the human capital theory.

Third, we have shown that unemployment for the lower educated is much higher than for the higher educated. Skilled individuals who cannot get a job in the skilled sector are by definition employed in the unskilled sector. This means that the general tendency towards overeducation – and therefore an increase in the amount of skilled labour supplied – leads to a further deterioration of the labour market position of unskilled labour, which among others leads to crowding out.

Finally, the statement that the rate of return to overeducation is positive can be observed from the skilled labour market. In the analysis above, we have shown that this holds for the worker with an ability higher than the marginal ability.

5 CONCLUDING REMARKS

This chapter is a contribution to economic theory to the extent that it provides a systematic approach to incorporate several labour market theories into one model. In addition, the model is able to explain several observations from the Dutch economy which could so far not be explained by the existing models.

Building a theoretical framework along the search-theoretic lines of Pissarides (1990) and extending this model with the human capital, labour queue, and screening theories, we have been able to explain four stylized facts. First we have provided a solid basis for the paradox that the returns to schooling have declined strongly while attainment remained the same. Our explanation is that individuals prefer to invest in schooling not only to maximize their life-time income (human capital theory) but to increase the chance (search theory) that they will obtain a proper job (job competition and screening theories). Combining these approaches, we can rather straightforwardly explain the general level of overeducation. In addition, it is clear from our analysis that the returns to overschooling are lower than the returns to the required level of schooling, but still positive.

In line with the observation that a general level of overschooling is prevalent in the Netherlands, we are able to explain that low-skilled workers have more difficulties in finding a job than their high-skilled colleagues. Since there are only a limited number of jobs, individuals who embody higher levels of human capital are in front of the labour queue, give the right signals to employers, and have therefore the best chances of becoming employed. As a result, low-skilled individuals face higher unemployment rates. This phenomenon is reinforced by the fact that high-skilled workers who cannot obtain a job in the high-skilled sector will be employed in the low-skilled sector, thereby crowding out low-skilled workers.

NOTES

1. In 1996, Groot and Maassen van den Brink (1996) triggered a discussion on overeducation in the Netherlands. They stated that overeducation did not increase between 1982 and 1995, on the basis of two different data sets for the Netherlands. This point is criticized by Groeneveld (1996, p. 511), who points out that overschooling may indeed have increased when differences between these sets are corrected. However, an interesting observation of Groot and Maassen van den Brink is that overschooling is concentrated in part-time workers, workers with interrupted careers and beginning workers. Hence, it is not necessarily crowding out of lower educated persons, but it may be compensation for the lack of experience. Oosterbeek and Webbink (1996) also criticize the results reported by Groot and Maassen van den Brink. They use a different analysis in which returns to overeducation are calculated and compared to normal returns for men and women in the Netherlands, 1982 and 1995. Their results show a decline for men in returns to overschooling, but the opposite for women.
2. Gelderblom et al. (1997) observe that education may be related to the opportunity of finding a job, which in turn may lead to crowding out of lower educated individuals. Van Ours and de Ridder (1995) find that no crowding out did occur in the Netherlands, but their results have been criticized by De Beer (1996) because Van Ours and Ridder assume that lower and higher educated persons have the same probability of being accepted in a low-skilled job.
3. For a survey of the empirical findings with respect to overeducation, see Hartog (1999).
4. To a certain extent, this is corroborated by Webbink (1996) who uses survey data for 1990 and 1995 to determine the extent to which the choice for a certain type of education is motivated by labour market perspectives. He finds that labour market perspectives definitely do matter. However, people often use stereotypes of labour market chances in this context. And an interesting observation is that the 1995 generation is more fixed on labour market perspectives than the 1990 generation.
5. An interesting overview of the sorting theory as opposed to the human capital theory is given in Weiss (1995). The labour queue theory was developed in Thurow (1979).

6. See, e.g. Schultz (1961) and Becker (1962) for the initial approaches of the human capital theory.
7. In this chapter we only make a distinction between skilled (L_s) and unskilled (L_u) labour. For a more elaborate model on skills, see, e.g. Van Zon, Muysken and Meijers (1998) and Hollanders and Ter Weel (1998).
8. Groot and Hoek (1997) illustrate the working of the labour market under the assumptions of the human capital and the labour queue theory. They stress the differences between the two theories.
9. In this context, Kettunen (1994) also uses a different argument from sorting: a higher educated person can perform a job at a lower level, but a lower educated person cannot perform a job at a higher level.
10. To large extent, we will follow the analysis as developed in Pissarides (1990), Chapter 1.
11. We assume the matching function to be linear and homogenous in unemployment and vacancies. Pissarides (1979), Blanchard and Diamond (1990), Layard et al. (1991), Van Ours (1991) and Romer (1996) show that constant returns to scale is a satisfactory approximation to reflect the matching process and to adopt an appropriate matching function.
12. As Pissarides (1990, p. 12) states: 'Workers are rewarded for the saving of hiring cost that the firm enjoys when a job is formed.' Burdett and Smith (1996) choose a different route by emphasizing that the outside option for firms increases when more workers are available.
13. θ_e is implicitly defined by the equality of the right-hand sides of equations (7) and (8).
14. For simplicity, we assume $A < \hat{s}$, hence anybody will follow some schooling.
15. Burdett and Smith (1996) use a somewhat related model to study the relation between matching and education – although they emphasize the bargaining process between (un)skilled workers and firms and pay no explicit attention to the duration of search.
16. This argument is also used by Kettunen (1994). However, he assumes that the matching probability will decrease again at higher levels of education, since he assumes that both the lump-sum costs and the variable costs of accepting another job also increase with education.
17. We assume that the elasticity of matching with respect to schooling at $\hat{s}$ to be sufficiently large:

$$\frac{1}{q}q_s > \frac{1}{\alpha d_e}\frac{e^{rj_e}}{e^{rj_e}-1}$$

where j_e is defined in equation (14) and d_e follows from Figure 5.1.
18. One might argue that this is inconsistent with rational expectations. However, in this case the employers state their wages in the context of a wage-bargaining process. Their claim will be that they demand wages consistent with a level of skills $\hat{s}$. And it is in their interest to keep the wages as low as possible because if they later demand more individuals because the hiring costs turn out to be lower, the resulting profits will be higher.
19. A similar argument is found in Groot and Hoek (1997), who argue that the decline in search and hiring costs can be explained from the labour queue theory. In a slack labour market, as is currently experienced in the Netherlands, labour queues are longer than job queues. In these relatively long labour queues, workers at the end of the queue remain unemployed. Now, a rise in the level of education in a slack labour market does not lead to higher wages but to lower hiring costs on the side of employers, because they face a better educated and therefore more employable work force.
20. In this sense, overschooling can be said to cause the chimney effects as discussed in Van Zon et al. (1998).
21. See various papers in Muysken and De Neubourg (1989).
22. An overview is presented in Muysken (1989).
23. The same holds for the impact of the demand shock resulting from the oil crises.

24. Van der Geest (1995) gives four reasons for the decline in the Netherlands. In the first place, he notes that large industrial firms with great numbers of unskilled workers have disappeared. This is attended by a decline in union membership. Second, a change in the composition of the labour force from un- and low-skilled male workers to a well-educated work force with many women and part-time workers, has led to a decline in union membership. Third, cultural changes such as individuality accompanied an adverse shock to union membership. Last, Van der Geest argues that due to decentralized wage bargaining the unions lost bargaining power.
25. For recent studies in the Netherlands, see Lever (1995), Van Lede (1995) and Koeman (1996). Kleinknecht (1996) counterargues with respect to the success of wage moderation that employment growth is only observed because of a lack of labour productivity relative to other OECD countries.
26. Sufficient conditions are that for duration $d_{s\theta}$, $d_{ss} < 0$ holds, and the right-hand side of equation (19) exceeds $1 + \alpha$.

REFERENCES

Becker, G.S. (1962), 'Investment in Human Capital: A Theoretical Analysis', *Journal of Political Economy* **70** (1), 9–49.

Blanchard, O.J. and P A. Diamond (1990), 'The Aggregate Matching Function', NBER Working Paper 4000, Cambridge MA.

Bruinshoofd, W.A. and B.J. ter Weel (1998), 'Skill-Biased Technical Change: On Technology and Wages in the Netherlands', *MERIT Research Memorandum 2/98-025*.

Burdett, K. and E. Smith (1996), 'Education and Matching Externalities', in A.S. Booth and D.J. Snower (eds), *Acquiring Skills. Market Failures, Their Symptoms and Policy Responses,*, Cambridge: Cambridge University Press, pp. 65–80.

CBA (Centraal Bureau Arbeidsvoorzieningen) (1995), *Hoe Werven Bedrijven*, Rijswijk.

CBS (Statistics Netherlands) (1995), *Enquête Beroepsbevolking*, The Hague: CBS.

De Beer, P. (1996), 'Laag Opgeleiden: Minder Kans op een Baan, meer Kans op Ontslag', *Economisch Statistische Berichten*, 06-11-1996, 908–12.

Gelderblom, A. and J. de Koning (1994), *Leren: Batig Investeren?* The Hague: OSA.

Gelderblom, A., J. de Koning and J. Odink (1997), 'Loont Studeren?', *Economisch Statistische Berichten*, 18-06-1997, 500–4.

Gottschalk, P. (1997), 'Inequality, Income Growth, and Mobility: The Basic Facts', *Journal of Economic Perspectives* **11** (2), 21–40.

Goux, D. and E. Maurin (1996), 'Changes in the Demand for Labour in France', *STI Review*, No. 18, OECD, Paris.

Groeneveld, S. (1996), 'Het Meten van Overscholing', *Economisch Statistische Berichten*, 05-06-1996, 511.

Groot, L. and A. Hoek (1997), *Job Competition in the Dutch Labour Market*, LOWER, London.

Groot, W. and H. Maassen van den Brink (1996), 'Overscholing en Verdringing op de Arbeidsmarkt', *Economisch Statistische Berichten*, 74–7.

Hartog, J. (1999), 'On Returns to Education: Wandering along the Hills of ORU Land', in H. Heijke and J. Muysken (eds), *Education and Training in a Knowledge Based Economy*, Basingstoke: MacMillan, pp. 3–45.

Hollanders, H. and B.J. ter Weel (1998), 'Skill-Biased Technological Change in an Endogenous Growth Model,' *MERIT Research Memorandum 2/98-019.*

Howell, D.R. and E.N. Wolff (1991), 'Trends in the Growth and Distribution of Skills in the US Workplace 1960-1985', *Industrial and Labour Relations* **44** (3), 486–502.

Kettunen, J. (1994), 'The Effects of Education on the Duration of Unemployment', *Labour* **8** (2), 331–52.

Kleinknecht, A. (1996), 'Potverteren met Loonmatiging en Flexibilisering', *Economisch Statistische Berichten*, 21-08-1996, 622–25.

Koeman, J. (1996), 'Loonmatiging en Macro-Economie', *Economisch Statistische Berichten*, 21-08-1996, 692–3.

Layard R., S.J. Nickell and R. Jackman (1991), *Unemployment*, New York: Oxford University Press.

Lever, M.H.C. (1995), 'Cao's en Werkgelegenheid', *Economisch Statistische Berichten*, 29-03-1995, 300–303.

Linbeck, A. and D.J. Snower (1986), 'Wage Setting, Unemployment, and Insider-Outsider Relations', *American Economic Review* **76** (2), AEA Papers and Proceedings, 235–39.

Muyksen, J. (1989), 'Classification of Unemployment: Analytical and Policy Relevance', *De Economist* **137** (4), 397–424.

Muyksen, J. and C. de Neubourg (1989), *Unemployment in Europe*, London: MacMillan.

OECD (1998), *Employment Outlook*, OECD, Paris.

Oosterbeek, H. and D. Webbink (1996), 'Over Scholing, Overscholing en Inkomen,' *Economisch Statistische Berichten*, 13-03-1996, 240–1.

Phelps, E.S. (1994), *Structural Slumps*, Cambridge MA: Harvard University Press.

Pissarides, C.A. (1979), 'Job Matching with State Employment Agencies and Random Search', *Economic Journal* **89** (3), 818–33.

Pissarides, C.A. (1990), *Equilibrium Unemployment Theory*, Oxford: Basil Blackwell.

Romer., D. (1996), *Macroeconomics*, New York: McGraw-Hill.

Schultz, T.W. (1961), 'Investment in Human Capital', *American Economic Review* **51** (1), 1–17.

Spence, A.M. (1973), 'Job Market Signaling', *Quarterly Journal of Economics* **87** (3), 355–74.

Thurow, L.C. (1975), *Generating Inequality*, New York: Basic Books.

Thurow, L.C. (1979), A Job Competition model, in: M.J. Priore (ed.), *Unemployment and Inflation: Institutionalist and Structuralist Views*, New York: White Plains, 17–32.

Topel, R.H. (1997), 'Factor Proportions and Relative Wages', *Journal of Economic Perspectives* **11** (2), 55–74.

Van Eijs, P. and H. Heijke (1996), *The Relation between the Wage, Job-related Training and the Quality of the Match between Occupations and Types of Education*, ROA, Maastricht.

Van der Geest, L. (1995), 'De Neergang van de Vakbeweging', *Economisch Statistische Berichten*, 23-08-1995, 729.

Van Lede, C.J.A. (1995), 'Werk Boven Inkomen: Wensdroom of Werkelijkheid?', *Economisch Statistische Berichten*, 04-10-1995, 876–80.

Van Ours, J.C. (1995), 'An Empirical Note on Employed and Unemployed Job Search', *Economics Letters* **49** (4), 447–52.

Van Ours, J.C. and G. Ridder (1995), 'Job Matching and Job Competition: Are Lower Educated Workers at the Back of Job Queues?' *European Economic Review* **39** (9), 1717–31.

Van Smoorenburg, M. and R. Van der Velden (1995), *Schoolverlaters tussen Onderwijs en Arbeidsmarkt*, ROA, Maastricht.

Van Zon, A., J. Muysken and H. Meijers (1998), 'Assymetric Skill Substitution, Labour Market Flexibility, and the Allocation of Qualifications', in H. Heijke and L. Borghans (eds), *Towards a Transparent Labour Market for Educational Decisions*, London: Avebury Publishers.

Webbink, D. (1996), *Arbeidsmarktverwachtingen en Opleidingskeuze*, ROA 10, Maastricht.

Weiss, A. (1995), 'Human Capital vs. Signalling Explanations of Wages', *Journal of Economic Perspectives* **9** (4), 133–54.

ACKNOWLEDGEMENTS

We thank both Lex Borghans and Andries de Grip for their comments on an earlier version of this chapter.

6. Overqualification Makes Low-wage Employment Attractive

Thomas Zwick

1 INTRODUCTION

Since the 1980s, skilled workers have earned an increasing rent from education. Although non-competitive rents can be earned when investing in schooling and training during more than one decade, nevertheless some workers still decide to stay unskilled and be employed for low wages. How can this be reconciled with individual rent maximization? In most OECD countries we observe the following:

- Skilled workers have enjoyed higher wage mark-ups in recent years.[1]
- Skilled workers have enjoyed lower relative unemployment rates in recent years.[2]

Both stylized facts lead to a non-competitive skill differential if we assume that investment costs in skills did not increase more than the benefits from being skilled.[3]

Increasing rents from education have stimulated much interest in the economic profession, especially because the rising wage inequality is associated with increased wage mark-ups on skills (Borjas, 1996, Johnson, 1997 and Topel, 1997 for recent references). Economic research concentrates on the question of how shifts in labour demand or supply and changes in wage setting may have caused the observed trend. Economists put forward a broad variety of arguments to explain the increased wage mark-ups of skilled workers. De-unionization, especially in Great Britain and the United States, may have had an adverse effect on the relative wages of unskilled workers (Freeman, 1993). Another argument is skill-biased technological change, which reduces the relative labour demand for unskilled workers (see Bound and Johnson, 1992; Katz and Murphy, 1992; or Brauer and Hickok, 1995, for recent data). Other arguments are immigration of unskilled workers, see Topel (1997), a slowdown in the rate of growth of the college educated population as described by Bound and Johnson (1992), Katz and Murphy (1992) and Davis (1992), the durable goods trade deficit, via the massive import of goods mainly produced by unskilled labour, see Borjas and Ramey (1994), and the internationalization that increased competition for goods that are produced with relatively unskilled labour (Murphy and Welch, 1989).

In the studies mentioned above, skilled and unskilled labour supply are assumed to be exogenous, or dependent on other factors, such as demographic structure or educational policy. This is at odds with the human capital investment literature, where agents invest in skills according to economic incentives. This chapter therefore treats the supply of skilled labour and the decision to perform a low-wage job as endogenous and as being influenced by the benefits and the costs of skills. The main economic incentives to invest in skills are the skilled wage mark-up and different unemployment levels of skilled and unskilled workers. In order to study the consequences of the empirical observations mentioned above on the skill investment decision within the theoretical model presented here, we study an increase in skilled wage mark-ups and higher relative unemployment incidence of unskilled workers. The main questions this chapter addresses are:

- What are the consequences of increased rents for skilled workers on the skill investment decision?
- Why do not more workers invest in skills as a consequence of persistent rents earned by skilled workers?
- Should we care about the consequences of rising wage mark-ups for skilled workers from a welfare point of view and what are possible remedies?

In order to answer these questions, a simple closed economic model is constructed including the demand and supply for different skills and unskilled low-wage labour. It is useful to distinguish several horizontally differentiated groups of skilled labour and homogeneous unskilled labour. If we assume in the tradition of the human capital theory that every worker is free to choose a skill, a worker will continue to invest in a certain skill as long as a rent is to be earned. The development of skilled wages suggests that skilled workers are increasingly able to charge a higher mark-up for their labour services, that is, they enjoy market power in the market for their skills. Combined with free entry on the skilled labour market, we face a situation familiar to the theory of monopolistic competition.

The approach to the interpretation of the labour market as monopolistically competitive is not new. All existing models that interpret the labour market as monopolistically competitive with differentiated skills (see, for example, Snower, 1983; Blanchard and Kiyotaki, 1987; Nishimura, 1989; Nielsen et al., 1995; Matsuyama, 1995), basically entail three flaws:

- All workers enjoy a rent, because the number of workers is assumed to be fixed and there are no unemployed workers underbidding the wage set collectively by the workers of one skill (or their union);
- Market power on the labour market is assumed to arise because there are different (but symmetric) types of labour. There are no costs for skill acquisition. Therefore, all workers are skilled and enjoy market power in these models without investment costs. Rent equalization takes place between different skills groups. Frequently, it is assumed that each worker has a unique skill that distinguishes him or her from all other workers;
- The models do not distinguish between unemployed and working persons, but assume that the working time of the entire labour force reacts on exogenous shocks. Therefore, unemployment is defined as under-utilization of total working time, while no one actually becomes unemployed as a result of an adverse shock or excessive wage demands.

The innovation of the model developed below is to draw the dividing line between skilled high-wage and unskilled low-wage labour, and to focus on the education decision. The model remedies the flaws noted above by explicitly introducing investment costs and two labour markets (skilled and unskilled) without entry barriers. In addition, conventionally unemployment and a rent differential between workers are possible.

It is assumed that the relationship between lifetime earnings and schooling is such that the supply and demand for workers of each schooling level are equal and no worker wishes to alter his or her schooling level (see the survey in Willis, 1986, p. 527). The data suggest that the first point does not hold, so it is not imposed here.

If we apply the Chamberlin (1933) model of monopolistic competition to the labour market, it can be characterized by the following elements:[4]

- Human capital is horizontally differentiated in various groups of workers that are not perfect substitutes. There is no difference in the level of skilled workers, but only in their specialization. Skilled workers are able to take advantage of their relative monopoly situation and determine wages themselves;

- The number of different human capital groups is so large that each group ignores its strategic interactions with other groups of workers. The wage setting of one skill group is negligible in the aggregate labour market;
- Entry to the skilled labour market is unrestricted and occurs until no unskilled worker can earn a rent by investing in human capital. The decision to train is based on a cost/benefit calculation, including the relative unemployment rate and the relative wage mark-up between unskilled low wages and skilled wages. There are no institutional barriers or market imperfections that would hinder educational investment among two equally able persons.

We have two labour markets and workers are free to choose which labour market to enter. This is a situation familiar from the theory of compensating wage differentials. It is well known from this theory that there must be a countervailing effect if one group of workers is to enjoy higher than compensating wages and free entry is possible for all groups of workers. Disagreeable job characteristics or different unemployment hazards between industries or skills groups have been identified as possible equilibrium mechanisms (see Layard et al., 1991, pp. 303–7; or Abowd and Ashenfelter, 1981). If we split the workforce into skilled and unskilled workers, however, and assume higher than compensating skilled wages, these arguments cannot be applied.[5]

2 LABOUR DEMAND

In this section, a firm's demand for skilled and unskilled labour is derived. For simplicity, it is assumed that we have one large firm representing the entire labour demand of the economy. The firm demands workers with different skill specializations and unskilled workers. There are k given groups of workers with horizontally differentiated abilities (with k large). The labour pool n per ability group is split into n_u unskilled and n_s skilled workers, while the number of workers choosing to train themselves is determined endogenously. In equilibrium, the entire labour force is made up of $\sum_{u=1}^{k} n_u = N_u$ unskilled and $\sum_{s=1}^{k} n_s = N_s$ skilled workers, with $N_u + N_s = N$.

The firm maximizes profits by requiring a number of skilled workers l_s (with $\sum_{s=1}^{k} l_s = L_s$) in each human capital category of abilities. The demand for unskilled workers is denoted by $L_u = \sum_{u=1}^{k} l_u$, with l_u being the unskilled labour demand per ability group. The profit function is assumed to be analogous to the Spence-Dixit-Stiglitz utility function, widely used in models of monopolistic competition:[6]

$$\pi = g\left(\sum_{u=1}^{k} l_u, \left(\sum_{s=1}^{k} l_s^{\rho}\right)^{\frac{1}{\rho}}\right) - \sum_{u=1}^{k} w_u l_u - \sum_{s=1}^{k} w_s l_s, \tag{1}$$

with $0 < \rho < 1$ for concavity and g homothetic in its arguments.

The parameter w_s is the wage demanded by the skilled workers of ability group s. The wage for unskilled labour is fixed at the minimum wage level either due to unions or minimum wage legislation, and is assumed to be equal to w_u. This minimum wage is higher than the outside option (or unemployment benefit) of unskilled workers. The closer ρ is to one, the more substitutable are the different human capital groups, that is other skills groups can be easily substituted for the same kind of job if their wage demand is lower. Each skill is hereby equally well substitutable by another. As $\rho < 1$ the firm shows 'love of variety', that is it employs all k different skills instead of employing all workers from a selected subset of skills. The price of the output is normalized to one.

    The firm maximizes its profits by deciding how many unskilled workers and how many skilled workers to employ per ability group. Maximizing the profit function (1) with respect to l_u and l_s yields the demand for skilled and unskilled workers within this group, respectively:

$$g_1 = w_u, \tag{2}$$

$$g_2\left(\sum_{i=1}^{k} l_s^{\rho}\right)^{\frac{1-\rho}{\rho}} l_j^{\rho-1} = w_s, \forall j = 1,...,k, \tag{3}$$

where g_1 and g_2 are the partial derivatives of g with respect to the first and second argument. Usually it is assumed that individual marginal productivity declines with the number of workers who have the same specialization while it is positive over the entire range (i.e. $g_2 > 0$).

    Therefore, labour demand for a specialization decreases if its wage level increases or production is strictly quasi-concave in all different skilled labour inputs. The same applies to unskilled workers ($g_1 > 0$) and therefore for aggregate labour demand. In order to derive the results reported below, we only need the assumption that labour demand decreases in wages but is always positive. For simplicity and without loss of generality, it is assumed that skilled labour demand is dependent only on the skilled wage, while unskilled labour demand is dependent only on unskilled wage, that is, there are no cross-wage elasticities ($\partial l_s / \partial w_u = 0$ and $\partial l_u / \partial w_s = 0$).

3 WORKERS' SURPLUS

All workers have uninhibited access to education. The decision to invest in skills or not is a rational intertemporal decision process under uncertainty. Uncertainty arises because workers do not know at the moment they invest in skills, whether they will find an adequate (skilled) job afterwards. As education takes time (often several years), skilled workers do not know if they will be chosen by the firm when the demand for their skill is lower than the supply. This crucial element can also be captured in a static set-up where all skilled workers face the same probability of failing to obtain an adequate job when there is an over-supply of skilled labour. Investment costs are assumed to be sunk, so that they cannot be recovered if the skilled workers do not find an adequate job.

Workers have the opportunity to invest in skills or not. If they invest in skills, they can choose from several horizontally differentiated specifications. Workers have different human capital investment costs. Only if the pay-off to training is higher than the training costs, will workers decide to train. For clarity of the exposition, we concentrate on one of the k horizontally differentiated ability groups. This representative group has n members, of which n_u workers decide to stay unskilled and n_s decide to be trained. Every ability group is assumed to have an identical education cost distribution. Assume that all workers in the ability group can be ranked by a strictly increasing human capital cost function. For simplicity, the investment costs have a special form for the i the worker in the ability group: $c_i = c / n_u^i$ with $n_u^i \in (1, n-1)$, the number of the remaining unskilled workers in the pool.

The worker with the lowest investment costs has therefore costs of $c / n - 1$, while c are the highest investment costs.[7]

Workers invest in human capital if their expected surplus increases as a result. Workers with low investment costs invest in skills, while above a certain level of investment costs training is no longer beneficial. The marginal skilled worker with rank $\hat{n}_s$ has costs of $c / n - \hat{n}_s$. This worker is indifferent between education or staying unskilled, while all workers with lower investment costs choose for education.

It is assumed that the skilled workers who cannot find an adequate job for their specialization, (i.e. the overqualified workers), are offered unskilled labour jobs at the minimum wage level. Skilled labour is therefore a perfect substitute for unskilled labour.[8] In order to introduce an economic reasoning for perfect substitutability, we assume (somewhat *ad hoc*) that overqualified skilled workers have a slightly higher productivity than unskilled workers. As a consequence, equation (2) changes to:

$$g_1 = w_u \qquad \text{if the worker is skilled,} \qquad (4)$$

$$g_1 + \delta = w_u \quad \text{if the worker is unskilled,}$$

with δ small. It will be shown that this additional assumption does not have an impact on the equilibrium results. The firm therefore prefers skilled workers to do these unskilled tasks, while the unskilled workers get the remaining vacancies for unskilled jobs.[9] Consequently, there may be two adverse effects on labour demand for unskilled workers. First, unskilled workers may be substituted directly by overqualified skilled workers. Second, if aggregate labour demand is lower than aggregate labour supply, some of the unskilled workers experience unemployment.

Suppose that $n_s - l_s = o$ skilled workers are overqualified (i.e. fail to find an adequate skilled job). These skilled workers crowd out unskilled workers. Then the n_u unskilled workers enjoy the following expected surplus:

$$s_u = \frac{l_u - o}{n_u} w_u + \left(1 - \frac{l_u - o}{n_u}\right) \bar{s} \quad \text{if } (l_u - o) > 0. \qquad (5)$$

That is, each unskilled worker earns the exogenous unskilled wage w_u (the minimum wage) when being employed. The outside option $\bar{s}$ (unemployment benefit) is earned by $n - l_u - l_s = u$ unemployed unskilled workers. Thus, u is the sum of both effects substitution by overqualified skilled workers o and a reduction in aggregate demand. If $(l_u - o)$ is negative, all unskilled workers are unemployed. For simplicity and without loss of generality, we will assume, however, that the number of skilled workers n_s is smaller than the total labour demand $l_s + l_u$ for this ability group, in short $l_u - o$ is always positive; overqualified skilled workers will always be able to find an unskilled job, and unemployment is only experienced by unskilled workers.

Human capital investment in a skill involves sunk costs. 'Sunk' means in this context that the investment costs cannot be realized if no adequate job is found. In equilibrium, every skilled worker is employed in his or her specialization or in a position that requires no specific skill. Skilled workers of one ability group face the same risk of being overqualified, if skilled labour demand l_s is smaller than labour supply n_s for 'their' skill.

In order to have a closed model, it is assumed that the skilled workers who work in an adequate skilled job (i.e. one paying more than the minimum wage), have to pay an unemployment insurance that is used for the unemployment benefit $\bar{s}$ of the unskilled workers. Skilled workers who find an adequate job in 'their' skill enjoy the following surplus given an investment cost of c_i:

$$s_s^i = w_s - \frac{\bar{s}u}{l_s} - c_i \text{ with } c_i = \frac{c}{n_u^i} \text{ and } n_u^i \in [1,N].$$

Here w_s is the skilled wage, which is equal for all skilled workers of the ability group. The unemployment benefit $\bar{s}$ which has to be paid for u unemployed unskilled workers is spread over the l_s adequately employed skilled workers. Skilled workers who do not find an adequate job and therefore work in unskilled jobs enjoy this surplus:

$$s_s^i = w_u - c_i.$$

Notice that the surplus of overqualified skilled workers is lower than that of employed unskilled workers if they work in a minimum wage job. Overqualification may thus lead to surplus equalization between the expected surpluses of skilled and unskilled workers. The expected surplus of skilled workers with investment costs c_i is:

$$s_s^i = \begin{cases} \dfrac{l_s}{n_s}\left(w_s - \dfrac{u}{l_s}\bar{s}\right) + \left(1 - \dfrac{l_s}{n_s}\right)w_u - c_i & \text{if } l_s < n_s \\[2em] w_s - \dfrac{u}{l_s}\bar{s} - c_i & \text{if } l_s \geq n_s \end{cases} \tag{6}$$

In this static set-up, it is assumed that, before the beginning of the period, skilled workers have to sink costs for a specialization in specific human capital and that, at the end of the period, equilibrium is attained. This assumes complete information on all sides. Prior to transacting, the workers know how many other workers specialize in 'their' human capital and there is no convergence process towards the equilibrium. In equilibrium, the expected surplus of the marginal skilled worker $\hat{n}_s$ equals the expected surplus of the unskilled workers.

4 THE FIRST-BEST SOLUTION

The first best solution maximizes the rent R of all market participants, which is the sum of workers' rents and firm's profits: $R = \pi + \sum_{u=1}^{k} n_u s_u + \sum_{i=1}^{n_s} \sum_{s=1}^{k} s_s^i$. Assuming symmetry between different skills, total rent or net output is:

$$ R = g \left(\sum_{u=1}^{k} l_u, \left(\sum_{s=1}^{k} l_s^\rho \right)^{\frac{1}{\rho}} \right) - k \sum_{i=1}^{n_s} c_i. $$

Notice that the level of wages influences only the distribution of rents between the agents, because the skilled workers pay the unemployment benefit $\bar{s}$ for the unemployed workers. Wages have no influence on total rent R, but total rent increases with the number of workers. Efficient total labour demand equals $l_s + l_u = L$, namely, the entire labour force. In the first-best solution which maximizes the rent, wages have to be set such that full and adequate employment is found for every worker.[10] This is made possible by reducing the wage level if labour demand is too low because the marginal productivity of all workers is positive (g_1 and $g_2 > 0$). Overqualification is inefficient because the investment in human capital is costly. The first-best solution for every skill group is $l_s = n_s$ with l_s according to (3) and $l_u = n_u$ with l_u according to (4). In the first-best solution, the expected surplus of skilled and unskilled workers in an ability group is changed (compare (5) and (6)):

$$ s_u = w_u , \tag{7} $$

$$ \hat{s}_s = w_s - \frac{c}{1 - \hat{n}_s} , \tag{8} $$

where (7) is the surplus of all unskilled workers and (8) is the surplus of the marginal skilled worker $\hat{n}_s$. All other skilled workers enjoy higher rents. The equilibrium condition for the number of skilled workers requires that the surplus of the marginal skilled worker $\hat{s}_s$ is equal to the surplus of the unskilled workers s_u. In other words, no additional expected rent can be gained from acquiring a skill. Only then will no unskilled workers be induced to invest in schooling. This is the case here, if:

$$ \hat{s}_s = w_s - \frac{c}{1 - \hat{n}_s} = w_u = s_u . \tag{9} $$

The skilled wage mark-up in (9) is called 'compensating', because the marginal skilled worker re-earns precisely his or her investment costs by the skilled wage premium. All unskilled workers cannot re-earn their investment because of their differential investment costs. All inframarginal skilled workers enjoy a rent, which is the difference between their individual investment costs c_i and $c/1 - \hat{n}_s$.

In order to obtain full employment, the minimum wage w_u has to decrease such that total labour demand $l_u + l_s$ is equal to total labour supply n in every ability group, taking (9) into account. The competitive unskilled wage that equates aggregate labour demand and supply is called w_u^c.[11] The situation for a representative ability group is shown in Figure 6.1.[12]

Figure 6.1   First-best equilibrium

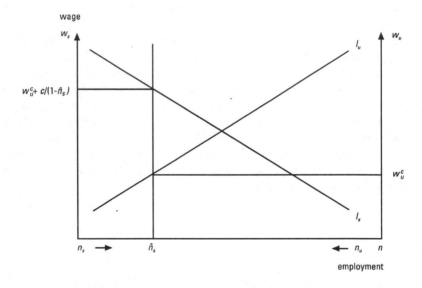

In Figure 6.1, unskilled wages and the skilled wage mark-up are such that skilled and unskilled labour demand l_u and l_s sum to n. In addition, all skilled workers n_s of the ability group depicted find adequate jobs, that is, there is no oversupply of skilled workers. In equilibrium, the marginal skilled worker with investment costs $c/1 - \hat{n}_s$ earns a net surplus of w_u^c.

5 MONOPOLISTIC COMPETITION

Next it is shown that a more than compensating mark-up for skilled workers arising from monopolistic market power necessarily leads to overqualification and a Pareto-inferior solution. Higher wages for skilled workers reduce skilled labour demand and therefore aggregate labour demand. This increases the unemployment of unskilled workers and the unemployment insurance payments of skilled workers.

It is assumed that all skilled workers are organized in a union that represents their interests and sets the monopolistic skilled wage mark-up.[13] An alternative interpretation is that one large union sets an individual wage for each ability group. In order to be able to compare the first-best solution with the monopolistic competition solution, we will assume that the wage for unskilled labour is still fixed at the level in the first-best scenario w_u^c. This can be motivated with a minimum wage set by unions.

According to the theory of monopolistic competition, it is assumed that skilled workers only take the demand function for their specialization into account, ignoring the effects of their wage demand on aggregate labour demand and labour demand for other skills groups. The basic assumption that skilled workers (or their unions) do not take into account the shift in their demand function resulting from wage setting, can be motivated from the large number k of skills. Here the actual impact of individual wage setting of one skill group indeed has a negligible impact on the total demand for labour. Since n and k are large, a change of l_s has little effect on total skilled labour demand and therefore little effect on g_1 and g_2. Hence it is assumed that all wage demands of the individual workers in an ability group move together and that the individually small effects add to a significant amount. The perceived skilled labour demand for the workers of a representative human capital group can be rewritten from (3):

$$l_s = \alpha w_s^{-\frac{1}{1-\rho}}, \tag{10}$$

with α being a positive constant. The labour demand for skilled workers of one ability group decreases with the wage demand of that group. This effect is the larger, the higher is the elasticity of substitution between the different abilities. If the perceived demand function for skilled workers of one specialization (10) is substituted into the expected surplus function of the skilled workers s_s (6), and this expression is maximized with respect to w_s, we obtain skilled wage demand. Unions set wages to maximize the expected skilled workers' surplus, taking labour demand (and overqualification) and unemployment benefit payments into account. This results in the well-known[14] optimal skilled wage mark-up:[15]

$$w_s = \frac{w_u^c}{\rho}. \tag{11}$$

Notice that the employment probability, the shift parameter in the perceived demand function α, as well as the individual sunk costs for the acquisition of skill c_i do not play a role in the monopolistic wage mark-up. The wage demanded increases with the outside option (i.e. the minimum wage w_u^c) and decreases with the substitutability of the different types of human capital. The workers demand a mark-up over their outside option because it is assumed that $0<\rho<1$. Analogous to other models of monopolistic competition, the necessity of employing workers with different skills ('love of variety') that cannot perfectly be substituted, gives skilled workers the opportunity to demand a monopolistic wage mark-up.

It is not clear whether the optimal monopolistic wage mark-up is higher or lower than in the first-best solution (where $w_s = w_u^c + c/1 - \hat{n}_u$). This model shows the consequences of a higher than compensating skilled wage mark-up.[16] It is thus assumed that the monopolistic wage mark-up is higher than the compensating mark-up in the social planner scenario. The mark-up of skilled workers also has to compensate for the unemployment benefit costs $\bar{s}$ that adequately employed skilled workers have to pay for the u unemployed unskilled workers. Therefore, in the remainder of this paper it is assumed that:

$$w_u^c \left(\frac{1-\rho}{\rho} \right) - \frac{u\bar{s}}{\hat{n}_s} > \frac{c}{1-\hat{n}_s}. \tag{12}$$

Notice that equation (12) has to apply for all levels of u. The equilibrium number of skilled workers is reached if the unskilled workers in the labour pool for a certain skill are not able to earn a rent by training. The traditional notion of monopolistic competition equilibrium would imply that there is no surplus above the competitive unskilled wage w_u^c achievable for the skilled workers; in other words, no additional rents from education can be earned by the skilled workers. This condition is analogous to the zero-profit condition in the goods market that rules out entry of additional firms. In the labour market, there is no such zero-profit condition, however, because the surplus of the unskilled workers falls below w_u^c if unskilled workers face the risk of becoming unemployed. In this case, the expected equilibrium surplus of all skilled workers also decreases and at least the marginal skilled worker enjoys an expected surplus which is lower than w_u^c.

It is shown below that overqualification is necessary to reach an equilibrium when the skilled wage is more than compensating. Skilled and unskilled labour demand l_s and l_u are directly derived from equations (2) and (3), dependent on w_u^c and ρ.

Overqualification and the number of unskilled workers are deduced from $\hat{n}_s$ and n. Notice that a necessary ingredient for this result is the assumption that overqualified skilled workers are not able to underbid their former colleagues in order to price themselves into the skilled labour market again. This follows from the assumption that the firm only employs workers with the same wage demand. Notice also that an equilibrium is only defined for overqualification (o is positive or zero), so that underqualification is not viable. With underqualification, skilled labour demand is higher than skilled labour supply. Therefore, all skilled workers earn a more than compensating wage differential with certainty, while unskilled workers can earn at most w_u^c. As a result, unskilled workers are induced to obtain skills. This cannot be an equilibrium, except at the corner solution defined by $\hat{n}_s = n$.

If we set the expected surplus for the marginal skilled worker equal to the surplus earned by an unskilled worker, the labour market equilibrium condition can be derived from the workers' surplus functions (5) and (6):

$$\frac{l_s}{\hat{n}_s} w_s - \frac{u}{\hat{n}_s} \bar{s} + \frac{o}{\hat{n}_s} w_u^c - \frac{c}{1 - \hat{n}_s} = \frac{l_u - o}{1 - \hat{n}_s} w_u^c + \left(1 - \frac{l_u - o}{1 - \hat{n}_s}\right) \bar{s} . \tag{13}$$

In order to show that overqualification o is necessary for an equilibrium in (13), this equation can be rewritten to make the effects of o on the surplus of unskilled workers and the marginal skilled worker transparent. The left-hand side, which is the expected surplus of the marginal skilled worker, can also be expressed as:

$$\hat{s}_s = -\frac{o}{\hat{n}_s}\left(w_s + \bar{s} - w_u^c\right) + w_s - \frac{(1 - \hat{n}_s) - l_u}{\hat{n}_s} \bar{s} - \frac{c}{1 - \hat{n}_s} . \tag{14}$$

The surplus of the unskilled workers (the right-hand side) can be rewritten as:

$$s_u = -\frac{o}{(1 - \hat{n}_s)}\left(w_u^c - \bar{s}\right) + \frac{l_u}{1 - \hat{n}_s} w_u^c + \left(\frac{1 - \hat{n}_s - l_u}{1 - \hat{n}_s}\right) \bar{s} . \tag{15}$$

In order to reach an equilibrium, (14) has to be equal to (15). Suppose there was no overqualification, and hence the number of skilled workers decreased symmetrically with the decrease in skilled jobs. In this case, equations (14) and (15) would become:

$$w_s - \frac{1-\hat{n}_s-l_u}{\hat{n}_s}\bar{s} - \frac{c}{1-\hat{n}_s}\frac{l_u}{1-\hat{n}_s}w_u^c + \left(\frac{1-\hat{n}_s-l_u}{\hat{n}_s}\right)\bar{s} \ . \tag{16}$$

As the right-hand side is smaller than w_u^c and the left-hand side is larger than w_u^c, this can never be an equilibrium (i.e. both sides cannot be equal). Therefore, overqualification has to equate both sides.[17] Overqualification reduces the expected surplus of both skilled and unskilled workers; compare (14) and (15). In order to reach an equilibrium, the surplus of the marginal skilled worker (14) has to decline faster than that of the unskilled workers (15), because the expected surplus of the unskilled workers is already lower than in the optimum due to the unemployment induced by higher skilled wages. In addition, the expected surplus of the skilled workers is higher than in the optimum because the skilled wage mark-up is higher than compensating. Overqualification reduces the surplus of the marginal skilled worker by the monopolistic wage mark-up over the outside option of the skilled workers minus the payment for an additional unemployed unskilled worker $1/\hat{n}_s(w_u^c/\rho +\bar{s}-w_u^c)$. The expected surplus of the unskilled workers is reduced by the difference between the wage in the unskilled labour market and the unemployment benefit $1/1-\hat{n}_u(w_u^c-\bar{s})$. This yields the following condition for an equilibrium with a more than compensating mark-up:

$$\frac{\hat{n}_s}{1-\hat{n}_s} < \frac{1-\rho-\varepsilon\rho}{\rho-\varepsilon\rho} \ . \tag{17}$$

The unemployment insurance cost burden has to be divided by the number of adequately employed skilled workers. Therefore the share of skilled workers in the workforce cannot be too large; otherwise, the expected reduction in surplus would be relatively too small per person. The larger the mark-up ρ, the smaller the relative share of skilled workers must be, because only the skilled workers benefit from a higher monopolistic mark-up.[18] The labour market is brought into equilibrium by the number of workers choosing education, $\hat{n}_s$.[19] As we assume a declining skilled labour demand in skilled wages, there is less skilled labour demand in the monopolistic wage scenario than in the optimum. As we have assumed that the cross-wage elasticity in labour demand is zero, unskilled labour supply is unaffected. It follows that, with a more than compensating monopolistic mark-up, overqualification has to be induced in order to reach an equilibrium in the labour market. The labour market power of skilled workers by virtue of their relative monopoly position causes labour market inefficiencies. The intuition is that if the costs of acquiring a skill are lower than the 'additional revenues' being skilled, it is in the interest of the unskilled workers to invest in education even if there is a risk of losing the investment costs because of the oversupply in their skill. The additional revenues are the more than compensating wage mark-up and the job guarantee for skilled workers. An excess supply of skilled workers will occur, if a low substitutability between skills groups and a low unemployment benefit allows a higher than compensating monopoly mark-up for skilled wages, provided the investment costs (and therefore the barriers to enter the skilled labour market) are low or if the minimum wage w_u^c is high. In addition, a high unemployment rate among unskilled workers (i.e. a high wage elasticity of aggregate demand) contributes to the waste of resources induced by overqualification.

Figure 6.2   Monopolistic competition

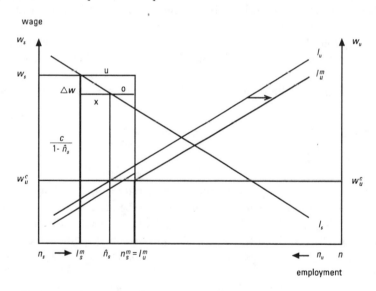

Unemployment of unskilled workers reduces the expected surplus of unskilled workers below w_u^c, which is the level obtained in the first-best equilibrium. Accordingly, the expected surplus of the marginal skilled worker is also lower than w_u^c. We find that the increase in surplus of adequately employed skilled workers by reason of a more than compensating mark-up has to be lower than the expected decrease in income of the skilled workers who are forced to work in unskilled jobs for the minimum wage $\bar{s}$. The monopolistic wage mark-up is the optimal strategy of skilled workers, taking the perceived labour demand curve for 'their' skill into account, although it generates an inefficiently low expected surplus for all workers if it is more than compensating. Therefore, the lack of a flexible wage coordination mechanism will lead to a suboptimal outcome even for the skilled workers if they enjoy enough market power. It is clear that the social rent is also smaller than in the first-best scenario, because the profits of the firm are reduced by the higher skilled wage and lower employment. The monopolistic competition situation may be depicted as in Figure 6.2.

From this analysis, it is clear that a more than compensating wage mark-up of skilled workers leads to overqualification if (17) holds. This means that $n_s^m > l_s$ at w_s. This difference is indicated by o in Figure 6.2. Notice that $w_s = w_u^c + c/1 - \hat{n}_s + \Delta w$, with Δw being the more than compensating part of the skilled wage demand. The labour demand function of unskilled workers shifts to the right by overqualification o, because the overqualified skilled workers substitute for unskilled workers. In addition, unskilled labour demand also shrinks due to lower aggregate labour demand, denoted by x in Figure 6.2. We know therefore that n_s^m is to the left of the new skilled labour demand l_s^m, while the difference between l_s^m and l_u^m equals the number of unemployed unskilled workers, $u = o + x = n - l_s^m - l_u^m$. Figure 6.2 is just one representation of many different possible equilibria in the monopolistic competition labour market.

6 REMEDIES

It is shown below how a social planner could avoid overqualification ($o = 0$), in the monopolistic competition scenario, where the more than compensating mark-up (12) is valid. In addition, a social planner solution proposed for example, by Dixit and Stiglitz (1977) in the unconstrained optimum section and by Tirole (1988) as 'first-best benchmark' is applied to this labour market model.

Two obvious possibilities for avoiding overqualification are to decrease the outside option of the skilled workers (the minimum wage w_u) or to increase the investment costs in human capital c. If the social planner has to respect the monopolistic mark-up of the skilled workers and free entry into the skilled labour market, full employment of skilled workers in skilled jobs can be achieved by decreasing w_u such that in the labour market equilibrium (13), aggregate skilled labour demand equals aggregated skilled labour supply $(l^m_s = \hat{n}^m_s)$. This is possible because a reduction in w_u reduces the expected surplus of the skilled workers more than that of the unskilled workers. This can be seen from equation (13), where the term on the left-hand side multiplied by w^c_s is larger than the term on the right-hand side which is also multiplied by w^c_u. The difference equals the investment costs in human capital frac $c/N - \hat{n}_s$. The solution for the unskilled wage is then:

$$w^P_u = \frac{c}{n - \hat{n}_s}\left(\left(\frac{1-\rho}{\rho}\right) - \frac{\left(1 - \hat{n}_s - l_u\right)\left(n\varepsilon - \hat{n}_s\right)}{\hat{n}_s\left(n - \hat{n}_s\right)}\right)^{-1}.$$

Figure 6.3   Reduction in the minimum wage

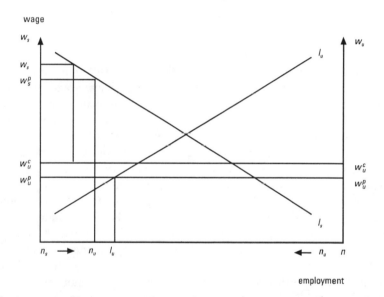

The level of the minimum wage w^P_u that is compatible with zero overqualification increases with the education costs and decreases with the mark-up between the minimum wage and skilled wage on the one hand, and the minimum wage and the unemployment benefit on the other hand. This social planner measure also leads to less unemployment of unskilled workers because aggregate labour demand increases with falling wages. The number of workers specializing in a certain skill is reduced, because it is no longer as attractive to invest in training. Notice that the social planner solution implies a lower surplus for both groups of workers than does the first-best optimum because $w_u^P < w_u^c$. The firm's profits increase in comparison to the monopolistic competition scenario. The mechanism can be illustrated in Figure 6.3.[20]

Here, the skilled workers ask the more than compensating mark-up according to (11). If the minimum wage is decreased, unskilled labour demand increases to l_u, while the number of unskilled individuals increases to n_u. Skilled labour demand increases to l_s in Figure 6.3. In the new equilibrium, then, $n_u - l_u$ workers are unemployed, while all skilled workers find work. No unskilled workers are replaced by overqualified skilled workers.

An increase in investment costs also reduces the attractiveness of investments in skills and hence reduces the number of workers deciding to obtain skills. In order to reduce overqualification to zero, the investment costs should be:

$$c^P = \left(n - \hat{n}_s\right)\left(\frac{1-\rho}{\rho}\right)w_u^c - \frac{(1-\hat{n}_s-l_u)(n\varepsilon - \hat{n}_s)}{\hat{n}_s} \ .$$

As education is commonly highly subsidized, an increase in investment costs could easily be achieved by a reduction in public subsidies for university education at times of overeducation. The inefficiencies incurred by the monopolistic skilled wage mark-up will still serve to reduce social welfare, however.

Dixit and Stiglitz (1977) and Tirole (1988) propose a different social planner solution. Here, the social planner does not allow for the exploitation of monopolistic market power by setting a more than compensating skilled wage demand. Instead, the social planner sets wages of skilled workers equal to the minimum level w_u. In addition, the schooling costs of the skilled workers employed in skilled jobs are borne by the firm. Marginal labour costs are therefore w_u for the unskilled jobs and $(w_u + c_i)$ for the skilled jobs. The demand for workers within the different skills groups l_s and the demand for unskilled workers per skills group l_u are determined from the first order conditions of the firm's profit function (2) and (3). The number of skilled workers n_s is determined by the no-entry condition, that is, unskilled workers earn no rent when training. Notice that the firm just pays the education costs for the skilled workers accepted, while the skilled workers who do not find an adequate job lose their investment costs. As a result, not all workers are attracted to invest in skills, because the investment costs will be lost if the worker does not get an adequate job.

In this case, the ex-post surplus function of the skilled workers is changed slightly. Skilled workers earn the basic wage with certainty (it does not matter whether they work in a skilled or unskilled job), but the education costs are only borne by the firm for those workers who have a job for which they specialized. If we again assume that the overqualified skilled workers are chosen randomly, we obtain the following expression for the marginal skilled workers' prime expected surplus:

$$\hat{s}^r = w_u - \frac{n\bar{s}}{l_s} - \frac{\hat{n}_s - l_s}{\hat{n}_s} \frac{c}{1 - \hat{n}_s}. \tag{18}$$

The surplus of the unskilled workers is not changed. They receive the remaining unskilled jobs and are paid the basic wage, while the unemployed unskilled workers just earn the outside option $\bar{s}$ (cf. (5)). If the surplus levels of both groups of workers are set to equal, the following condition for the labour market equilibrium is derived instead of (13):

$$w_u - \frac{o}{\hat{n}_s(n - \hat{n}_s)} c - \frac{u}{\hat{n}_s} \bar{s} = \frac{l_u - o}{1 - \hat{n}_s} w_u + \frac{u}{1 - \hat{n}_s} \bar{s}. \tag{19}$$

From the equilibrium condition above, it can be seen immediately that this social planner rule only leads to adequate employment for all skilled workers ($u = 0$) if all unskilled workers find work ($1 - \hat{n}_s = l_u - o$) or if the outside option of the unskilled workers is equal to the minimum wage $w_u = \bar{s}$. Otherwise, there is a continuum of equilibria with overqualified workers. The results of this scenario are equal to the first-best optimum if $w_u = w_u^c$. Therefore, the social planner also achieves full and adequate employment by giving the firms the right to pay education costs while all workers earn the minimum wage paid in the optimum.

Notice that this measure is associated with a different distribution of rents with respect to the optimum. The firm now earns the entire rent created by the investment in human capital, whereas in the first best optimum all inframarginal skilled workers enjoy a surplus which is higher than the minimum wage w_u^c.

7 CONCLUSIONS

We are able now to answer the three questions posed in the introduction.

- What are the consequences of increased rents for skilled workers on the skill investment decision? Workers are attracted to invest in skills even when they face a certain risk to be overqualified.
- Why do not more workers invest in skills as a consequence of persistent rents earned by skilled workers? First, if workers have different education costs, benefits may still be lower than costs for workers with high education

costs even if skilled workers enjoy rents. Second, under the condition that overqualification reduces the expected rents of skilled workers more than that of unskilled workers, overqualification is a surplus-equalizing factor when skilled workers in adequate jobs demand a wage mark-up which is higher than compensating.

• Should we care about the consequences of rising wage mark-ups for skilled workers from a welfare point of view and what are possible remedies? This model shows that a more than compensating skilled wage mark-up, made possible by market power of skilled workers, leads to a Pareto-inferior labour market equilibrium. Market power of skilled workers arises because they are specialized in a certain skill and cannot be replaced without a cost either by skilled workers with another specialization or by unskilled workers. In contrast to comparable models with compensating wage differentials, the monopolistic wage mark-up enjoyed by the skilled workers is not compensated by a higher incidence of unemployment or amenities, but by the risk of becoming overqualified. The labour market equilibrium induced by a more than compensating wage differential provides a lower surplus for both groups of workers and reduced profits for the firm. It follows that skilled workers are also on average worse off with their monopolistic wage mark-up, while skilled workers in skilled jobs are better off. Workers use skills as a weapon in job competition, which is made possible by the ease of substituting unskilled workers by skilled workers. This induces an additional incentive for overeducation in times of unemployment that makes schooling partially ineffective (compare Van Ours and Ridder, 1997).

An important question for future research is whether the consequences of increased wage inequality predicted by this model are observed in reality. We should find increasing overeducation at the end of the 1980s and the beginning of the 1990s in all countries with large rents for skilled workers. Mincer (1994) estimates the lag between the appearance of rents for schooling and a higher supply of skilled workers at eight years. This model proposes three solutions to the overqualification problem. First, a reduction in unskilled wages leads to full and adequate employment of skilled workers, because it makes unskilled work relatively more attractive. But the equilibrium surplus of both groups of workers is lower than in the optimum. A second step to reduce overqualification is to increase education costs or reduce the substantial subsidies to education. Higher education costs make it naturally less attractive to invest in skills. Third, the social planner can set the wage for all workers at the minimum level, so that skilled workers are not able to exploit their market power. In order to stimulate workers to invest in human capital, firms now pay for the education costs of those workers they hire. This solution leads to the first-best equilibrium with full and adequate employment for all workers, if the unskilled wage is at the market-clearing level in the first best scenario. In this case, the firm earns the entire rent generated by the workers and all workers just earn the minimum wage. By contrast, in the first best optimum all inframarginal adequately employed skilled workers enjoy rents above the minimum wage.

NOTES

1. Empirical studies indicate that returns to schooling are more than compensating and have been increasing in recent years, see Ashenfelter and Krueger (1994) and Juhn et al. (1993), Topel (1997, p. 58), as well as the country surveys in Davis (1992).

2. Unemployment rates for unskilled workers are roughly three times higher than those for skilled workers (see e.g. Mincer (1991), or the survey in Layard et al. (1991, pp. 286–92)).

3. This is certainly the case for the 1980s, while the evidence is mixed for recent years (see e.g. Blackburn et al. (1991, p. 8)).

4. Compare also Benassy (1991) and Matsuyama (1995).

5. Note that Layard et al. (1991, p. 305) assume a less than compensating wage differential for skilled workers in order to obtain a higher equilibrium unemployment rate for unskilled workers. They argue that the wage bargaining power of skilled workers does not allow for a compensating wage mark-up.

6. Compare e.g. Blanchard and Kiyotaki (1987), Tirole (1988), Nishimura (1989) and Matsuyama (1995).

7. Note that the additional costs of education increase from worker to worker. The differences in costs between skilled workers are therefore relatively small in contrast to those between unskilled workers.

8. The extreme assumption of complete substitutability and zero unemployment for skilled workers is made for simplicity. If some costs are associated with employing skilled workers in unskilled jobs and skilled workers face some unemployment probability which is lower than that of the unskilled workers, the results derived below would not change qualitatively.

9. This is in accordance with the empirical observation that skilled workers can easily be substituted for unskilled workers and during recessions firms hoard skilled workers, see Nickell and Bell (1995, p. 41) or Van Zon et al. (1998).

10. Compare Layard et al. (1991, p. 319).

11. We have to assume that investment costs c are such that the difference $l_s - l_u$ equals c/n_u at n_s. This 'heroic' assumption is made for the convenience of presentation and does not have an impact on the results derived below.

12. Compare the analogous Figure 9 in Layard et al. (1991, p. 320). Labour demand is depicted linearly decreasing for expository purposes. The productivity advantage δ of overqualified skilled workers does not play a role here, because all workers find an adequate job.

13. This construction is frequently used (see Snower (1983), Nishimura (1989) and Nielsen et al. (1995)).

14. The price setting behaviour is identical in Tirole (1988) equ. (7.19) on p. 299 and Dixit and Stiglitz (1977) equ. (15) on p. 299.

15. The expression below is only valid for $l_s < n_s$, or overqualification. It will be shown that this is the case with a more than compensating monopolistic skilled wage mark-up.

16. If the skilled wage mark-up were lower than compensating, aggregate labour demand would be higher than aggregate labour supply and there would be fewer skilled workers than in the optimum. This situation could be the consequence of a low market power of the skilled workers produced by a high substitution elasticity ρ.

17. Equilibrium overqualification is equal to:

$$
o = \frac{\dfrac{\hat{n}_s - l_u}{\hat{n}_s}\bar{s} + \dfrac{l_u}{\hat{n}_s}w_u^{\,c} - w_s + \dfrac{\hat{n}_s - l_u}{\hat{n}_s}\bar{s} + \dfrac{c}{\hat{n}_s}}{\dfrac{w_u - \bar{s}}{\hat{n}_s} - \dfrac{w_s + \bar{s} - w_u}{\hat{n}_s}}
$$

18. If $\rho > 0.5$, the share of skilled workers has to be smaller than the share of unskilled workers $n_s / n_u < 1$

19. Equation (13) determines the number of skilled workers n_s in the market equilibrium with monopolistically competitive wages w_s:

$$
\hat{n}_s = n\left(\frac{\epsilon u - l_s\left(\dfrac{1-\rho}{\rho}\right)}{u - l_s\left(\dfrac{1-\rho}{\rho}\right) - \dfrac{c}{w_u^{\,c}}}\right)
$$

20. As there is no overqualification, δ is ineffective again.

REFERENCES

Abowd, J. and O. Ashenfelter (1981), 'Anticipated Unemployment, Temporary Layoffs, and Compensating Wage Differentials', in Sherwin Rosen (ed.), *Studies in Labor Markets*, Chicago: University of Chicago Press.

Ashenfelter, O. and A. Krueger (1994), 'Estimates of the Economic Return to Schooling from a New Sample of Twins', *American Economic Review* **84**, 1157–73.

Benassy, J.P. (1991), 'Monopolistic Competition', in Werner Hildenbrand and Hugo Sonnenschein (eds), *Handbook of Mathematical Economics*, Vol. IV, Amsterdam: North-Holland.

Blackburn, McK., D. Bloom and R. Freeman (1991), *Changes in Earnings Differentials in the 1980s: Concordance, Convergence, Causes, and Consequences*, NBER Working Paper Series No. 3901.

Blanchard, O. and N. Kiyotaki (1987), 'Monopolistic Competition and the Effect of Aggregate Demand', *American Economic Review* **77**, 647–66.

Borjas, G. (1996), *Labor Economics*, New York: McGraw-Hill.

Borjas, G. and V. Ramey (1994), 'Time-Series Evidence on the Source of Trends in Wage Inequality', *American Economic Review* **84**, Papers and Proceedings, 10–16.

Bound, J. and G. Johnson (1992), 'Changes in the Structure of Wages in the 1980s: An Evaluation of Alternative Explanations', *American Economic Review* **82**, 371–92.

Brauer, D. and S. Hickok (1995), 'Explaining the Growing Inequality in Wages across Skill Levels', *Economic Policy Review* 1, 61–75.

Chamberlin, E. (1933), *The Theory of Monopolistic Competition*, Cambridge, MA/: Harvard University Press.

Davis, S. (1992) 'Cross-Country Patterns of Change in Relative Wages', in Olivier Blanchard and Stanley Fischer (eds), *NBER Macroeconomics Annual*, Cambridge, MA: MIT Press.

Dixit, A. and J. Stiglitz (1977),'Monopolistic Competition and Optimum Product Diversity', *American Economic Review* 67, 297–308.

Freeman, R. (1993), 'How much has De-unionization Contributed to the Rise in Male Earnings Inequality?', in Sheldon Danziger and Peter Gottschalk (eds), *Uneven Tides*, New York: Russell Sage, 133–63.

Johnson, G. (1997), 'Changes in Earnings Inequality: The Role of Demand Shifts', *Journal of Economic Perspectives* 11 (2), 41–54.

Juhn, C., K. Murphy and B. Pierce (1993), 'Wage Inequality and the Rise in Returns to Skill', *Journal of Political Economy* 101, 410–42.

Katz, L. and K. Murphy (1992), 'Changes in Relative Wages, 1963–1987: Supply and Demand Factors', *Quarterly Journal of Economics* 107, 35–78.

Layard, R., S. Nickell and R. Jackman (1991), *Unemployment-Macroeconomic Performance and the Labour Market*, Oxford: Oxford University Press.

Matsuyama, K. (1995), 'Complementarities and Cumulative Processes in Models of Monopolistic Competition', *Journal of Economic Literature* 33, 701–29.

Mincer, J. (1994), *Investment in U.S. Education and Training*, NBER Working Paper No. 4844.

Murphy, K. and F. Welch (1989), 'Wage Premiums for College Graduates: Recent Growth and Possible Explanations', *Educational Researcher*, 18, 17–26.

Nickell, S. and B. Bell (1995), 'The Collapse in Demand for the Unskilled and Unemployment across the OECD', *Oxford Review of Economic Policy* 11 (1), 40–62.

Nielsen, S., L. Pedersen, and P. Sørensen (1995), 'Environmental Policy, Pollution, Unemployment, and Endogenous Growth', *International Tax and Public Finance* 2, 185–205.

Nishimura, K. (1989), 'Indexation and Monopolistic Competition in Labor Markets', *European Economic Review* 33, 1606–23.

Snower, D. (1983), 'Imperfect Competition, Underemployment and Crowding Out', *Oxford Economic Papers* 35, suppl., 245 70.

Spence , M. (1976), 'Product Selection, Fixed Costs, and Monopolistic Competition', *Review of Economic Studies* 47, 217–35.

Tirole, J. (1988), *The Theory of Industrial Organization*, Cambridge, MA: MIT Press.

Topel, R. (1997), 'Factor Proportions and Relative Wages: The Supply-Side Determinants of Wage Inequality', *Journal of Economic Perspectives* 11, 55–74.

Van Ours, J. and G. Ridder (1997), 'Job Matching and Job Competition: Are Lower Educated Workers at the Back of Job Queues?', *European Economic Review* 39, 1717–31.

Van Zon, A., H. Meijers and J. Muysken (1998), 'Asymmetric Skill Substitution, Labour
    Market Flexibility, and the Allocation of Qualifications', in H. Heijke and L.
    Borghans (eds), *Towards a Transparent Labour Market for Educational Decisions*,
    Aldershot: Ashgate.
Willis, R. (1986), 'Wage Determinants: A Survey and Reinterpretation of Human Capital
    Earnings Functions', in Orley Ashenfelter and Richard Layard (eds), *Handbook of
    Labour Economics*, Amsterdam: Elsevier, 525–602.

ACKNOWLEDGEMENTS

This chapter greatly benefited from comments by John Addison, Lex Borghans,
Andries de Grip, Joan Muysken, Ralph Olthoff, and Winfried Vogt.

7. Overeducation and Crowding Out in Britain

Harminder Battu and Peter Sloane

1 INTRODUCTION

There has been a rapid increase in the numbers holding various levels of educational qualifications in Britain. Thus Robinson and Manacorda (1997), using Labour Force Survey data, show that the increase in the proportion of the working population holding qualifications has been dramatic over the period 1984–1994. Those with higher education qualifications as a percentage of the employed workforce rose from 14.9 per cent in 1984 to 23.1 per cent in 1994, while those without any qualifications fell from 35.2 per cent in 1984 to 17.2 per cent in 1994. It follows that unless the demand for skills has risen at the same rate or more than the increase in supply, then those with higher education qualifications must accept jobs formerly held by those with lower qualifications or face the possibility of unemployment.

The aim of the chapter is twofold. First, we attempt to establish whether this increase in qualifications is reflected in a rise in overeducation, in the sense that some workers at particular occupational levels hold qualifications not required to gain employment or perform tasks in those occupation levels, and whether this has led to a movement of workers, with the previously requisite level of qualifications in that occupational level, into jobs which previously required a level of entry level qualification lower than those of the new entrants. Second, we attempt examine the determinants of overeducation and we attempt ascertain whether larger establishments and particular industrial sectors are more likely to exhibit overeducation, as predicted by Van der Meer and Wielers (1996).

Earlier work has shown that a substantial number of those with qualifications are overeducated in the sense of being in jobs which do not require the level of education they currently possess. Thus, using the Social Change and Economic Life Initiative (SCELI) dataset Sloane et al. (1999) found that in 1986, 31 per cent of the sample were overeducated, whereby lower qualifications than they currently possessed were required of current applicants. Battu et al. (1999), using data for graduates only, found that approximately 40 per cent of graduates reported that in 1996 they were in jobs for which a degree was not a requirement. Given the substantial increase in the number of workers with qualifications this is suggestive of a bumping down process operating in the labour market with workers holding qualifications traditionally required in certain occupations being forced to accept jobs previously requiring lower qualifications than they currently possess, as those with superior qualifications take an increasing share of jobs at their own educational level. Those with no formal qualifications may as a result of this process be forced out of employment altogether.

The associated question of bumping rights in the USA, whereby some workers are protected more than others from enforced downward mobility, was emphasized by Doeringer and Piore's (1971) analysis of the internal labour market. Bumping rights are closely related to workers' ability and seniority which define the sequence in which workers displace one another when downgrading or lay-offs are required in the recession. Chain bumping is the most extreme case in which a bump by one worker initiates a series of consecutive bumps with the lowest ranked worker facing a lay-off. Kato (1986) suggests that this type of behaviour, which he claims is prevalent in the USA, can be explained in terms of an implicit contract model. However, there is no evidence that such behaviour is widespread in Britain. Further, bumping down as a consequence of an increase in educational qualifications would seem to result more in the upswing when new recruits are hired.

There is also evidence that the relative position of the least qualified deteriorated in the UK during the 1980s. Glyn (1995) reported that relative employment (the ratio of employment to population) fell by 12 per cent for this group between 1979 and 1991, while the relative ratio of employment to the labour force fell by 17 per cent. There are a number of explanations why the unskilled or uneducated might have higher rates of unemployment than the rest of the working population. Nickell and Bell (1995), for example, have four explanations. First, the skilled can do many of the tasks undertaken by the unskilled, and this makes it easier to hoard skilled workers during recessions. Second, the lack of specific skills reduces the attachment to the firm of unskilled workers and raises their rates of turnover. Third, higher unemployment benefit replacement ratios reduce the incentive to work of the unskilled. Fourth, any floor on wages will reduce the relative demand for unskilled workers and increase their relative supply as this will reduce the incentive to acquire skills. As Kraft (1994) points out, technical progress may have a differential effect on the two groups with the unskilled more likely to be replaced by capital equipment. Robinson and Manacorda (1997) note that the skill-biased technical change argument implies that any increase in the demand for more qualified labour should vary significantly by occupation depending on the degree to which particular occupations are subject to technical change or to overseas competition. They find, however, little support for this in their analysis of Labour Force Survey data. Saint-Paul (1996) has shown that firing restrictions tend to depress the demand for unskilled workers relative to the skilled because they create an option value for keeping a vacancy open until it is filled by a skilled worker rather than an unskilled worker, which suggests that the increase in the number of educated workers may have contributed to the unemployment problem, particularly in countries with high firing costs. Together these factors suggest that the employment of skilled workers relative to the unskilled will vary counter-cyclically.

An alternative approach is that of Van der Meer and Wielers (1996), who argue that educational credentials will grow in importance as productivity of workers becomes harder to measure and the employment relationship is influenced by the need for trust. A typical characteristic of job classification is that the higher the job level (linked loosely to educational qualifications) the greater the autonomy and discretion afforded the worker. The degree of such autonomy is likely to be manifested more in the service sector than it is in manufacturing. Similarly large organizations find it more difficult to measure the output of each worker than do small. They note that when there is an increase in the supply of educated labour the wages of both highly and lowly educated workers will fall. Further, some highly educated workers will bump less educated workers and the latter will become unemployed as their costs per unit of labour are now above the market clearing rate. The hypothesis is, therefore, that the first signs and the stronger effects of crowding out will appear in the high trust sectors rather than in low trust sectors (i.e. in services and in large organizations). Hence, larger establishments and the service sector are more likely to display overeducation.[1] This we test using a logit model.

The above studies neglect, however, the behaviour of wage rates for various educational qualifications within broad occupational groups. Earlier work on over-education suggests that overeducated workers can earn more than those who are educationally matched in the same occupation, implying that the former are more productive than the latter (Sicherman, 1991). However, there still exists a penalty for being overeducated since those who have a higher but fully utilized level of education earn a wage premium over those whose higher education is not fully utilized (they are in a lower level job). As Robinson and Manacorda (1997) note, ideally we should also pay attention to the widening earnings distribution which has occurred over the period and establish whether this is a consequence of intra- or inter-occupational wage changes.

The main hypothesis of the chapter, as outlined above in section 2, is that as the proportion of the labour force with various educational qualifications rises some of the educated move into lower prestige jobs (generating over-education) and the less educated are bumped down, so that the mean education level rises in all occupations and presumably some of the uneducated lose their jobs. This will have the effect of widening wage differentials overall, thus offsetting the tendency for the educated wage differential over the uneducated to fall with the increase in the supply of qualifications. Though we do not test this aspect, the earnings distribution in Britain has widened significantly over the period analysed.

The chapter has the following structure. In Section 2 we outline various measurement issues associated with our two datasets and our empirical approach. Section 3 offers some stylised facts and some empirical findings with respect to the determinants of overeducation. Section 4 has a conclusion.

2 METHODOLOGY

The data used are the 1986 Social Change and Economic Life Initiative (SCELI) dataset and waves A (1991) and E (1995) of the British Household Panel Study (BHPS). The SCELI dataset contains information on both actual education and required education, and these two measures can be used to generate a measure for overeducation.

Both the SCELI and the BHPS dataset provide the Hope-Goldthorpe prestige ranking for the respondent's occupation (Goldthorpe and Hope, 1974). This enables us to make a direct comparison of the extent to which those with a given level of education have, over the time period covered by these datasets, changed the nature of their employment as proxied by the prestige of their occupation. As Goldthorpe and Hope note, the validity of occupational prestige scales depends crucially on the extent to which different evaluators concur in their assessment of occupations. It appears that regardless of socio-economic group, age, residential type or region, the evaluations are remarkably similar. The scale values they adopt, ranging from 18 to 82, reflect the median of the scale values for the constituent occupations.

The availability of the Hope-Goldthorpe scale in both datasets allows us to estimate the extent of overeducation in the BHPS. Overeducation is typically measured by comparing actual education with the educational requirements of the job. SCELI respondents were asked '. . . if they were applying today, what qualifications, if any, would someone need to get the type of job you have now?'. Respondents would then indicate which of nineteen education qualifications were required for their job. These nineteen educational qualifications were then categorized into a hierarchy of six education levels – No Qualifications; Apprenticeship, Clerical and Commercial Qualifications; Qualifications less than the Ordinary Level (Other); Ordinary level or equivalent; Advanced level or equivalent; and finally Higher Education or equivalent Professional Qualifications.

No information on educational requirements for the job were provided in the BHPS. However, it was possible to determine, for each of the points on the Hold-Goldthorpe scale, the average educational requirements for such jobs using the individual observations within SCELI. This information could then be used to generate for BHPS respondents, a required education term based on the relevant point on the Hope-Goldthorpe scale. Thus, each BHPS respondent would be given, as their educational requirement level, the average educational requirements of SCELI respondents with the same Hope-Goldthorpe scale.

Though the estimated required level of education must have the same mean as the original required level of education, the standard deviation for the estimated measure is less than that for the original measure. The reason for this 'compression' of the required education scale is because of overestimation when required education is no qualifications (or, to a lesser extent, basic qualifications) and underestimation when required education is a degree or professional qualification (or, to a lesser extent, A level or equivalent). This is not surprising – any errors when required education is no qualifications must be positive, while errors when required education is degree or professional qualifications must be negative.

The validity of this exercise was indicated by the fact that the new estimated required education measure is positively related to the original required education measure. Using the new estimated required measure and the original actual education measures from SCELI and the two waves of the BHPS made it possible to obtain estimates of overeducation for the years 1986, 1991 and 1995. In essence, both the SCELI and the BHPS respondents were given, as their measure of required education, the average level of required education reported by SCELI respondents in their Hope-Goldthorpe category.

In both datasets overeducation is determined by comparing actual education with either the original required education or the estimated required education. How do the aggregate levels of overeducation compare? Using the estimated required education measure indicated that no individuals were adequately educated. The reason for this stems from the fact that our estimation method, based on arithmetic averages, provides estimates of required education that are rarely integers; actual education, on the other hand, is always an integer; thus, our method artificially restricts adequate education to be low or zero.

So long as a 'match' (i.e. adequately educated) is defined as being an exact match, respondents will almost always be classified as either overeducated or undereducated. This problem is overcome by widening the extent of inequality permitted between actual education and required education before a respondent is classified as mismatched. Thus, adequate education is now defined as a range encompassing one point either side of the estimated required education measure for that respondent. This might be seen as an arbitrarily-imposed criterion. However, it was found using the SCELI data that this definition of adequate education provided an estimate of adequate education that is very similar to that obtained when using the original measures for actual and required education (see Table 7.2).

In addition to the above approach a regression analysis is attempted. Following Blackburn et al. (1991) Schmitt (1995), Van der Meer and Wielers (1996) and Robinson and Manacorda (1997) there are two distinct approaches to explaining variations in overeducation. First a shift-share decomposition of changes in educational differentials over time and second a regression based approach. A shift share approach is not possible using the Hope-Goldthorpe occupational scale. This stems from the fact that for many of the occupational scores there exist either very few or no individuals in each of our six educational categories. An econometric approach was then taken in which a cross-section equation is estimated at three points in time.

Prior econometric analysis has focused on explaining the mean level of earnings controlling for industry and educational qualifications (Schmitt, 1995) or the probability of exceeding a given educational level (Van der Meer and Wielers, 1996). Here we attempt to explain the probability of being overeducated across segments using the Hope-Goldthorpe scale. Thus, the estimating equation is

$$Oe_i = a + b_1 J_i + b_2 W_i + b_3 Age_i + b_4 Gender + b_5 Ten + b_6 EstSize_i + b_7 Ind_i + b_8 Reg_i + \epsilon_i$$

where

Oe_i = dummy variable according to whether overeducated or not
J_i = occupational level measured by the Hope-Goldthorpe scale
W_i = mean level of hourly earnings
Gender = a dummy for male
Ten = tenure
$EstSize_i$ = establishment size measured in terms of employment
Ind_i = industry dummies
Reg_i = regional dummies
and ϵ_i = error term

This equation is estimated separately for 1986, 1991 and 1995. The specification is uncontroversial except for the fact that we have incorporated the HG scale as an independent variable to test whether higher occupational levels are associated with greater over-education. Hourly earnings are expected to increase, given occupational level, as the proportion of the overeducated rises in line with Sicherman's stylized facts. This is to be interpreted as indicating that overeducated workers are more productive than appropriately matched workers, and employers are prepared to pay a premium to attract and/or retain the former. Implicitly we assume that the proportion of the workforce undereducated remains constant within occupational groups. The age terms allow for the fact that workers with no qualifications tend to be older than those with qualifications (Schmitt interacts the age terms with qualifications). The gender variable attempts to deal with Schmitt's (1995) observation that new female employees may have competed disproportionately with low-skilled male workers, thus helping to widen skill differentials. The inclusion of tenure as an explanatory variable is intended to capture the substitutability hypothesis whereby different components of human capital are regarded as substitutes. For instance a large number of overeducation studies have established that those who are overeducated also tend to have lower tenure and experience (proxied here by age).[2] The incorporation of establishment size and industrial dummies is intended to test Van der Meer and Wielers (1996) notion that high trust sectors (those in services and in large establishments) are more likely to exhibit overeducation.

3 RESULTS

3.1 Education and Occupational Prestige 1986–1995: Some Stylized Facts

Across our three data points, the increase in the proportion of educated workers in the British workforce has been dramatic. Table 7.1 lists qualification levels in 1986, 1991, and 1995. It should be borne in mind that the SCELI data are not strictly comparable as they relate to only six local labour markets, but in practice they seem to be reasonably representative of Britain as a whole over a number of dimensions. The BHPS data are also subject to attrition and the unemployed may be particularly prone to this. Notwithstanding, the rise in the proportions in the sample educated to degree level is dramatic increasing from 23.8 per cent in 1986 to 30.4 per cent in 1991 and 38.4 per cent in 1995. Correspondingly the proportion of the labour force lacking any educational qualifications, declines from 30 per cent in 1986 to 22.1 per cent in 1991 and 15.9 per cent in 1995.

Table 7.1   Qualification levels across the three data years

Qualification	SCELI 1986 %	BHPS I 1991 %	BHPS 1995 %
No qualifications	30.0	22.1	15.9
Apprent/commer	5.9	0.8	0.7
Other	11.8	10.0	9.0
O Level	19.3	24.7	22.9
A level	9.2	12.0	13.1
Higher education/Professional	23.8	30.4	38.4
N	3,678	5,004	4,410

Note: The disaggregated educational qualification classification system (the 19 'raw' categories) in SCELI is not 100 per cent the same as that in the BHPS. One of the effects of this is that apprenticeship and commercial qualifications are less common in the BHPS datasets. In general, there is not an exact match-up.

Table 7.2 provides our estimates of overeducation. In column 1 we have reproduced our estimates from an earlier study using SCELI (Sloane et al., 1999) and the next column has the reworked estimates using the estimated rather than actual required education variable. The final two columns present estimates from the 1991 and 1995 tranches of the BHPS using the estimated required education variable generated from SCELI. The estimates reveal quite clearly a rise in overeducation from SCELI to the BHPS and across the two waves of the BHPS. Two factors need to be borne in mind. First, we make the assumption that required education has not changed since 1986. Second, estimates of mismatch are contingent upon the method of measurement. Other UK studies which employ a standard deviation (a worker is defined as overeducated if his or her education is more than one standard deviation above the average for his or her occupation) approach tend to find fairly low levels of overeducation (for example, see Groot, 1996).

Table 7.2   Extent of mismatch

	SCELI 1986[a] %	SCELI 1986[b] %	BHPS I 1991[c] %	BHPS 1995[d] %
Overeducated	30.5	28.0	40.5	44.1
Adequately educated	52.5	55.4	48.5	44.9
Undereducated	17.1	16.6	11.0	11.0

Notes:
[a] SCELI estimates from Sloane, et al. (1999).
[b] Reworked SCELI estimates using estimated required education.
[c] 1991 BHPS estimates using estimated required from SCELI.
[d] 1995 BHPS estimates using estimated required from SCELI.

To ascertain the extent to which those with a given level of educational qualifications have changed their distribution of employment across the Hope-Goldthorpe occupational scale we charted each level of education across the HG scale for our three data points. Figure 7.1 which plots the cumulative percentage of unqualified workers against the Hope-Goldthorpe scale shows remarkable stability over time with approximately 60 per cent of this group in lower-level manual occupations. It does not appear that the increase in qualifications has led to a displacement of this group towards lower level occupational prestige jobs. The Apprenticeship chart (Figure 7.2) shows a more confused picture with the curves for 1986, 1991 and 1995 intersecting one another. If anything this group has gained from a rightward

Figure 7.1   Cumulative percentage of unqualified workers against the Hope-Goldthorpe scale

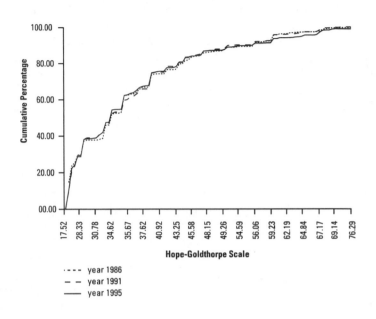

shift in the occupational prestige of jobs. The situation for workers with other qualifications (Figure 7.3) is much clearer as the cumulative percentage curves for 1991 and 1995 everywhere lie above the 1986 curve, so that the mean occupational prestige of jobs for this group has fallen, with the decline being concentrated in the period 1986–1991. In the case of O-level holder employees (Figure 7.4) there is a discontinuity in the distribution between manual and non-manual occupations. To the left of this discontinuity the distributions are very similar at each of the three dates, but thereafter the 1995 and 1991 distributions diverge from 1986, again reflecting a movement towards lower prestige jobs for this group. Workers with A-levels (Figure 7.5) have a similar discontinuity at the top of the manual and bottom of the non-manual division and in this case there is a leftward shift towards lower prestige occupations throughout the distribution. Finally, for those employees with higher education and or professional qualifications (Figure 7.6) there is a sharp discontinuity at the occupational prestige scale representing lower grade salaried professionals which includes school teachers, nurses and lower

Figure 7.2   Cumulative percentage of workers with apprenticeship level or commercial qualifications

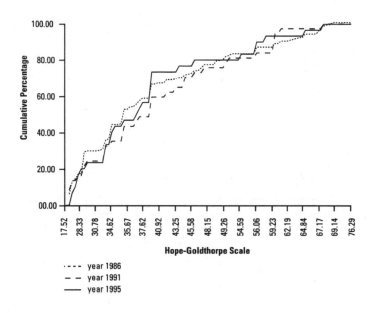

Table 7.3   Mean Hope-Goldthorpe score across education groups

Qualification	SCELI 1986	BHPS I 1991	BHPS 1995
No qualifications	35.34	35.63	35.54
Apprenticeship/Commercial	39.42	40.44	39.64
Other	43.02	38.76	39.13
O Level	43.54	42.39	42.29
A level	49.20	48.10	46.41
Higher education/Professional	59.26	57.61	56.51
All	45.06	45.83	46.90

level civil servants. To the left of the discontinuity there is a clear movement over time into jobs of lower occupational prestige, while to the right of the discontinuity the change is in the opposite direction reflecting less of a sharp divide between graduate and non-graduate jobs.

Causes of Underutilization

Figure 7.3   Cumulative percentage of workers with other qualifications

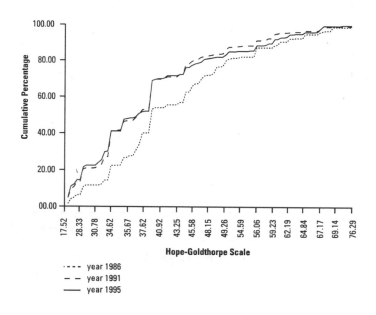

Table 7.3 confirms the above by showing that the mean Hope-Goldthorpe score has remained constant for low levels of attained education (no qualifications and apprenticeship), but fallen for the higher educational levels. Overall, the mean Hope-Goldthorpe score has risen between 1986 and 1995 refuting the sociological notion that there has been a deskilling of jobs. However, the rise in the supply of educated manpower has caused an increase in the share of this group among the unemployed in our sample (Table 7.4). While in 1986 those with the highest qualifications comprised 12.4 per cent of the unemployed by 1995 this had risen to 27.5 per cent. In contrast the share of those without any qualifications among the unemployed fell from 43.8 to 29.9 per cent. To conclude, the evidence points strongly towards skill bumping or the crowding out of educated workers, such that the median level of the occupational prestige values has declined for most educational levels. It remains to be determined whether this in turn will lead to a re-evaluation of jobs in prestige terms with individuals increasing their rating of the prestige rankings of jobs in which educational levels have risen.

Figure 7.4   *Cumulative percentage of workers with O-level qualifications*

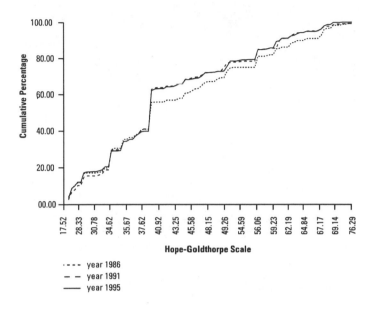

Table 7.4   *Educational qualifications of the unemployed*

Qualification	SCELI 1986 %	BHPS I 1991 %	BHPS 1995 %
No qualifications	43.8	37.8	29.9
Apprenticeship/Commercial	8.9	1.7	0.5
Other	10.5	13.8	10.1
O Level	17.4	21.1	23.2
A level	7.0	9.0	8.8
Higher education/Professional	12.4	16.6	27.5

Figure 7.5   Cumulative percentage of workers with A-level qualifications

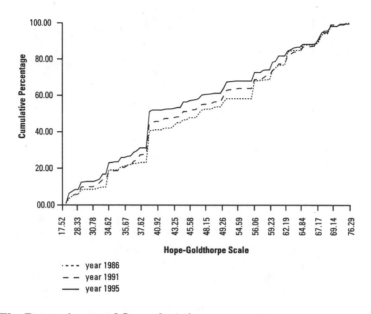

3.2 The Determinants of Overeducation

The logit estimates are given in Table 7.5. As expected the probability of being overeducated is positively related to one's position in the Hope-Goldthorpe rating scale. Similarly, as the level of required education increases the probability of being overeducated rises. Overeducation is also positively associated with earnings for 1991 and 1995. This is consistent with Sicherman's (1991) finding that there is a premium in pay associated with being in a job which does not require as much education as the worker possesses, relative to matched and undereducated workers.

Men are significantly more likely to be over-educated than women and since marriage is not associated with the probability of being overeducated these results lend no support to Frank's theory of differential overqualification. According to Frank (1978) married females are more likely to be overeducated in non-urban areas since for couples the search for a pair of jobs which will optimize family income will be spatially constrained. Only by chance will both husband and wife maximize their incomes in the same labour market. The husband, being a primary earner makes smaller compromises than the wife when changing jobs, resulting in differential overeducation.

Table 7.5   Logit equations for over-education

	1986		1991		1995	
	Coeff	*t*-stat	Coeff	*t*-stat	Coeff	*t*-stat
Constant	0.927	(1.64)	0.955**	(2.02)	1.112*	(1.95)
Male	0.348***	(4.51)	0.315***	(3.81)	0.505***	(5.07)
Married	−0.087	(−1.06)	0.054	(0.62)	0.019	(0.19)
White	0.050	(0.18)	−0.432	(−1.93)	−0.126	(−0.47)
Age	−0.028***	(−7.36)	−0.050***	(−13.42)	−0.045***	(−9.85)
Required education	−0.430***	(−14.76)	−1.302***	(−16.10)	−1.436***	(−14.40)
Hope-Goldthorpe score	0.002**	(2.05)	0.056***	(8.09)	0.057***	(6.87)
Hourly earnings	0.008	(1.23)	0.111***	(8.52)	0.089***	(6.95)
Tenure	−0.005***	(−6.85)	−0.002**	(−2.48)	−0.002***	(−3.38)
Temporary	−0.284**	(−2.30)	−0.051	(−0.34)	0.041	(0.22)
Establishment size (25–99 employees)	−0.350***	(−3.65)	−0.143	(−1.47)	0.015	(0.13)
Establishment size (100–499 empl.)	−0.299***	(−3.00)	−0.097	(−0.96)	−0.096	(−0.80)
Establishment size (500 plus empl.)	−0.051	(−0.51)	0.0004	(0.003)	−0.139	(−0.99)
Manufacturing	0.667	(1.41)	0.044	(0.12)	−0.081	(−0.19)
Energy	1.066**	(2.19)	0.365	(0.94)	0.322	(0.69)
Construction	0.555	(1.12)	0.288	(0.71)	0.277	(0.54)
Distribution	0.865*	(1.84)	0.257	(0.71)	0.041	(0.09)
Services	0.835*	(1.77)	0.308	(0.85)	0.166	(0.38)
N	4596		3895		2813	
Log likelihood	−2,480.822		−2,198.368		−1,573.511	
Pseudo R^2	0.103		0.169		0.188	

Note: Levels of significance *:10%, **:5%, ***:1%.

In accordance with the substitutability hypothesis (i.e. the idea that different types of human capital can be substituted for one another) there is a strong negative association between age (a proxy for experience) and tenure and the probability of being overeducated. Though no strong association between the size of establishment and overeducation for 1991 and 1995 is detected, for 1986 larger employers are associated with lower overeducation. On the whole this contradicts the hypothesis entertained by Van der Meer and Wielers (1996) that larger employers unable to monitor employee productivity take on more educated workers affording them greater autonomy and discretion. There is also no support for Van der Meer and

Wielers educational credentials theory at an industrial level. No discernible relationship between area or region and over-education is evident from our data (not reported in table).

Figure 7.6   Cumulative percentage of workers with professional qualifications

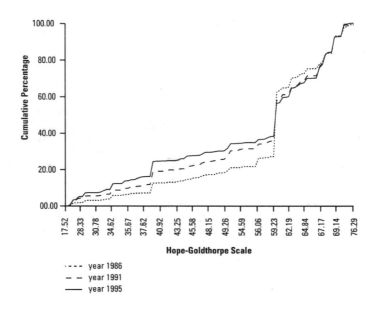

4 CONCLUSIONS

There has been a substantial increase in the proportion of the British workforce which is qualified at particular education levels since the mid-1980s, and this is particularly marked at degree level. Using the Hope-Goldthorpe occupational prestige ranking scale we find clear evidence of skill bumping at the more highly educated levels, but this does not extend down to the less or no educational qualifications categories, so that there is no evidence that any of the unqualified have been forced out of the labour market as a consequence of an increase in the proportion of the workforce who are overeducated. The probability of being overeducated is strongly associated with personal characteristics such as gender, age and job tenure. There is however, no strong link between overeducation and structural unemployment characteristics, such as region or industry. Given the basis of our data we have had to assume that the nature of jobs has remained unaltered over the decade analysed. That this assumption may not be valid is supported by the fact that the rate of return to education, including that at degree level does not appear to have declined. However, further work is needed to establish the extent to which jobs have been modified to take advantage of this influx of highly educated labour and whether in these cases there is a salary premium on offer to the overeducated compared to those workers who only have the required level of education in those jobs.

NOTES

1. It is also possible that smaller firms may not take on graduates and where they do they may find it difficult to find them work commensurate with their education.
2. For details see Sloane et al. (1999).

REFERENCES

Battu, H., C.R. Belfield and P.J. Sloane (1999), 'Over-education Among Graduates: A Cohort View', *Education Economics* **17** (1), 1–18.

Blackburn, M., D. Bloom, and R. Freeman (1991), 'The Declining Economic Position of Less Skilled American Males', in G. Burtless (ed.), *A Future of Lousy Jobs?*, Washington DC: Brookings Institution.

Doeringer, P.B. and M.J. Piore (1971), *Internal Labour Markets and Manpower Analysis*, Lexington, MA/D.C. Heath and Co.

Frank, R.H. (1978), 'Why Women Earn Less: The Theory and Estimation of Differential Overqualification', *American Economic Review* **86**, 280–84.

Glyn, A. (1995), 'The Assessment: Unemployment and Inequality', *Oxford Review of Economic Policy* **11** (1), 1–25.

Goldthorpe, J.H. and K. Hope (1974), *The Social Grading of Occupations: A New Approach and Scale*, Oxford: Clarendon Press.

Groot, W. (1996), 'The Incidence of, and Returns to Overeducation in the UK', *Applied Economics* **28**, 1345–50.

Kato, T. (1986), 'Bumping, Layoffs and Worksharing', *Economic Inquiry* **24**, 657–68.

Kraft, K. (1994), 'Wage Differentials between Skilled and Unskilled Workers', *Weltwirtschaftliches Archiv* **130** (2), 329–49.

Nickell, S. and B. Bell (1995), 'The Collapse in Demand for the Unskilled and Unemployment Across the OECD', *Oxford Review of Economic Policy* **11** (1), 40–62.

Robinson, P. and M. Manacorda (1997), *Qualifications and the Labour Market in Britain,1984–1994: Skill Biased Change in the Demand for Labour or Credentialism?*, LSE Centre for Economic Performance Discussion Paper 330.

Saint-Paul, G. (1996) 'Are the Unemployed Unemployable?', *European Economic Review* **40**, 1510–19.

Schmitt, J. (1995) 'The Changing Structure of Male Earnings in Britain, 1974–1988', in R. Freeman and L.F. Katz (eds), *Differences and Changes in Wage Structures*, Chicago and London: University of Chicago Press, pp. 177–204.

Sicherman, N. (1991), 'Over-education in the Labor Market', *Journal of Labor Economics* **9**, 101–22.

Sloane, P.J., H. Battu and P. Seaman (1999), 'Over-education, Undereducation and the British Labour Market',*Applied Economics* **31**, 1437–1453.

Van der Meer, P. and R. Wielers (1996), 'Educational Credentials and Trust in the Labour Market', *Kyklos* **49** (1), 29–46.

8. The Effect of Bumping Down on Wages: an Empirical Test

Ides Nicaise

1 INTRODUCTION

The purpose of this chapter is to investigate the effects of 'bumping down' on wages and employment. To this end, we integrate insights from three theories into a single model explaining the simultaneous distribution of employment and wages. Human capital theory is taken as the general framework, whereas search theory and the 'bumping-down' (or 'crowding out') hypothesis[1] are used to explain selectivity in employment and the resulting bias in wage regressions.

Our key question relates to the impact of bumping down and crowding out on wages and employment. If it is true, as the bumping-down hypothesis claims, that highly skilled job seekers tend to poach the jobs of the lower-skilled when jobs are scarce overall, then the former will earn wages 'below their normal level of remuneration'. These lower wages are regarded as the price to be paid for a higher employment probability. Put differently, either one holds on to the 'normal' wage that corresponds to one's level of human capital, running a higher risk of unemployment; or one sacrifices part of this wage in exchange for greater job security. The argument holds for different levels of schooling, work experience and post-school education: at given levels of human capital, there is a trade-off between better remuneration and a higher employment probability. Of course, at the bottom of the skill distribution, where further crowding out of lower categories is impossible, low wages and high unemployment go hand in hand. The argument may sound obvious; yet we will see that it is diametrically opposite to what search theories of labour supply predict.

In the literature about 'overeducation', the bumping-down phenomenon is usually measured by inserting the number of years of overeducation as a separate variable into a human capital earnings function. It is generally found that the rate of return to years of overeducation is positive but lower than the 'normal' rate: in other words, overeducated individuals earn more than what their job normally pays, but less than what their school degree normally pays. Unemployment is left aside in this type of analysis.

Our chapter adopts a different approach, by estimating the probability of employment and earnings simultaneously. The treatment of selectivity bias in earnings functions, proposed by Heckman (1979) and by now widespread in search-theoretical models of labour supply and earnings, is given a broader interpretation here. We take account indeed of selectivity bias on the demand and supply side of the labour market. Moreover, our method can be applied to data sets that do not contain explicit information on overeducation.

2 TWO COMPETING THEORIES: RESERVATION WAGES AND BUMPING DOWN

Heckman (1979) was the first to comment that observed earnings are not a true reflection of the potential earnings distribution in a situation of full employment, because of the existence of selection bias. Indeed, the search theory holds that unemployed people only accept a job if the earnings are higher than their 'reservation wage', i.e. the minimum earnings they will request in order to give up benefits and take paid employment. The same applies *mutatis mutandis* for persons of active age who have withdrawn from the labour market – in practice mainly women with children, for whom the opportunity costs of re-entering the

Figure 8.1   Upward bias in OLS-regression: the reservation wage (or opportunity cost) hypothesis

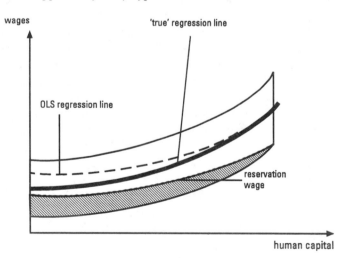

labour market (mainly child care costs) may outweigh the benefits unless wages
are sufficiently high. For both groups, inactivity is more or less voluntary and
'supply-driven'. The resulting (observed) distribution of earnings – of those
actually working – would be upwardly biased compared to a situation in which
all individuals in active age were employed.

The bold line in Figure 8.1 represents the 'unbiased' regression line between
wages and a hypothetical index of productivity or human capital (HC); the
shaded area around this line represents the confidence interval. Now suppose
that potentially active individuals have a reservation wage (reflected by the
dotted line) below which they do not (re)enter the labour market, then all
observations below the reservation wage disappear. In Ordinary Least Squares
(OLS) regressions, this will result in an upward bias of the HC wage regression
(see the dashed line).

The search theory is implicitly associated with voluntarily unemployed
people – at any level of human capital – who turn their noses up at jobs which
are too lowly paid in their view, something which sounds counter-intuitive in
a context of massive involuntary unemployment. In such a context, one would
rather expect inactivity to be forced by constraints on the demand side of the
labour market, and a struggle for jobs to take place, where individuals compete
with each other by bidding down on wages or by accepting jobs below their
level of qualification.

Figure 8.2   Downward bias in OLS regression: the bumping-down hypothesis

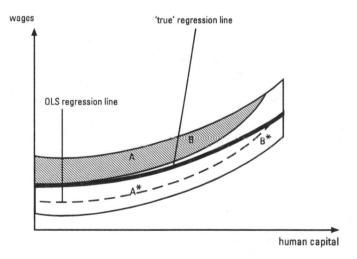

In Figure 8.2, individuals A and A* have identical HC levels but different wages for reasons unexplained by HC. In periods of high unemployment, people like A (situated above the regression line) may well be replaced by people like A*. Similarly, people like B tend to be displaced by people like B*, who cost the same wage but have higher levels of HC. Individuals like B* will prefer to take these jobs below their level of qualification rather than falling into unemployment. Consequently, observations on top of the dotted curve (the relatively well-paid and the less educated– say, those in the dark shaded area in Figure 8.2) will be particularly at risk of being displaced, bearing the burden of unemployment of other categories ('bumping-down' or 'crowding out' theory). From this perspective, one would rather expect the observed distribution of wages (or the one estimated with OLS) to underestimate the potential distribution in a situation of full employment.

In the model developed below, we incorporate elements from both theories and let the data show which type of selection bias turns the scale.[2] The estimates apply to a representative sample of the Belgian active population (the CSP database) in 1985.[3] The data set contains cross-section information on 6,471 households and 18,322 individuals, of whom 10,134 are of active age. Data are available on a number of individual and household characteristics such as age, gender, level of education, employment status, number of hours worked, net monthly earnings, etc.

3 THE MODEL

The starting point for our analysis is the well-known human capital (HC) model, which relates earnings to education, training and work experience. This earnings function is accompanied by a double selection function, on the supply and demand side. A generalized version of Heckman's model would comprise the following: let the estimated earnings function be represented in abbreviated form by:

$$y_i = a'x_i + e_i \qquad\qquad (1)$$

where:
y_i stands for earnings;
x_i for a vector of individual characteristics;
a for the corresponding vector of parameters and
e_i for the error term, with standard deviation σ_e.

Earnings are only observed in so far as the individual actually presents himself or herself on the labour market, while an analogous condition applies in connection with involuntary inactivity. In other words, equation 1 is conditional with respect to a 'supply constraint'.

$$b'z_i + u_i > 0 \qquad \text{or else: } u_i > -b'z_i \qquad (2)$$

where:
z_i represents a vector of individual characteristics;
b' is a row vector of parameters; and
u_i an error term and a 'demand constraint': [4]

$$v_i - g'z_i \qquad (3)$$

where:
v_i is again an error term; and
g a vector of parameters.

Assuming that the error terms e_i, u_i and v_i are correlated, the OLS-estimators of the observed earnings function are not consistent because

$$Ey_i = a'Ex_i + E\left(e_i | u_i > -b'z_i, v_i > -g'z_i\right) \qquad (4)$$

where the expectation of the error term may differ from zero, because all observations in which the individual is not working are omitted. Now assume that the probabilities of staying at home, being involuntarily inactive and being employed are determined by a multinomial probit distribution, then (4) is equivalent to

$$Ey_i = a'Ex_i + E\left(e_i | w_i > -d'z_i\right) \qquad (5)$$

where:
w_i is an error term, with standard deviation σ_w;
d a vector of parameters; and
$Pr(d'z_i + w_i > 0)$ determines the probability of employment.

In other words, the multinomial probability model can be reduced to a binary model (being employed or not – whatever the reason of non-employment). If w_i and e_i are jointly normally distributed, then the latter term of (5) can be written as:

$$\rho_{ew} \sigma_e \; \frac{\varphi(d'z_i)}{\Phi(d'z_i)} \tag{6}$$

(see Greene, 1993, p.709) where:

ρ_{ew} is the covariance between the error term of the earnings function w_i;

φ its density function; and

Φ its cumulative distribution function.

So a 'two-stage, probit – OLS' estimation procedure would yield unbiased estimates of the parameters in the earnings function: after fitting the probit model, $\varphi(d'z_i)/\Phi(d'z_i)$ (the 'inverse Mills ratio', usually represented by $\chi\lambda$ and therefore also called 'Heckman's lambda') can be calculated and used as a regressor in the earnings function (the parameter of this term would equal $\rho_{ew}\sigma_w$). Let us now further specify the earnings and employment function. A somewhat heuristic version of the HC-earnings function is being used, which predicts the distribution of earnings much better than the standard semi-logarithmic specification.[5]

$$y_i = \alpha_0 + \alpha_1's_i + \alpha_2's_i\exp_i + \alpha_3's_i\exp_i^2 + e_i \tag{7}$$

where:

y_i is the absolute value (rather than the logarithm) of net monthly earnings (in BEF, and corrected for hours worked, i.e. converted into full-time equivalent earnings);

s_i is a vector of dummies reflecting diploma levels, and α_1, α_2 and α_3 are the corresponding vectors of parameters. Six types of diplomas are distinguished (primary, lower secondary vocational, lower secondary technical or general, upper secondary, higher non-university, and university);

$\exp_i$ stands for work experience, used as a proxy for post-school investments in HC;[6] with respect to interactions between schooling and experience, the number of resulting age–earnings profiles is limited to four[7] (primary, lower secondary, upper secondary and higher education).

As regards the employment function, we included the same HC variables (with the exception of the interaction between schooling and experience) because the two tested theories predict a positive relation between an individual's level of HC and his/her employment probability. On the other hand, the search theory predicts a negative effect of unearned income on labour supply. Further, we expect the number of children to restrict female employment on the supply side (because of the existing intra-family division of work patterns) and on the demand side (because of possible discrimination against women with children).

The interaction between the number of children and experience allows for attenuation of the effect of family burden as the family grows older. Finally, we assume no simultaneity between the employment functions of married couples.[8]

4 EMPIRICAL RESULTS

The results of our empirical test are displayed in Table 8.1, where the selection function (a binary probit model) is combined with OLS into a two-stage approach.[9] The resulting earnings profiles by gender, level of education and age group, corrected for selection bias, are depicted in Figures 8.3 and 8.4.

First of all, looking at the employment function, one can observe a contrast between men and women with respect to the effects of unearned income and number of children. The male employment probability is fairly insensitive to unearned income, and rises with family size.[10] Women's employment, on the contrary, is negatively affected by both factors, which suggests a relatively stronger effect of supply side constraints on employment.

Further, the employment probability of both sexes is positively related with HC (measured by educational levels and a concave function of work experience). Note that this in itself does not say anything about the predominance of supply or demand constraints: as noted earlier, crowding out theory as well as search theory can explain that people with lower HC stocks tend to participate less in the labour market.

The estimates relating to the earnings functions are consistent with the predictions of the HC-theory, as earnings appear to increase with an individual's level of education, and to be a concave function of experience on the labour market. Women appear to earn significantly less than men; unfortunately the data do not allow for a distinction between discrimination and other causes (as for example differences in true work experience). For a more detailed discussion of the results, we refer to Nicaise, 1999.

As regards the impact of sample selection on the earnings function (the effect of λ) it turns out insignificant for women but significant for men. Let us start by analysing the results for men. As λ is positive for employed individuals (its average value being 0.25 for men), the negative sign of its coefficient indicates a negative covariance between the error terms in the employment and wage functions. This implies that, even at given HC-levels, the more expensive workers (i.e. those 'above the wage regression line') are relatively more likely to be out of employment, while the cheaper ones tend to remain in employment, just as the crowding out theory predicts. This is also consistent with the expectation that unemployment exerts a downward pressure on wages. At the same time, the findings contradict the reservation wage hypothesis – or at least put it into perspective – which claims that the observed wages of employed individuals are on average higher than those of the overall population. The observed wages of employed individuals are not higher, but lower than the underlying 'true' wage distribution.

Why, then, are the results different for women? Here, the coefficient of λ turns out insignificant. A possible explanation is that women are probably much more led by family considerations than are men: their non-employment is thus more often determined by supply-side constraints, which tend to counterbalance the bumping-down effects on wages. For men, crowding out effects are not offset, due to the (near) absence of supply constraints.

Figure 8.3   Earnings profiles by level of education: men (Belgium, 1985, corrected for selection bias)

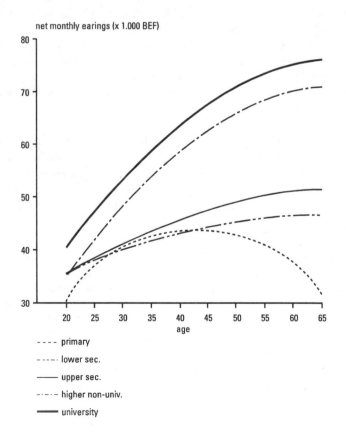

net monthly earings (x 1.000 BEF)

age

```
---- primary
----· lower sec.
——— upper sec.
--·-· higher non-univ.
━━━ university
```

Figure 8.4   Earnings profiles by level of education: women (Belgium, 1985, corrected for selection bias)

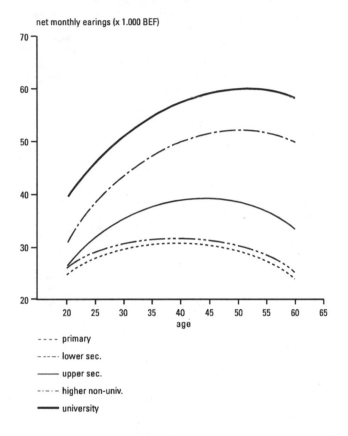

net monthly earings (x 1.000 BEF)

- - - - primary
- - - - - lower sec.
———— upper sec.
- - · - - higher non-univ.
——— university

The question of selectivity bias can be looked at from a different angle, by examining the nature and strength of the selection effect on the observed returns on HC. The net effect of a particular educational degree on earnings consists of two partial effects: a direct effect (the α-coefficients in earnings function 1) and an indirect effect via employment selection. These effects can be calculated as follows (Greene, 1993, p. 709):

$$\frac{E\left(y_i \,|\, w_i > -d'z_i\right)}{x_i} = \alpha + \delta\rho_{ew}\sigma_w\left(\lambda_i^2 + d'z_i\lambda_i\right) \qquad (8)$$

Table 8.1   Sample selection effects on the earnings function (Belgium, 1985)

Independent variables	Men Employment function (probit model)	Men Two-stage earnings function (probit-OLS)	Women Empl. function (probit model)	Women Two-stage earnings (probit-OLS)
Intercepts				
Primary	−0.121 *	23.54	0.058 *	21.65
	(0.102)	(5.81)	(0.096)	(7.87)
Lower sec. vocational	−0.156 *	33.90	0.339	23.84
	(0.106)	(4.59)	(0.093)	(3.80)
Lower sec. techn./gen.	0.128 *	33.97	0.551	24.73
	(0.095)	(4.25)	(0.088)	(3.98)
Upper secondary	0.296	33.95	0.806	25.54
	(0.085)	(4.06)	(0.077)	(3.28)
Higher non-university	0.550	38.07	1.23	34.95
	(0.102)	(3.85)	(0.089)	(3.09)
University	0.707	43.29	1.354	42.82
	(0.160)	(3.82)	(0.159)	(3.47)
Experience	0.112	-	0.032	-
	(0.007)		(0.007)	
Squared experience	−0.0025	-	−0.0013	-
	(0.0001)		(0.0002)	
Unearned income	0.0014 *	-	−0.0068	-
	(0.0009)		(0.0008)	
Number of children	0.1711	-	−0.298	-
	(0.057)		(0.042)	
N° of children * experience	−0.004	-	0.0044	-
	(0.002)		(0.0018)	
Primary * experience	-	1.45	-	0.79 *
		(0.39)		(0.55)
lower sec. * experience	-	0.47	-	0.74
		(0.28)		(0.28)
upper sec. *exp.	-	0.71	-	1.15
		(0.30)		(0.20)
higher * experience	-	1.42	-	1.24
		(0.36)		(0.28)
Primary * exp.^{2}	-	−0.025	-	−0.016 *
		(0.006)		(0.01)
lower sec. * exp.^{2}	-	−0.004 *	-	−0.016
		(0.006)		(0.006)
upper sec. * exp.^{2}	-	−0.007 *	-	−0.023
		(0.007)		(0.005)
higher * exp.^{2}	-	−0.016 *	-	−0.022
		(0.009)		(0.01)
λ	-	−32.86	-	(12.68)
	-	−6.83 *		
Number of observations	5,272	4,148	4,862	2,321
model (χ^2 (L.R.) /adj. R^2	3,168	0.78	1,050	0.81

The figures in parentheses are t-values. Figures marked with asterisks are NOT significant at 95% level (non-marked figures are significant at 95% level or higher).

where α_i is the coefficient of the selected schooling dummy in the earnings function and δ_i its coefficient in the employment function. These calculations are presented in Table 8.2, together with the (biased) single-stage OLS-estimates for comparison. Calculations relate to men only, as our regressions did not indicate selectivity bias among women. The figures suggest that the pure (direct) earnings effect of schooling is much higher than what is actually observed. The indirect effect (via employment selectivity) is negative. This again suggests that employment is gained at the expense of under-utilization of HC and displacement of less educated workers.

Table 8.2   Direct and indirect earnings effects of education (two-stage model, Belgium 1985, in thousands BEF – men only)

Level of education	(biased) OLS	Direct effect (two-stage)	Indirect effect (two-stage)	Overall effect (two-stage)
Primary	18.80	23.54	-0.83	22.71
Lower sec. - vocational	24.60	33.90	-4.57	29.33
Lower sec. - techn. or general	25.60	33.97	-5.87	28.10
Upper secondary	24.67	33.95	-7.32	26.63
Higher non-university	29.93	38.07	-8.43	29.64
University	35.91	43.29	-7.28	36.01

Note that the calculations only reflect effects on the schooling intercepts and not on the interactions between schooling and experience. Hence, the results hold only at the start of the career.

5   CONCLUSION

Our analysis confronts empirically the reservation wage hypothesis and the bumping-down hypothesis, using data for Belgium, 1985. A Heckman-type two-stage probit-OLS model has been developed with two sources of selection rather than one (one on the supply side and one on the demand side of the labour market). The resulting employment function shows that the probability of employment is positively related with one's human capital stock. This finding is consistent with both theories and, hence, does not prove the dominance of either. However, the wage function tends to confirm that observed wages for men are negatively affected by selection; in other words, the reservation wage constraint appears not to be 'binding' while the bumping-down theory is supported. Observed wages for men appear to lie far below potential earnings under full employment, which may be attributed to bumping-down mechanisms in wages or to the fact that the more educated men accept jobs below their level of qualification in order to escape from unemployment. As a result, mainly low-skilled workers are displaced and the burden of unemployment is shifted to the bottom of the labour market.

As concerns women, no significant selection effect is found, which may indicate that supply and demand constraints outweigh each other. It is of course not excluded that some other, omitted variables can explain the non-employment of relatively expensive workers. In technical terms, the correlation between the error terms in the employment and earnings function can point to a set of similar influences of omitted variables on both functions. Although we have no intuitive reasons for suspicion in this regard, estimations with other data and specifications would be welcome.

NOTES

1. As in other contributions to this book, we will use the term 'bumping down' to denote the fact that more skilled people (are forced to) accept jobs at lower levels, while 'crowding out' relates to workers being displaced from suitable jobs. However, both phenomena are closely linked and, consequently, both terms will be used throughout this contribution.

2. We deliberately abstract from other types of selection problems such as the possible bias resulting from omitted ability and endogenous schooling decisions. Recent debates in the literature (Angrist and Krueger, 1995; Blackburn and Neumark, 1995; Harmon and Walker, 1995) have raised doubts as to the nature and direction of this bias.

3. The data were kindly provided by the Centre for Social Policy (Centrum voor Sociaal Beleid, hereafter abbreviated to CSP) of the UFSIA (University of Antwerp).

4. Note that the vector of determinants z is supposed to be identical on the demand and supply sides, which obviously does not necessarily imply that all corresponding coefficients are significant, nor even that they have the same sign in the demand and supply constraint.

5. See Nicaise (2000) for a justification of the method.

6. Note that the variable 'work experience' is not actually measured; it has been estimated as the difference between an individual's age and his/her (theoretical) school-leaving age. This approximation inevitably implies an overestimation of actual work experience, especially among women.

7. This restriction is imposed in order to avoid inconsistent (crossing) age–earnings profiles within each 'level', namely between vocational and other options in secondary education.

8. Put differently, we assume that one of the partners (in practice, usually the husband) decides first on his labour supply, independently of his spouse's intentions. Other arguments for our assumption of independence are (a) that many individuals in the sample are unmarried, and (b) that the employment functions reflect supply and demand influences, while employers do not take account of the division of work between partners.

9. Admittedly, the two-stage procedure does not yield efficient estimates (i.e. with minimum variance). A more sophisticated method with simultaneous estimation of both functions by means of a maximum-likelihood procedure (LISREL) may yield still better results.

10. The positive effect of family size on fathers' employment can be explained by the greater financial needs and/or the greater sense of responsibility induced by additional children.

REFERENCES

Angrist, J.D., A.B. Krueger (1995), 'Split-Sample Instrumental Variables Estimates of the Return to Schooling', *Journal Business of Economics and Statistics* **13** (2), 225–35.

Blackburn, M.L. and D. Neumark (1995), 'Are OLS Estimates of the Return to Schooling Biased Downward? Another look', *Review of Econimics and Statistics* **77** (2), 217–30.

Greene, W.H. (1993), *Econometric Analysis*, New York/Oxford: Maxwell Macmillan.

Harmon, C. and I. Walker (1995), 'Economic Return to Schooling for the UK', *American Economic Review* **85**, 1278–86.

Heckman, J.J. (1979), 'Sample Selection bias as a Specification Error' , *Econometrica* **47**, 153–61

Nicaise, I. (2000), *Poverty and Human Capital*, Aldershot, Ashgate.

PART THREE

Consequences of Underutilization of Skills

9. Low Wages, Skills and the Utilization of Skills

Lex Borghans, Allard Bruinshoofd and
Andries de Grip

1 INTRODUCTION

Although the criterion for low wages is a rather arbitrary one and is related to
the wage distribution within the country concerned, a substantial part of the
labour force in many OECD countries seems to be unable to earn a
reasonable income. The low wage incidence varies between one quarter of all
full-time workers in the USA and Canada and 6 per cent in Finland and
Sweden (Keese et al. 1998). These people have earnings that are far below
the median income, which raises questions about the social desirability of
such wages within a country.

Education is generally regarded as an important determinant for the
labour market position of workers. People with more education tend to get
better jobs and will therefore reduce their probability of low-wage employment. The major economic reason for this is that education increases productivity. Since income is related to productivity, more education will also
imply better pay. Education and training are therefore regarded as important
policy instruments to combat low pay employment and unemployment.

This relationship between education and wages, however, may be
complicated by the functioning of the labour market. The link between
education and wages implicitly assumes an equilibrium on the labour market.
The human capital theory, for example, regards education as a deliberate
investment in skills that was done because the returns to the investment will
outweigh the costs. The costs of the investments are therefore directly related
to the returns in the form of wages on the labour market. The concept of
human capital represents at the same time the skills that someone possesses
and their value on the labour market. Educational investments are, however,
surrounded by great uncertainties. People may invest in education, but

experience difficulties in finding a job that pays accordingly. Therefore, surpluses or shortages of certain types of skilled labour may influence the wages people receive. As a consequence, education or the skills that people have, are not the only determinants of their wages. Despite a good educational background, labour market conditions may have a negative effect on payments.

Within economic theory, we can roughly distinguish two types of answers to the question why some people earn low wages. On the one hand, starting from the human capital assumption that wages reflect productivity, one could say that these people do simply not possess enough skills to enable them to earn reasonable wages. On the other hand, a malfunctioning labour market, may prevent people from getting adequate jobs. Therefore their skills are not fully utilized or their efforts are not rewarded according to their productivity. This observation makes it possible to define low wages in terms of the skills people possess. Low wages are defined as *The wage below the payment that people receive who completed a level of education that is regarded socially as a minimum qualification for a good labour market position, when their skills are utilized and paid for by their employer.*

The aim of this chapter is to analyse the definition and the incidence of low wages from the perspective of skills and skill utilization. We will analyse which factors cause school-leavers to earn less than this minimum normal wage. Three main reasons can be distinguished. First, the human capital point of view that a lack of adequate skills leads to low payment. Second, people may be unable to find jobs that require their educational level and they are crowded out to low-paid jobs at a level where their skills are underutilized. Third, even if people find adequate jobs, excess competition may put a downward pressure on wages since too many people are competing for these adequate jobs.

The focus on the relationship between skill level, skill utilization and wage level enables us to assign the actual occurrence of low wages to three causes. First, people may have low wages because their skill levels do not meet the education required for adequately participating in the labour market. Second, underutilization of the skill level of people whose educational background is sufficient may lead to low wages. Third, excess supply of people with a particular educational background may lead to low wages, even if these people have a job that makes full use of their skills.

The empirical analyses presented in this chapter are based on data about school-leavers in the Netherlands. A wage equation will be estimated in which we include not only the standard variables used in analyses on the earnings effect of underutilization (Hartog, 1999), but also some variables concerning the situation on the labour market (Smits and Willems, 1999). First, we include the difference in the level of the job and the level of a person's educational background, indicating whether someone's skills are underutilized. Furthermore, the result of the market mechanism may be that if supply exceeds demand on a segment of the labour market, and consequently many school-leavers are unable to find jobs on the appropriate level, not only those who are underutilised, but also people with appropriate jobs earn less than in a situation of a balanced labour market. Therefore two variables have been included concerning the probability of being unemployed and the probability of finding a job below one's educational level. These probabilities indicate the tension on the labour market in a market segment, independent of the actual position of a person. The wage equation shows separately the effects of both the underutilization of a person's skills and the labour market conditions in the market segment that is relevant for this person.

2 THE WAGE EQUATION

To investigate the influence of educational attainment, utilization of skills and the actual situation on the labour market segment concerned, we will introduce a wage equation (explaining the log of the hourly wage) with – in addition to the standard control variables such as sex, race and age – three main groups of explanatory variables. First, wages depend on the educational attainment of workers. Second, the underutilization of this educational attainment may reduce the wages. Third, if workers have an educational background for which supply exceeds demand – and hence there are relatively many people with the same educational background who are unemployed or have a job below their educational level, wages may also decrease even if the workers themselves have found work on a level that fits their educational attainment.

The wage-reducing effect of underutilization has often been investigated in the literature (e.g. Alba-Ramirez, 1993; Groot, 1996; Hartog, 1985, 1999; Hartog and Jonker, 1998). Empirical results unequivocally show that people in jobs below their educational level earn less than those who found a job at their own level, but still more than people in this lower-level job with an appropriate (and therefore lower) educational background. Years of education that are not utilized therefore still yield returns, but these returns are lower than they would have been if an appropriate job had been obtained.

The neo-classical human capital theory (cf. Becker, 1962 and Mincer, 1974), however, predicts that individuals with the same personal characteristics and hence the same educational background, will earn the same wages, irrespective of the type of job they obtain. The reason for this is that if there are only a limited number of jobs available that require this educational background, competition among these individuals will reduce wages to the wage level that can be obtained in less favourite jobs. Excess supply will therefore – according to the neo-classical theory – reduce wages both for those who underutilize their level of education and for those who have the same educational background, but were able to find a job at their own educational level. To estimate this influence on wages – which is generally ignored in empirical studies about the relationship between skills and wages – by means of a logit model, estimates of the probability of unemployment and underutilization are calculated. The predictions of these probabilities for each individual to be unemployed or underutilized are used as variables that represent the market situation. The logit model includes dummies for each combination of educational level and field of study. Altogether, 116 types of education are distinguished. The logit regressions also include regional variables, which distinguishes the twelve provinces of the Netherlands.

Variables such as age, race and sex will in general influence the labour market position, but do in our opinion not indicate different market segments. For that reason they are not included in the logit analyses explaining the probability of unemployment and the probability of underutilization.

3 DATA

The analyses presented in this chapter refer to school-leavers in the Netherlands. We used the data of the school-leavers survey of 1996. This survey provides information on about 20,000 school-leavers who left school in 1995, collected approximately 1.5 years after they finished school. The data used concern all levels of education. But university graduates are only partly covered by the survey (Economics, Business Administration and Technology and Engineering). Hardly any dropouts were included. The survey includes questions about gross wages, educational background (level and field), age, sex, ethnicity and employment status. Ethnicity is indicated by the definition of 'ethnic minorities' that is used by Statistics Netherlands: people from the countries named in the 'Promotion of Balanced Employment Participation by Members of Ethnic Minority Act' (WBEAA). The WBEAA countries include the Dutch Antilles, Morocco, Surinam and Turkey. The school-leavers also provide information about the level of the job they have and about the question of whether this job is within the field of their studies. Five levels of education can be distinguished:

- Low-level education (Lower General Secondary Education, MAVO), and Preparatory Vocational Education, VBO);
- Intermediate-level education: general education and short vocational courses (Higher General Secondary Education, HAVO,VWO), and Short Intermediate Vocational Education, KMBO);
- Intermediate-level: long vocational courses (Intermediate Vocational Education, MBO);
- Higher vocational education (HBO); and
- University education.

4 RESULTS

Table 9.1 shows the estimation results for the Dutch wage equation. The dependent variable is the (logarithm of the) gross hourly wages of the school-leavers (Ln W/hour). The first column provides the estimation results for the total group of school-leavers. Since academics are covered only partially by the survey, they have been excluded from this analysis. All parameters have the expected signs. Ethnic minorities and other non-Dutch individuals earn less than Dutch citizens. Men earn more than women, and every year of education provides 4.5% higher wages. Wages increases with age, and jobs with management tasks imply higher wages.

For our purpose, the important variables concern the effects of under-utilization and overutilization, having a job related to the field of study (type of work), and the degree of excess supply of school-leavers with the educational background concerned, i.e. the unemployment and underutilization probabilities. All variables have the expected signs. In the equation in which all types of education are included, individuals whose skills are overutilized earn above average, while those whose skills are underutilized earn less. The reduction in wages resulting from underutilization exceeds the premium of overutilization. This corresponds to earlier findings by Hartog (1999). The separate equations for underutilized workers, individuals with jobs at the regular level for people with their educational background, and overutilized workers, show that the probability of unemployment and the probability of underutilization affects not only the wages of those who are actually

Table 9.1 Wage equation for school-leavers in the Netherlands, total group* and by category of utilization

		Utilization		
	Total	Under	Regular	Over
Constant	2.331	2.629	2.152	2.548
	(0.039)	(0.074)	(0.047)	(0.309)
Ethnic minorities	−0.029	−0.056	0.005	−0.209
	(0.018)	(0.033)	(0.023)	(0.125)
Other Non-Dutch	−0.032	−0.083	−0.012	0.284
	(0.050)	(0.055)	(0.036)	(0.420)
Sex	−0.028	−0.035	−0.024	−0.079
	(0.005)	(0.010)	(0.006)	(0.060)
Education	0.046	0.024	0.056	0.037
	(0.002)	(0.004)	(0.002)	(0.016)
Age				
17	−0.788	−0.847	−0.757	−
	(0.038)	(0.074)	(0.044)	
18	−0.573	−0.662	−0.577	−0.432
	(0.028)	(0.045)	(0.039)	(0.224)
19	−0.491	−0.598	−0.446	−0.542
	(0.022)	(0.034)	(0.033)	(0.166)
20	−0.337	−0.448	−0.285	−0.374
	(0.014)	(0.026)	(0.018)	(0.133)
21	−0.244	−0.336	−0.202	−0.301
	(0.013)	(0.025)	(0.015)	(0.128)
22	−0.151	−0.207	−0.129	−0.168
	(0.011)	(0.023)	(0.013)	(0.122)
23	−0.083	−0.126	−0.065	−0.141
	(0.009)	(0.018)	(0.010)	(0.127)
24	−0.063	−0.081	−0.050	−0.378
	(0.008)	(0.017)	(0.009)	(0.117)
25	−0.044	−0.056	−0.040	0.106
	(0.008)	(0.018)	(0.009)	(0.133)
Above 25	0.021	0.019	0.022	0.028
	(0.001)	(0.002)	(0.001)	(0.009)
Management tasks	0.002	0.001	0.002	0.001
	(0.000)	(0.001)	(0.000)	(0.002)
Type of job	−0.054	−0.082	−0.042	0.156
	(0.006)	(0.010)	(0.008)	(0.066)
Overutilization	0.037	−	−	−
	(0.019)			
Underutilization	−0.089	−	−	−
	(0.006)			
P(Unemployment)	−0.214	−0.436	−0.097	−0.627
	(0.085)	(0.169)	(0.098)	(0.795)
P(Underutilization)	−0.157	−0.041	−0.209	−0.168
	(0.021)	(0.041)	(0.026)	(0.231)
N	12,605	3,676	8,703	226
R^2	0.502	0.474	0.484	0.374

Notes:
The dependent variable is LnW/hour.
* Excluding academics

Table 9.2   *Wage equation for school-leavers in the Netherlands, total group and by level of education*

	Total	Low level	Medium level: short	Medium level: long	Higher vocational	University
Constant	2.350	1.960	4.745	2.991	3.155	2.996
	(0.028)	(0.171)	(0.838)	(0.043)	(0.008)	(0.066)
Ethnic minorities	-0.035	-0.117	-0.041	-0.010	-0.043	-0.109
	(0.018)	(0.178)	(0.071)	(0.037)	(0.023)	(0.063)
Other Non-Dutch	-0.034	0.274	-0.129	-0.101	-0.007	-0.063
	(0.030)	(0.209)	(0.242)	(0.058)	(0.037)	(0.153)
Sex	-0.027	-0.133	-0.105	-0.052	-0.010	-0.003
	(0.005)	(0.063)	(0.031)	(0.012)	(0.006)	(0.017)
Education	0.045	–	–	–	–	–
	(0.001)					
Age						
17	-0.796	–	-1.150	–	–	
	(0.037)		(0.425)			
18	-0.580	0.204	-0.905	-0.712	–	–
	(0.027)	(0.075)	(0.260)	(0.083)		
19	-0.496	0.229	-0.835	-0.502	–	–
	(0.021)	(0.086)	(0.252)	(0.052)		
20	-0.340	0.221	-0.672	-0.310	–	–
	(0.014)	(0.144)	(0.251)	(0.038)		
21	-0.247	0.321	-0.660	-0.209	-0.163	–
	(0.012)	(0.194)	(0.252)	(0.037)	(0.067)	
22	-0.152	0.429	-0.555	-0.139	-0.110	–
	(0.011)	(0.327)	(0.254)	(0.037)	(0.015)	
23	-0.082	0.684	-0.488	-0.049	-0.094	-0.067
	(0.009)	(0.261)	(0.267)	(0.038)	(0.009)	(0.072)
24	-0.063	–	-0.430	0.011	-0.075	-0.083
	(0.008)		(0.292)	(0.040)	(0.008)	(0.029)
25	-0.042	–	-0.415	0.014	-0.049	-0.020
	(0.008)		(0.292)	(0.048)	(0.008)	(0.018)
Above 25	0.022	–	-0.054	0.015	0.021	0.038
	(0.001)		(0.071)	(0.005)	(0.001)	(0.004)
Management tasks	0.002	0.012	0.003	0.002	0.001	0.004
	(0.000)	(0.013)	(0.001)	(0.001)	(0.000)	(0.001)
Type of job	-0.051	-0.019	-0.018	-0.035	-0.068	-0.016
	(0.006)	(0.064)	(0.035)	(0.014)	(0.007)	(0.018)
Overutilization	0.035	0.334	0.029	0.091	-0.008	–
	(0.019)	(0.128)	(0.050)	(0.041)	(0.030)	
Underutilization	-0.089	-0.023	-0.019	-0.068	-0.108	-0.091
	(0.006)	(0.072)	(0.041)	(0.013)	(0.006)	(0.015)
P(Unemployment)	-0.238	-0.545	-0.038	-0.472	-0.080	-0.959
	(0.084)	(0.621)	(0.456)	(0.214)	(0.096)	(0.601)
P(Underutilization)	-0.153	0.082	-0.200	-0.238	-0.163	0.540
	(0.019)	(0.408)	(0.126)	(0.061)	(0.024)	(0.126)
N	13,823	220	498	3,340	8,547	1,218
R^2	0.504	0.159	0.157	0.188	0.233	0.154

Note: The dependent variable is LnW/hour

underutilized, but also the wages of those who acquired a job at their own educational level or even higher. A larger probability of unemployment seems mainly to affect the position of both underutilized and overutilized workers. A larger probability of underutilization, however, mainly affects the workers with regular jobs and the overutilized. This confirms the hypothesis that more underutilization of workers with a particular educational background leads to increased competition for jobs that provide normal wages. As a consequence, the wages in these regular jobs will also be pushed down to some extent.

It is important to note that the effect of a higher probability to be underutilized only represent changes in the wages of the different groups. People in jobs in which their skills are underutilized will on average always earn less than people who have jobs for which their skills are required, but a deterioration of the labour market position will affect the wages of these regular jobs more than the wages of the people who are underutilized. Borghans and Smits (1997) show that heterogeneity of the workers within a certain level can explain these modest wage effects for underutilized workers. Due to increased underutilization within the group as a whole, more people with relatively high productivity levels are pushed into these less attractive jobs, changing the composition of the group of underutilized workers. As a result, the consequences of such a change in composition may easily offset lower wages due to labour market pressures; so even a positive effect is possible.

Table 9.2 presents similar estimation results for each level of education separately. The effect of underutilization on wages is found at each level of education. Only for the school-leavers of the short courses at medium level, no significant effect is found for underutilization.

5 THE DEFINITION OF LOW WAGES

In general, the literature about low pay uses a definition of low wages which is based on people's relative position in the wage distribution (cf. the various studies presented in Bazen et al., 1998). In various studies, wages lower than 66 per cent of the median of the wage distribution are considered to be low. By focusing on the relationship between skills, skill utilization and wages, the model presented in this chapter enables us to apply a – less arbitrary – skill-related definition of low wages. Wages that are lower than *the wages expected for persons (i) who completed their vocational education, (ii) with an appropriate job, (iii) in a market without excess supply* are defined as low wages. For the Netherlands, the government considers school-leavers with at least a diploma at the medium level of education – i.e. Intermediate Vocational Education (MBO): short or long courses – as adequately educated for the labour market.

In order to determine the wage level which demarcates the low wages based on the above definition, the actual earnings have to be corrected for both the underutilization at the individual level and the general labour market imbalance for the people with the appropriate skill level in the two countries. Table 9.3 presents the means of the log wages (in Dutch guilders and dollar cents) for school-leavers with these minimum required educational levels, both before and after correction. Since wage differentials also exist within a group of school-leavers in which we control for underutilization, the demarcation between low wages and normal wages has to be chosen in a pragmatic way. In this chapter, we take the mean of the log wages minus 1.282 times the standard deviation. After adjustment for the standard deviation, the minimum normal wage for the Netherlands equals $5.29.

Table 9.3   The mean and standard deviation of the wages for Dutch IVE graduates (in Dutch guilders)

	Mean of ln wage	Standard deviation	Low wages
IVE without correction	2.6739	0.2982	
IVE after correction	2.7847	0.2931	2.4089 = fl.11.12 = appr.\$ 5.29

6   SKILL-RELATED CAUSES OF LOW WAGES

On the basis of this definition of low wages and the estimated wage equation, it is possible to assign the actual occurrence of low wages to three skill-related causes. First, people may have low wages because their educational background does not meet the standard educational background introduced above. Second, even if the educational background is sufficient, under-utilization of these skills may lead to a low paid job. Third, even if people find a job at their own (sufficient) educational level, excess supply may have a negative effect on the labour market conditions and therefore give rise to low wages.

Table 9.4 shows that for the Dutch school-leavers, low wage incidence would reduce from 21.6 per cent to 9.5 per cent if everybody met the three criteria. The remaining 9.5 per cent represents unexplained variation in wages. Insufficient educational attainment only accounts for 4.9 percentage point of this 12.1 percentage point gap and work in a field not related to the study for 1.5 percentage points of the gap. Imbalances on the market account for 4.0 percentage point and individual underutilization for 1.7 percentage point of this gap. These results indicate that for Dutch school-leavers, having an educational level lower than Intermediate Vocational Education and underutilization at the market level are the main causes for low wages. However, underutilization at the individual level only has a modest impact on the incidence of low wages.

Table 9.4　　Predicted incidence of low wages, Netherlands and US

	Incidence %
Uncorrected	21.6
Adequate skill level	16.7
& required field	15.2
& no underutilization	13.5
& balanced market	9.5

The educational level of people remains an important determinant for wages. Table 9.5 presents low wage incidence and its components for the different educational levels. Among school-leavers with low level education – which is below the minimum required educational level – 69.5 per cent of the workers earn low wages. The table shows that both a more adequate educational background and a balanced market with an appropriate job for everyone, would reduce low wage incidence for these school-leavers substantially, by 18 percentage points and 16 percentage points, respectively. Additional training as well as labour market policies that increase the number of jobs of this skill level therefore seem to be appropriate policy instruments which can improve the labour market position of these people.

For the school-leavers with a medium level education, underutilization and excess supply in this market segment are the most important causes of low wages. As could be expected, hardly any of the school-leavers with a high-level educational background earn low wages.

Table 9.5   Predicted incidence of low wages for different educational groups

	Low level	Medium level: short	Medium level: long	Higher vocational	University
Uncorrected	69.5	33.1	8.0	0.8	0.2
Adequate skill level	51.8	22.5*	8.0	0.8	0.2
& required field	47.7	21.0	6.9	0.8	0.2
& no underutilization	45.6	16.0	5.8	0.7	0.2
& balanced market	33.1	10.6	3.8	0.6	0.2

* Formally, not all workers in this category have the required level of education as this category also includes the school-leavers of general education (HAVO,VWO) who are not considered to have the minimum (vocational) qualification for a good start in the labour market.

7   CONCLUSIONS

In this chapter, we presented an analysis of the causes of low wages that can be related to skills. The analysis of data on school-leavers in the Netherlands shows that a large probability of becoming unemployed mainly affects the wages of people who work below their own educational level. The probability of working below the educational level seems to put downward pressures on wages. This effect is mainly felt in regular jobs, which require a particular educational background of school-leavers.

The main cause for low wages is the acquired skill level. Excess supply on the labour market segments for the people with an appropriate educational background is another major cause of low wages. The underutilization at the individual level is a much less important cause of low earnings.

REFERENCES

Alba-Ramirez, A. (1993), 'Mismatch in the Spanish Labor Market: Overeducation?', *Journal of Human Resources* **27** (2), 259–78.

Bazen, S., M. Gregory and W. Salverda (eds) (1998), *Low Wage Employment in Europe*, Cheltenham, UK, Northampton, MA: Edward Elgar.

Becker, G.S. (1962), 'Investment in Human Capital: A Theoretical Analysis', *Journal of Political Economy* **70**, 9–49.

Borghans, L. and W. Smits (1997), *Underutilization and Wages of HVE Graduates*, paper presented at the LVII conference of the Applied Econometrics Association on Education and Training.

Groot, W. (1996), 'The Incidence of, and Returns to Overeducation in the UK', *Applied Economics* **28**, 1345–50.

Hartog, J. (1985), 'Earnings Functions, Testing for the Demand Side', *Economics Letters* **19**, 281–5.

Hartog, J. (1999), 'On Returns to Education: Wandering on the Hills of ORU land', in H. Heijke and J. Muysken (eds), *Education and Training in a Knowledge Based Economy*, Basingstoke/Mac Millan.

Hartog, J. and N. Jonker (1998), 'A Job to Match your Education: Does it Matter?', in H. Heijke and L. Borghans (eds), *Towards a Transparent Labour Market for Educational Decisions*, Aldershot: Ashgate, 99–118.

Keese, M., A. Puymoyen and P. Swaim (1998), 'The Incidence and Dynamics of Low-Paid Employment in OECD Countries', in R. Asplund, P.J. Sloane and L. Theodossiou (eds), *Low Pay and Earnings Mobility in Europe*, Cheltenham, UK: Edward Elgar.

Mincer, J. (1974), *Schooling, Experience and Earnings*, New York: NBER.

Smits, W. and E. Willems (1999), 'Low Wages of School-Leavers of Vocational Education in the Netherlands', in S. Bazen, M. Gregory and W. Salverda (eds), *Low-Wage Employment in Europe*, Cheltenham, UK, Northampton, MA: Edward Elgar, pp. 177–92.

10. Do More High-skilled Workers Occupy Simple Jobs During Bad Times?

Pieter Gautier

1 INTRODUCTION

The relatively high unemployment rate for low-skilled workers in most OECD countries is one of the most important economic policy issues. Table 10.1 shows that the Netherlands is no exception. In this chapter, I will focus on the crowding out explanation for this fact. According to this explanation, the position of the low-skilled workers has worsened because more high-skilled workers occupy simple jobs. We would expect that if crowding out is an important phenomenon, it will be concentrated in recessions since that is a time when high-skilled workers find it difficult to find jobs at their own level. We will therefore test for workers with a given education, whether the mass of the job complexity distribution at the lower job levels increases in periods when the total supply of jobs is relatively low. If crowding out is a temporary phenomenon, only new workers will flow in below their skill level. Therefore the analysis will also be done for this group separately.

Some researchers have mistakenly concluded from the fact that some workers with a higher education occupy simple jobs, that crowding out is the main reason for the high unemployment rates of low-skilled workers. Education is, however, an imperfect measure of true productivity. An academic degree is no guarantee for higher marginal productivity and little formal education does not imply that one lacks skills which are highly valued in the labour market. In addition, we should realize that job complexity levels change over time, and that education may serve as compensation for a lack of other skills.

A conventional piece of wisdom is that when there is crowding out, there is no need for extra education since well trained workers would occupy simple jobs anyway. This view is also typically based on a static and mechanical view of the labour market. If crowding out is, for example, the result of search frictions, better education will lead to the opening of more complex vacancies and also to more contacts and lower overall unemployment. The last reason for concern about crowding out is the fact that the burden of unemployment is concentrated in a particular group of low-skilled workers, which can lead to a variety of social problems. It is therefore important not only to look at changes in the fraction of skilled workers at simple jobs, but also to pay attention to the total stock of simple jobs. When the relative number of skilled workers in simple jobs increases, but at the same time more low-skilled workers (in absolute terms) find a job, the position of low-skilled workers has still improved. In other words, when there are no victims it does not make much sense to talk about crowding out.

Table 10.1   Unemployment rates for different education classes

	Unemployed %	Share of labour force %
Primary	15	8
Lower Secondary (LGSE, PVE)	9	22
Higher Secondary (HGSE, IVE)	6	44
Higher Vocational	5	17
University	6	8
Total	7	100

Source: EBB, Statistics Netherlands (1996).

From a welfare point of view, crowding out can never be a first best solution since potential productivity is not used. In the Netherlands it is therefore often argued that the government should follow a 'drawing chimney policy'. The idea behind such a policy is that when the government stimulates the creation of jobs at the top segment, workers with surplus skills in simple jobs will leave those jobs and unemployed low-skilled workers can fill up the vacancies they leave behind. In this chapter it is argued that such a policy is not a good idea. First of all, it is unclear why there would be too few complex jobs in equilibrium and secondly, I find little empirical evidence for crowding out.

The first objective of this chapter is to build a framework in which crowding out at the aggregate level is an equilibrium outcome and the result of optimizing behaviour of individual businesses and workers at the micro level. I will assume that it takes some time before job searchers and businesses with vacancies find each other. Crowding out occurs when unemployed high-skilled workers temporarily accept simple jobs. As long as the wages on those jobs are higher than the income when unemployed, they will accept those jobs because they can continue searching for complex vacancies anyway. In this respect, crowding out is a temporary phenomenon. The main role of employers in this model is to decide how many vacancies to open. The equilibrium stock of vacancies will depend on the relevant number of employed and unemployed job searchers and on the profitability of complex and simple jobs. Thus the model has the long-term property that both the supply and composition of jobs adjust to the supply and composition of workers. The model also allows for a different explanation of the relatively high unemployment rate for low-skilled workers. This explanation is based on differences in adjustment costs. When the profitability of simple jobs becomes lower than for complex jobs (e.g. because of skill-biased technological changes), unemployment rates for low-skilled workers will be higher than for high-skilled workers (because relatively more low-skilled workers occupy those simple jobs). This process may take place without crowding out (i.e. more high-skilled workers occupying simple jobs).

The second objective of this chapter is to test for the empirical relevance of crowding out in the Netherlands in the mid 1990s. To avoid most of the pitfalls I discussed before, I will compare differences of job complexity distributions over the cycle for workers within given education classes. The advantage of this method over simple cross tables at a point in time is that our model is not sensitive to the fact that education is an imperfect measure for true ability (as long as unmeasured ability is constant over time).

The chapter is organized as follows. Section 2 starts with an equilibrium search model which allows for crowding out. Section 3 describes our data, and in Section 4 I will test for the empirical relevance of crowding out in the Netherlands. Lastly, Section 5 lists the conclusions.

2 THEORY

One reason for the popularity of crowding out is that the labour market is often regarded as a closed system. If this were true, crowding out is a very plausible story. If there are a fixed number of jobs and an excess supply of labour, it is likely that high-skilled workers who cannot find a job that match their capabilities will accept jobs below their level at the cost of workers with intermediate skills, who will in turn accept low-skilled jobs. At the end of the line are the low-skilled workers who are forced into unemployment.

Fortunately, the labour market is not a closed system. The supply and composition of jobs will of course adjust after some time to the supply and composition of the labour force! That is why there are more jobs in the US than in the Netherlands, why there are more skilled jobs in Korea than in Bangladesh and why most countries with a good education system have more complex jobs in 1997 than in 1957. Still, there are more sophisticated explanations for the occurrence of crowding out. One is that for some reason the supply of jobs does not immediately adjust to the composition of the labour force, because of such factors as credit or information constraints, and that therefore too few jobs are created. In such cases, it may happen that some workers find jobs that match their capabilities and others are forced to accept jobs below their skill level. In addition, it is sometimes argued that when employers pay efficiency wages in the complex sector, some high-skilled workers become unemployed and could decide to search for simple jobs. It is, however, not *a priori* clear why this would result in higher unemployment rates for low-skilled workers. An additional requirement is that the simple job sector should not clear either. Another reason for crowding out may be that the probability of a bad simple job match is higher for low-skilled workers and that employers therefore statistically discriminate against this group.[1] An additional requirement would then still be that the simple job segment of the labour market does not clear. In this chapter, I will focus on search frictions as the reason for crowding out. When it takes time for workers and vacancies to come together, a possible strategy for high-skilled workers is to temporarily accept a simple job and continue searching for a complex job that pays more. The advantage of this approach is that it is relatively easy to allow for on-the-job searching of skilled workers who occupy simple jobs. Moreover, there are hardly any other models that allow for an analysis that includes labour market flows. The model implies that the process of crowding out is a temporary one and driven by either variation in the supply of high-skilled workers or shocks in the relative profitability of high-skilled jobs.[2] How important temporary crowding out is remains an empirical question, which I will also try to answer in Section 3.

2.1 A Simple Framework for the Analysis of Crowding Out

One of the first models of job competition and crowding out was developed by Thurow (1975). In this model, the labour market is not a market where the demand and supply of various job skills are matched but one where trainable individuals and training ladders are matched. In addition, the marginal product is associated with jobs rather than with workers. In this model, employers prefer skilled workers (who require lower training costs to reach a certain level of output). Consequently, the best jobs will go to the best workers and the worst jobs will go to the worst workers. In this respect, the model does not differ from traditional neo-classical models of the labour market. Thurow also assumes that wages are fixed. In bad times, workers at the end of job queues who have the highest training costs will therefore not get job offers. When the supply of skilled workers increases, the skilled workers will accept more simple jobs and the unskilled workers at the end of the queue remain unemployed. Since this is a partial equilibrium model, the composition of vacancies does not adjust to compositional changes in the labour force. This is a severe shortcoming of the model.

This section presents an alternative crowding out model. In this model, search frictions in the labour market prevent the supply of jobs from adjusting instantaneously to the supply of workers. Crowding out in this model is an equilibrium phenomenon that occurs when high-skilled workers temporarily accept simple jobs. Van Ours and Ridder (1995) also assume that crowding out is caused by search frictions. In their model, high-skilled workers either search for simple or they search for complex jobs. Here they look for both.

In earlier economies, complex tasks could be performed by either a high-skilled worker or a sufficient number of low-skilled workers. Currently, it seems more appropriate to assume that certain complex tasks can only be performed by high-skilled workers. In particular if we think about such tasks as flying an aeroplane, teaching students, managing a company, performing brain surgery, or programming computers. For all those activities there is a minimum amount of skills necessary to be able to perform the tasks and a larger amount of labour input can simply not compensate for any lack of skills.[3]

Figure 10.1   Labour market flows

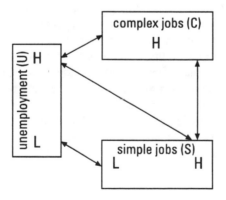

H: high-skilled workers
L: low-skilled workers

Therefore, in our model, complex vacancies can only be filled by high-skilled workers while simple job vacancies can be filled by both high and low-skilled workers. Since workers will take any position that improves their current state, unemployed high-skilled workers also search for simple jobs and high-skilled workers employed in the simple sector continue searching for complex jobs. Sometimes it is argued that high-skilled workers will not accept simple jobs because of a negative signalling effect, see McCormick (1990). I abstract from that here.[4] Workers and vacancies meet according to a Constant Returns to Scale (CRS) matching function which increases by the relevant amount of searchers and vacancies. All of this is captured in Figure 10.1. The pools of unemployment (U) and simple employment (S) consist of two types of workers, high-skilled (H) and low-skilled (L). The pool of complex jobs (C) contains only high-skilled workers. The arrows give the possible flows between the different states.

Assume furthermore that complex jobs produce output y_c while simple jobs occupied by a low-skilled worker produce output $y_{sl} = \psi y_c$, where $0 < \psi < 1$ and simple jobs occupied by a high-skilled worker produce output $y_{sh} = \mu y_{sl}$, $0 < \mu < 1/\psi$ Thus, the output at complex jobs is job-specific and always higher than the output at simple jobs, while high-skilled workers either produce more or less on simple jobs than low-skilled workers. We have no reasons *a priori* to set μ either greater or smaller than 1. Arguments can be given for both cases. One can on the one hand imagine that high-skilled workers do not perform better (or even worse) than low-skilled workers on simple repetitive activities. University professors do not have an absolute advantage over low-skilled workers when it comes to hamburger flipping. On the other hand, there are simple occupations where a higher education may increase one's productivity. Think about a waiter who speaks many languages or a nurse with a great deal of medical knowledge. I will return to this issue later. In this version of the model, I will not explicitly model the wage process. I will just assume that wages support efficient mobility. With this I mean that the quasi rents of complex jobs are higher than of simple jobs and the quasi rents of a simple job are higher than the quasi rents associated with the state of unemployment.[5] Furthermore assume that unemployed high-skilled workers and high-skilled workers employed in simple jobs search equally efficiently.

When workers know beforehand whether a vacancy requires a high or a low-skilled worker, the rate at which simple jobs and unemployed workers meet is:

$$x_s = x_s\left(v_s^+\left(y_s^+, \mu^+, (u_h + u_l)^+, (u_h/u_l)^\pm\right), (u_h + u_l)^+\right) \tag{1}$$

Where x_s is a crs matching function, increasing in both its arguments and concave, v_s is the simple vacancy rate and u_l represents low-skilled unemployment. The equilibrium supply of simple vacancies, in turn, increases its output, the productivity of high-skilled workers in simple jobs, the number of relevant searchers (which influences the rate at which a vacancy is filled), and the ratio of high and low-skilled workers, which is less obvious but I will return to that issue later. The intuition behind this is that the asset value of a simple job is likely to differ with the type of worker (high and low-skilled) who occupies the job because the two types of workers have different productivities and quit probabilities. At the moment when the business opens the vacancy, it does not know which type of worker will arrive at the vacancy first so it has to form its expectations on the basis of the aggregate ratio of unemployed low and high-skilled workers.[6]

The number of contacts between complex jobs and workers is also an increasing function of vacancies and relevant searchers and is given by:

$$x_c = x_c\left(v_c^+\left(y_c^+,(u_h+e_{sh})^+\right),(u_h+e_{sh})^+\right) \qquad (2)$$

Where v_c represents complex vacancies (also increasing in expected productivity and relevant number of job searchers), u_h is the unemployment rate for high-skilled workers and e_{sh} stands for the number of high-skilled workers occupying simple jobs but who continue searching for higher paying complex vacancies. All variables are expressed as fractions of the labour force. Note that I implicitly assume that employed and unemployed high-skilled workers search equally efficiently for complex jobs.

The rates at which low and high-skilled unemployed workers find simple jobs is given by: $p_s = x_s/(u_h + u_l)$ and $p_c = x_c/(u_h + e_{sh})$. Given the properties of the matching technology, p_s and p_c are increasing in vacancies and decreasing in the number of job seekers. Furthermore, I will define the firing rates for simple jobs to be equal to $s_{sl}(y_s^-)$ for low-skilled workers and $s_{sh}(\mu y_s^-)$ for high-skilled workers and the redundancy rate for high-skilled workers at complex jobs to be equal to $s_c(y_c)$, where both $s_{sl}'(y_s)$ and $s_c'(y_c) < 0$. There are several reasons why redundancy rates for simple and complex jobs may differ. The most uncontroversial one is that complex jobs require more sunk investments in company specific human capital, which gives both the company and the worker more incentives to continue their relation. But it could also be the case that the evolution of technology structurally leads to net job creation of complex jobs and net job destruction of simple jobs.

We can now write down the five differential equations for the different worker states.

$$\frac{du_l}{dt} = s_{sl}e_{sl} - p_s u_l \tag{3}$$

$$\frac{du_h}{dt} = s_c e_c + s_{sh}e_{sh} - \left(p_s + p_c\right)u_h \tag{4}$$

$$\frac{de_{sl}}{dt} = p_s u_l - s_{sl}e_{sl} \tag{5}$$

$$\frac{de_{sh}}{dt} = p_s u_h - \left(p_c + s_{sh}\right)e_{sh} \tag{6}$$

$$\frac{de_c}{dt} = p_c\left(u_h + e_{sh}\right) - s_c e_c \tag{7}$$

In the steady state, all those differential equations will of course be equal to zero and they can be solved for equilibrium low and high-skilled employment and unemployment rates. First note that both high and low-skilled unemployment rates are decreasing in the hiring probability and increasing in the redundancy probabilities (both depend on the job-specific productivity).

The conventional idea is that increased competition of high-skilled workers is always bad for low-skilled workers. This view is, however, based on partial equilibrium arguments whereas we should be interested in the general equilibrium effects of high-skilled workers looking for simple jobs. In Gautier (1998), I show that the smaller the output ratio of high and low-skilled workers at *simple jobs*, μ, is, the more unemployed low-skilled workers will be harmed by competing high-skilled workers. The intuition behind this result is the following: profit maximizing companies will open simple vacancies as long as the quasi rents of a simple vacancy are positive. The quasi rents of a vacancy simply depend on the number of relevant searchers and the expected output of a filled vacancy. As μ increases, the expected quasi rents of a vacancy will also increase. Consequently, more vacancies will be opened (until the point is reached where the quasi rents of opening an additional vacancy will be zero again). Since employers do not know beforehand whether they will meet a high or a low-skilled worker, low-skilled workers benefit as much from a high μ as do high-skilled workers. When μ is equal to one, employers prefer low-skilled workers in simple jobs because high-skilled workers have a probability p_c to quit and leave to the complex sector. But there exists a value for μ (> 1) for which employers with simple vacancies are indifferent between a low and a high-skilled worker. Call this value μ^*. When $\mu = \mu^*$, the higher productivity of the high-skilled worker exactly compensates employers for his positive quit probability. When $\mu < \mu^*$, employers will prefer low-skilled workers in simple jobs and the supply of simple vacancies will therefore decrease in u_h/u_l. When $\mu > \mu^*$, the opposite holds.

Some authors have suggested that there is crowding out because low-skilled unemployment rates are higher than high-skilled unemployment rates. According to this model, this is not a very useful approach because low-skilled unemployment rates will always be higher than high-skilled unemployment rates, simply because unemployed high-skilled workers have the same probability to meet a simple vacancy but also have a positive probability to meet a complex vacancy.

It is also sometimes argued that changes in the unemployment rates of different skill categories can give us information on crowding out. If the fraction of workers with a lower education at simple jobs decreases when unemployment rises, they conclude that there is crowding out. However, there is ample evidence from e.g. Pfann and Palm (1993) and Gautier et al. (1998) that redundancy rates for low-skilled workers increase much more in bad times than the redundancy rates of high-skilled workers without evidence of there being more high-skilled workers who occupy simple jobs, a necessary requirement for crowding out. Oi (1962) gives a number of plausible reasons for this. When the sunk costs required to create simple jobs are lower than for complex jobs, we expect redundancy rates for low-skilled workers to also be higher. In addition, the above-mentioned explanation of skill-biased technological change may explain the observed differences in unemployment rates.

In our framework, low-skilled unemployment may increase for a number of reasons. In addition to the above mentioned higher redundancy rates for low-skilled workers, low-skilled unemployment will also increase when the productivity of simple jobs falls and fewer simple vacancies are opened. In both cases there is no crowding out. Hence, changes in unemployment rates over time do not provide us with sufficient information either, to be able to distinguish crowding out from other theories of low-skilled unemployment. When low-skilled unemployment increases because of crowding out, the origin of the shocks often lies in the complex sector. Crowding out occurs when relatively many high-skilled workers occupy simple jobs ($de_{sh}/dt > de_c/dt$). The source of this process may be a fall in productivity (or profitability) of complex jobs, which in turn leads to more job destruction (s_c rises) and to a lower stock of complex vacancies (p_c falls). When crowding out takes place, policy makers should therefore focus on distortions in the complex sector.

In Section 4 we will use a matched company–worker data set to test to what extent the relatively high unemployment rates for low-skilled workers in the beginning of the 1990's were the result of crowding out. But first we will describe our data in the next section.

3 DATA

For this chapter, we have used the AVO (ArbeidsVoorwaarden Ontwikkeling) data over the period 1992–95 from the Ministry of Social Affairs. This is a company–worker data set. The data were collected from administrative records of a sample of companies by means of a stratified two-step sample procedure. In the first step a sample of companies was drawn from the Ministry's own database (which is roughly similar to the company statistics collected by Statistics Netherlands), while in the second step a sample of workers was drawn from each of the companies. The number of workers drawn from a particular company depended on the size of the company.

Each year (October), in the first step a sample of companies (about 2,000 per year) is drawn from the population of companies with 1 or more employees.[7] In the second step, a sample of workers (around 25,000 a year) is drawn from the records of companies selected in the first step. The population of companies was allocated over a number of strata (80 in 1993, 280 in 1994, and 312 in 1995). The strata were based on combinations of sectors and size classes. In particular the number of companies with fewer than 10 employees was underrepresented. This was corrected by reweighting.

The number of workers drawn depends on the company's size (from companies with fewer than 10 employees, all workers were drawn, from the larger companies, the sampling probability decreased with company size), and whether the employees had a collective wage agreement or not. Lastly, a distinction was made between employees who were present at both sampling moments (stayers), workers who were only present at the first sampling moment (outflow) and workers who were only present at the second sampling moment (inflow). More than 75 per cent of the workers were present at both sampling moments. When workers were only present at $t - 1$ and not at t (leavers), information was obtained on the new labour market status of the worker. The fractions of workers entering and leaving which were sampled in a particular period are consistent with the macro figures. We have information on seven job complexity levels (which vary as to the experience required, the complexity of the activities and the amount of supervision required for the job) and seven types of education. In general, the first three education levels are considered to be low. For a description of the job complexity and education levels I refer to the Appendix.

In the reweighting process, every company gets a weight equal to the inverse of the probability of being sampled. All companies within each of the strata have the same probability of being drawn and consequently receive the same weight. The 'Statistiek van het ondernemersbestand 1994' of Statistics Netherlands was used for this procedure. For the determination of the weights of the employees, the Statistics Netherlands statistic: 'Banen van werknemers' (jobs of workers) was used. Since different worker types are distinguished within a company (with or without collective wage agreements, and new staying and leaving workers), individual workers have different probabilities as to be selected in the sample. As a result it is possible that within a stratum workers can have different weights.

The data were collected by the Labour Inspectorate office of the Department of Social Affairs. Information on wages, hours worked, days worked and a number of other variables were collected from the wage administration. Lastly, it is useful to mention that the response rates are very high. Job complexity levels were for example reported for more than 99 per cent of the workers.

Disadvantages of the data are that the sampling strategy is quite complex and that the number of strata from which companies were drawn change over time. In addition, the data contain no information on output, investment and profits. For more information on the data, see Venema (1996) and Gautier (1998).

4 MEASURING THE IMPORTANCE OF CROWDING OUT

4.1 Testing Crowding out with Micro Data

I will test for crowding out by measuring changes over time in the fraction of high-skilled workers in simple jobs and I have used education as a proxy for worker skills. The 'true' skills of a worker, however, depend on education plus some observed and unobserved characteristics. The identifying assumption is that these unobserved characteristics are constant over time but that crowding out is not. In order to clarify this, it is useful to introduce a shorthand notation for the distribution of new workers with a given level of education over the various job levels. We label this distribution $f(i)$, where i stands for the level of education. Crowding out implies that in a bad year, more workers accept jobs below the level that corresponds to their skills, i.e. $f(i)$ in a bad year lies to the left of $f(i)$ in a good year.[8] On the other hand, if the seemingly imperfect match between job level and educational level is due to unobserved differences between workers, then $f(i)$ should *not* depend on the state of the labour market. Hence, the fraction of workers with a higher education who occupy simple jobs and who have unobserved characteristics which do not make them more productive than low-skilled workers (e.g. because they choose the wrong field) is assumed to be constant over the cycle. This could be a restrictive assumption if people anticipate adverse labour market conditions and therefore choose studies with higher job probabilities. However, the time lags between the beginning of an education and the time one enters employment are so large that we can reasonably rule this option out. Also note that what we observe are equilibrium outcomes. Crowding out could be either caused by employers who demand more skills for given jobs when employment is low or because more high-skilled workers arrive at low-skilled jobs. In this chapter, I will define the following operational condition for crowding out to take place.

Condition 1
Crowding out occurs when in periods of low employment, more high-skilled workers occupy simple jobs.

The next issue is to find two years in our sample period in which employment opportunities differed. Table 10.2 shows that in 1993 unemployment rose sharply and that few vacancies were opened, while in 1995 unemployment fell and many vacancies were opened. Moreover, the V/U ratio for almost all education groups, and in particular for those with only primary school was lower in 1993 than in 1995. In what follows, we will therefore consider 1993 to be a bad year and 1995 to be a good year in terms of employment opportunities.

Table 10.2 Labour market conditions in 1993 and 1995

Indicator	1993	1995
Unemployment change	22.7	−6.7
Employment change		
persons	−0.1	2.1
man years	−0.5	2.1
New vacancies × 1000	383	526
Filled vacancies × 1000	396	508
Employment (priv. sector × 1000)	5,754	5,897

Table 10.2 Continued

V/U ratios	1993	1995	1993/1995
Primary	0.002	0.030	0.067
Lower Secondary (LGSE)	0.169	0.038	4.408
Lower Secondary (PVE)	0.068	0.133	0.511
Higher Secondary (HGSE)	0.025	0.075	0.328
Intermediate Vocational	0.076	0.172	0.574
Higher Vocational	0.099	0.003	0.574
University	0.035	0.075	0.465

Source: EBB (Statistics Netherlands) and AVO (Labour Inspectorate 1997).

4.2 Stylized Facts

In this section we will start with some key statistics on the magnitude and composition of employment. The analysis will be on both detailed job complexity levels (F1–F7) and less detailed job complexity levels: *low* (F1, F2), *intermediate* (F3–F5) and *high* (F6, F7). An additional advantage of the last method is that the results are less vulnerable for measurement errors due to the always subjective definition of job complexity levels and the fact that I have used different samples. A disadvantage is however that some detailing is lost.

Table 10.3 Allocation of workers with a certain education over different jobs for 1993 and 1995

Job complexity level	Low		Intermediate		High		Total
Stock	1993	1995	1993	1995	1993	1995	
Education							
Low	27.0	27.8	72.7	72.1	0.4	0.1	100
Intermediate	3.3	3.9	94.6	95.6	2.1	0.5	100
High	0.2	1.0	69.9	77.9	29.9	21.2	100

Source: AVO (Labour Inspectorate 1997).

We will now turn to some simple tests. Remember that if an increase in low-skilled unemployment is the result of crowding out, we expect that in the shrinking employment year 1993, given the job level, a smaller fraction of the workers has a lower education.

We see in Table 10.3 that both the workers with an intermediate and a higher education occupied relatively more simple jobs in the high employment year. Moreover, the fraction of high-skilled workers at intermediate jobs was 10 percentage points higher in 1995 than in 1993. If the reduction of employment opportunities for low-skilled workers was the result of crowding out, we would expect the opposite.

We repeated this exercise for the stocks of one sample to make sure that our results were not driven by sample differences or the fact that the economy behaved in a fundamentally different way in 1993 than in 1995. Table 10.4 gives the results for 1992–93 (employment was higher in 1992 than in 1993) and Table 10.5 gives the results for 1994–95 (employment was lower in 1994). We have to be careful interpreting these results, since job complexity levels were only measured once (in October $t-1$ for all workers who were present in period t and in October t for the new workers). Hence the shifts are partly driven by changes in job complexity levels between inflow and outflow. In general, we would expect that job-leavers who are included in period $t-1$ occupied more complex jobs than new workers who were present in period t. If we compare 1994 with 1995, we see in Table 10.5 that in the relatively low employment year 1994 in the group of intermediate employed workers, 0.8 percentage points less occupied a simple job (in the case of crowding out, we would expect more of those workers of to be employed at a simple job), while in the group of employed workers with a higher education, 0.7 percentage points more occupied a simple job. This is an upper bound of the crowding out effect because the stocks of 1994 and 1995 only differed as to outflow$_{95}$ (included in 1994) and inflow$_{95}$ (included in 1995). The tests for 1992 and 1993 give similar results. Again, we did not find evidence for a crowding out effect.

*Table 10.4   Allocation of workers with a certain education over different jobs based on the 1992–1993 sample**

Job complexity level	Low		Intermediate		High		Total
	1992	1993	1992	1993	1992	1993	
Education							
Low	29.5	30.2	70.2	69.5	0.3	0.3	100
Intermediate	3.7	4.0	94.3	94.1	2.0	1.9	100
High	0.2	0.3	70.6	71.0	29.2	28.8	100

Note: *   Based on stocks. In 1992, employment and employment growth was higher than in 1993.
Source: AVO (Labour Inspectorate 1997).

Table 10.5   Allocation of workers with a certain education over different jobs based on the 1994–1995 sample*

Job complexity level	Low		Intermediate		High		Total
	1994	1995	1994	1995	1994	1995	
Education							
Low	29.9	30.4	70.1	69.5	0.1	0.1	100
Intermediate	4.3	5.1	95.2	94.4	0.5	0.6	100
High	1.6	0.9	77.8	77.8	20.7	21.3	100

Note: * Based on stocks. In 1995, employment and employment growth was higher than in 1994.
Source: AVO (Labour Inspectorate).

4.3 Ordered Logit Estimates

4.3.1 Estimates for low, intermediate and high complexity jobs

Still, we cannot rule out that a labour market in a boom behaves fundamentally different from a labour market in a recession. Female participation may differ, the age distribution of the labour force may differ, and some sectors (such as the chemical sector) are more vulnerable for cyclical movements than others. Moreover, unions and employer organizations may behave differently in tight labour markets. In this section, I will try to correct for this by estimating the probabilities from an ordered logit for workers with a certain type of education and other characteristics of being employed at different job complexity levels.

Let f^* be an index of job complexity, which depends on a vector x of characteristics, such as occupation, education, sector, age, sex and tenure. Where ϵ has a logistic distribution and the mean and variance of ϵ are normalized to zero and one. We do not observe f^* but we do observe that

$$f^* = \beta'x + \epsilon$$

$$f = 1 \qquad if \ 0 \leq f^* < \mu_1$$

$$f = 2 \qquad if \ \mu_1 \leq f^* < \mu_2$$

$$f = 3 \qquad if \ \mu_2 \leq f^* < \mu_3$$

$$\vdots$$

$$f = 7 \qquad if \ \mu_6 \leq f^*$$

The probabilities for $f=1...7$, can be calculated in the standard way. I will calculate those probabilities separately for a high and for a low employment year. If the probabilities for the 'average worker' with a certain type of education of being employed at a low complexity job are higher in the low employment year, this would be evidence in favour of crowding out. I will estimate our model for detailed (F1–F7) and rough (1–3) job complexity levels and both with and without wages. On the one hand, the gross hourly wage (including overtime payments, profit shares, etc.) is a good measure of a worker's true productivity, but on the other hand we have to worry about endogeneity issues. It is possible that wages are linked institutionally to different job complexity levels. Table 10.6 shows, however, that there is quite some wage dispersion within each of the first five job complexity levels. The issue of including or excluding wages is also related to the degree to which crowding out is a matter of substitution or not. When skilled workers earn higher wages in simple jobs, it partly reflects substitution. In the estimates which include the wage effect, we thus measure the pure crowding out effect.[9]

Table 10.6 Gross hourly wages (including overtime payments, etc.)

	<10	10–15	15–20	20–25	25–30	30–35	35–40	>40	Total
F1	14.6	42.8	33.4	4.1	1.8	1.2	1.1	0.9	100
F2	16.2	30.9	32.3	9.5	3.0	1.9	1.9	4.3	100
F3	1.2	10.7	27.0	26.6	11.7	4.1	5.7	13.1	100
F4	0.1	1.8	8.1	20.0	21.5	9.9	6.4	32.3	100
F5	0.0	0.5	1.6	5.0	14.2	13.2	11.9	52.5	100
F6	0.1	0.1	0.6	1.1	1.8	2.8	5.5	88.1	100
F7	0.0	0.0	0.0	0.3	0.0	0.0	0.2	99.5	100

Source: AVO (Labour Inspectorate).

In Table 10.7, the estimation results are printed for 'rough' job complexity levels. All variables are highly significant. The probability of being employed in a complex job increases with education, age, tenure, productivity (measured as hourly wages), and is also higher for workers in growing companies, males, creative and managerial occupations, and for full-time workers. Our results appear to be qualitatively invariant with respect to the inclusion or exclusion of hourly wages.

Table 10.7 Estimation results: ordered logit estimates with and without wages 1993/1995

Variable	Coefficient[b]		Coefficient[c]		Mean
Intercept	5.37	(0.008)	4.79	(0.008)	
Intercept intermediate	-3.20	(0.006)	-4.39	(0.007)	
Year=1995	-0.08	(0.002)	-0.09	(0.002)	0.53
Lower education	-4.96	(0.006)	-4.72	(0.006)	20.72
Intermediate education	-2.94	(0.005)	-2.83	(0.006)	65.91
Age	0.04	(0.000)	0.03	(0.000)	35.80
Female	-0.75	(0.003)	-0.67	(0.002)	0.40
Tenure	0.01	(0.000)	0.004	(0.000)	7.53
Gross hourly wage			0.03	(0.000)	31.11
Shrinking company	-0.11	(0.002)	-0.06	(0.002)	0.28
Growing company	0.07	(0.002)	0.10	(0.002)	0.32
Company size 10–19	-0.31	(0.004)	-0.37	(0.004)	0.09
20–49	-0.34	(0.003)	-0.42	(0.003)	0.12
50–99	-0.42	(0.004)	-0.55	(0.004)	0.09
100–199	-0.40	(0.004)	-0.47	(0.004)	0.08
200–499	-0.37	(0.004)	-0.52	(0.003)	0.13
≥ 500	-0.50	(0.003)	-0.66	(0.003)	0.33
Part-time	-1.24	(0.003)	-1.14	(0.003)	0.28
Sector					
Agriculture/fishing	-0.42	(0.006)	-0.36	(0.006)	0.02
Construction	0.74	(0.004)	0.77	(0.004)	0.13
Trade	-0.23	(0.003)	-0.16	(0.003)	0.13
Hospitality	-1.13	(0.005)	-1.04	(0.005)	0.11
Transport/communication	0.64	(0.004)	0.61	(0.004)	0.06
Financial	0.28	(0.004)	0.17	(0.004)	0.11
Health	0.22	(0.003)	0.37	(0.003)	0.17
Occupation					
Simple technical	-0.18	(0.003)	-0.18	(0.003)	0.29
Administrative	0.99	(0.003)	0.91	(0.003)	0.15
Computer	0.58	(0.008)	0.55	(0.009)	0.02
Management	1.84	(0.005)	1.58	(0.005)	0.07
Commercial	0.38	(0.004)	0.37	(0.004)	0.11
Creative	1.67	(0.008)	1.75	(0.009)	0.01
Log likelihood:	-4,010,560.9		-3,900,061.6		

Notes:
[a] Standard error in brackets, reference groups/states, year=1993, higher education, male, companies which do not change size, companies with 0–9 employees, full-time, IT sector, non-technical service occupations.
[b] Excluding gross hourly wage.
[c] Including gross hourly wage.

Table 10.8 Simulated probabilities of being employed at a certain job complexity level[a]

Job complexity level Education	Low	Intermediate	High
Low			
Including wages	21.7	78.2	0.0
1993	20.9	79.0	0.0
1995	22.5	77.5	0.0
Excluding wages	24.8	75.2	0.1
1993	24.8	75.1	0.0
1995	26.3	73.6	0.0
Male	19.9	80.1	0.0
Female	34.4	65.6	0.0
Full-time	18.6	81.3	0.1
Part-time	44.2	55.8	0.0
Intermediate			
Including wages	4.0	95.7	0.2
1993	3.8	95.8	0.4
1995	4.2	95.6	0.2
Excluding wages	4.5	95.3	0.1
1993	4.1	95.4	0.4
1995	4.6	95.2	0.1
Male	3.2	96.2	0.6
Female	6.5	93.2	0.3
Full-time	3.0	96.4	0.6
Part-time	9.5	90.3	0.2
High			
Including wages	0.2	95.7	4.0
1993	0.2	95.5	4.2
1995	0.2	95.9	3.9
Excluding wages	0.2	92.2	7.7
1993	0.2	92.0	7.7
1995	0.2	92.6	7.2
Male	0.2	90.0	9.9
Female	0.4	94.9	4.7
Full-time	0.2	89.7	10.1
Part-time	0.6	96.2	3.2

Note:
[a] The probabilities are based on ordered logit estimates of Table 10.7 evaluated at the mean characteristics of the workforce.

From a statistical point of view, we must reject the hypothesis that low-skilled workers were crowded out in 1993. The 1995 dummy is negative and highly significant, which means that in the high employment year, workers performed on average less complex tasks. If we transform the coefficients into probabilities, we also see in Table 10.8 that differences in job complexity levels for a given education are much larger between males and females and part-time and full-time workers than between different years.

Table 10.9 The relevance of crowding out; probabilities based on ordered logits for different years and different education groups[*]

Job complexity level	Low		Intermediate		High	
	all	inflow	all	inflow	all	inflow
Education						
Low						
1993	22.1	56.5	69.0	43.5	0.0	0.0
1995	24.5	61.1	75.4	38.9	0.0	0.0
Difference	6.8	−4.6	−6.4	4.6	0.0	0.0
Intermediate						
1993	0.5	7.0	98.4	92.9	0.1	0.0
1995	4.9	3.3	95.1	96.7	0.0	0.0
Difference	−4.4	3.7	3.3	−3.8	0.1	0.0
High						
1993	0.2	0.4	87.3	95.2	12.5	4.4
1995	0.5	0.7	81.9	96.0	17.6	3.3
Difference	−0.3	−0.3	5.4	−0.8	−5.1	1.1

Note:
[*] The estimates are excluding wages and the probabilities of both 1993 and 1995 are based on average characteristics of the 1993 worker.
Source: AVO (Labour Inspectorate).

In the previous specification I implicitly assumed that the effects of the different variables was the same for all job complexity levels. Table 10.9 presents probabilities based on 2 × 3 separate ordered logit estimates for 1993 and 1995, and for each of the different education groups to reach optimal flexibility. The transformation of coefficients into probabilities is done over the average characteristics of the 1993-worker (for both 1993 and 1995). In this table, I also included information for new workers only since it is likely that crowding out is concentrated in this group. In the case of crowding out, we would expect a positive sign in the differences between 1993 and 1995 at low job complexity levels and a negative sign at high job complexity levels. There is some evidence that more workers with an intermediate education entered at low job complexity levels in 1993 and more high-skilled workers entered at intermediate jobs. If we consider the whole sample, however, we see no evidence for crowding out. On the contrary, a larger fraction of the high-skilled workers occupied complex jobs in the low employment year 1993.

In Table 10.10, the stocks of different skill groups are compared for the 1995 sample. Again we do not find that in the relatively low employment year 1994, more workers with an intermediate or higher education occupy simple jobs. The results are robust for the inclusion and exclusion of gross hourly wages.

Table 10.10 Crowding out; different probabilities based on stocks of the 1995 sample[*]

Job complexity level	Low		Intermediate		High	
	excl. w	incl. w	excl. w	incl. w	excl. w	incl. w
Education						
Low						
Low employment (1994)	22.1	16.8	77.8	83.1	0.0	0.0
High employment (1995)	21.0	18.0	79.0	81.9	0.0	0.0
Difference	1.0	−1.2	−1.2	1.2	0.0	0.0
Intermediate						
Low employment (1994)	3.4	2.9	96.2	96.9	0.0	0.0
High employment (1995)	3.4	3.2	96.3	96.6	0.3	0.1
Difference	0.0	−0.3	−0.1	0.0	−0.3	0.1
High						
Low employment (1994)	0.1	0.1	92.3	95.6	7.6	4.3
High employment (1995)	0.1	0.1	90.1	95.2	9.7	4.7
Difference	0.0	0.0	2.2	0.4	−2.1	−0.4

Note:
[*] The probabilities of 1995 are based on average characteristics of the 1993 worker.
Source: AVO (Labour Inspectorate).

4.3.2 Estimates for detailed job complexity levels

We now turn to a more detailed description of job complexity levels. Instead of considering only three job levels, we will now distinguish seven levels. For greater clarity, I have decided to present the results in a graphical form. Figure 10.2 shows how for given education classes, the distribution of job complexity levels changed between 1993 and 1995. The probabilities are again based on

ordered logit estimates (different ones for 1993–95, where the 1995 probabilities were obtained from the 1995 coefficient estimates and the average 1993
population averages), with the same variables (excluding wages) as in the
previous section. Remember that we would expect for all different education
classes to find more mass at low complexity jobs in 1993 than in 1995. First of
all, we see from all graphs that only workers with a primary education occupy
simple jobs at F1, both in 1993 and 1995, which suggests that there is no
crowding out in this segment.

Figures 10.2 and 10.3 show that in the low employment year there is a shift
in mass from job complexity level 3 to job complexity level 2, which is
consistent with crowding out. For workers with a higher secondary education
and a university degree, the shift is in the opposite direction, which is
inconsistent with crowding out. For the other groups, the distributions overlap.

If we look at the distributions of the inflow of workers (Figure 10.3), we see
some evidence that crowding out took place. Three out of seven education
groups exhibit a small leftward shift in the low employment year. Only the
workers with university degrees occupied on average more complex jobs in
1995 than in 1993. We may conclude therefore that only for the inflow of new
workers there is weak evidence for crowding out. In 1993, relatively many
workers with a higher secondary education occupied job complexity levels 2
and 3 and relatively few workers from this education class occupied job
complexity level 4. For the workers with a lower secondary education and the
workers with no more than primary education, we see a shift from job
complexity level 3 to job complexity level 2.

4.4 Inflow and Outflow

In the previous sections, we established that in a year of low employment, the
fraction of skilled workers occupying simple jobs did not increase. We did,
however, find some evidence that during bad times, new skilled workers were
recruited more frequently for low-skilled jobs. But the differences are small and
cannot explain the disproportionally large share of low-skilled workers who are
unemployed in recessions. The previous section also suggested that the companies who use bad times to improve the quality of their workforce mainly do
so by firing relatively underqualified workers. In this section, we will collect
more stylized facts on the firing and hiring behaviour of companies over
different segments of the labour market.

Figure 10.2   Shifts in job complexity distributions based on ordered logits for different education groups

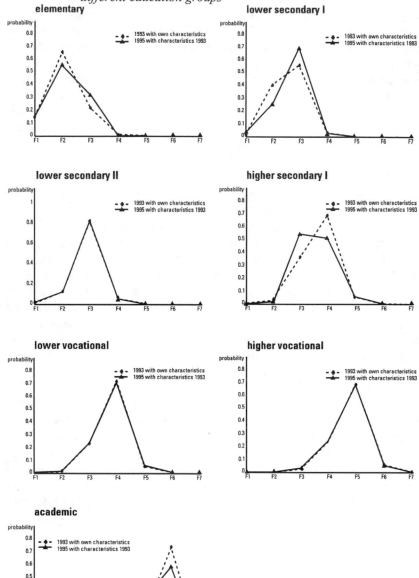

Figure 10.3   Shifts in job complexity distributions for employment inflow based on ordered logits for different education groups

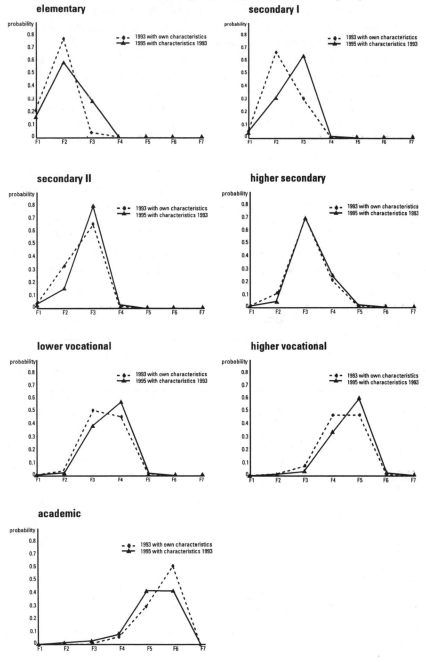

For an unemployed job searcher, at least three issues are relevant: the probability of getting a job, the expected duration of the job, and the net increase in wealth as a result of the job. The probability of getting a job is determined by the relevant stock of competing job searchers and total hirings. Table 10.11 shows that both hiring and firing rates are always higher in simple jobs. The cyclical behaviour of firing and hiring rates for simple and complex jobs is different, however. In bad times, relatively many workers are fired from simple jobs and relatively few workers are hired from complex jobs. This is consistent with Pfann and Palm's (1993) finding based on aggregate data. We also see for all job types that there are fewer job-to-job movements in bad times, which is a well known fact.

Hence the fact that the stock of low-skilled unemployed workers is relatively high in recessions, seems to be mainly caused by increased outflow and to a much lesser extent to a reduction of inflow. Note that both processes can take place with or without crowding out. In the crowding out hypothesis, more high-skilled workers occupy simple jobs, which results in either an increased outflow of low-skilled workers, a decreased inflow, or a combination of both. On the other hand, fewer low-skilled workers can be hired and more low-skilled workers can get fired without an increase of the fraction of high-skilled workers in simple jobs.

Table 10.11 Hiring and firing rates for different job complexity levels

Job complexity level		Firing	Hiring	Disability	Job to job
Low	1993	10.6	19.0	0.5	1.2
F1–F2	1995	4.3	21.8	0.3	7.1
	ratio	2.5	0.9	1.6	0.2
	difference	6.3	−2.8	0.2	−5.9
Intermediate	1993	7.1	8.8	0.3	1.0
F3–F5	1995	2.7	11.5	0.2	5.2
	ratio	2.6	0.8	1.5	0.2
	difference	4.4	−2.7	0.1	−4.2
High	1993	4.9	5.4	0.0	0.3
F6–F8	1995	1.5	15.0	0.1	5.3
	ratio	3.3	0.4	0.0	0.1
	difference	3.4	−9.6	−0.1	−5.0

Source: AVO (Labour Inspectorate).

5 CONCLUSION

In this chapter, I have presented a bare bone matching model in which low-skilled unemployment may rise relatively sharply due to either crowding out, or a decrease in the profitability of simple jobs. For policy makers it is important to know how important crowding out is, because it has implications for the labour market segments that economic policies should be focused on. In general, crowding out occurs when either the supply of high-skilled workers rises or the supply of complex jobs falls and some high-skilled workers compete with low-skilled workers for simple jobs.

The main empirical question was whether more high-skilled workers occupied simple jobs in the beginning of the 1990s in the Netherlands. This was tested with a combined company/worker data set. It turns out that there is weak evidence that new workers (with a lower education) enter in less complex jobs in bad times than in good times. For new workers with a higher education, there is no such evidence. Moreover, if we consider the entire stock of workers, we do not find more mass at low job complexity levels for any education group during bad times.

The message for policy makers is that labour market policies that stimulate job creation at the top segment of the labour market will be less effective in reducing low-skilled unemployment than policies that focus directly on the bottom segment.

APPENDIX
JOB COMPLEXITY AND EDUCATION LEVELS

We have used the following classification (see Venema, 1996) of job complexity levels.

Low

F1 Very simple activities that do not change over time. No schooling and only limited experience are required. The activities are under direct supervision.

F2 Simple activities that are generally repetitive. Some (lower) administrative or technical knowledge and experience is required. In general, the activities take place under direct supervision.

Intermediate

F3 Less simple activities that do not repeat themselves continuously. Administrative or technical knowledge is required, and the activities are partly done without direct supervision.

F4 More difficult (non-repetitive) activities, for which an intermediate level of education is required. In general, the activities take place without direct supervision.

F5 Activities within a certain field that require a higher level of knowledge and experience. The activities take place without direct supervision.

High

F6 Managerial activities of an analytical, creative or contactual nature, which are undertaken independently and require an academic or comparable level.

F7 Managers of intermediate companies or comparable businesses, departments, etc., who also participate in decision-making and managers of large companies or comparable businesses or departments.

In this chapter, F7 and F8 are merged because F8 contained too few observations to treat it as a separate group. We have used the following education scheme:

Primary/elementary	Low
Lower secondary	Low
Preparatory vocational	Low
Higher secondary	Intermediate
Intermediate vocational	Intermediate
Higher vocational	High
University	High

NOTES

1. See, for example, Aigner and Cain (1977) for a treatise on statistical discrimination.
2. For a comparison of the efficiency wage and the search model with and without crowding out, see Gautier and Pomp (1999).
3. Other models, such as Pissarides (1994) and the simulation model of den Butter and Gorter (1998), assume that jobs are heterogeneous but workers are not.
4. McCormick (1990) assumed that unemployed high-skilled workers have a higher probability of finding a complex job because they have more time to devote to searching. Therefore, the best workers will decide to remain unemployed rather than accept a simple job. Workers with lesser skills, however, also have incentives for not accepting simple jobs because accepting a simple job gives a bad signal. In my model, I assume that employed workers search exactly as effectively as unemployed workers. Therefore, there are no incentives for this type of signalling. Of course arguments can be given for more efficient searching by either unemployed workers (more time) or employed workers (better network), but the evidence on this issue is still inconclusive. Moreover, one may also imagine that the temporary acceptance of a job below one's level signals a strong motivation to work.
5. In Gautier (1998) and Gautier and Pomp (1999), explicit wages are derived by a Nash bargaining over the match surplus.

6. Remember that there is a CRS production technique and there is free entry of vacancies. This implies that the company accepts both types of workers as long as there is a positive match surplus. If there is still a surplus, a new vacancy will be opened.

7. The sample was drawn from the company register of the Department of Social Aff airs, which contains roughly the same information on companies as 'Statistiek van het ondernemingsbestand' of Statistics Netherlands.

8. This can be viewed as a supply approach. Gautier et al. (1998) followed a more demand-orientated approach to test whether companies upgraded their workforce during recessions. Their results are consistent with the ones in this chapter.

9. Van den Berg et al. (1998) showed that workers with more schooling than their direct colleagues at the same job level in the same company do not earn higher wages. They do tend to select themselves into high wage companies.

REFERENCES

Aigner and Cain (1977), 'Statistical Theories of Discrimination in Labor Markets', *Industrial and Labor Relations Review*, **30** (2), 175–187.

Den Butter, F.A.G. and C. Gorter (1998), 'Vacancy Chains and Labour Market Dynamics', Free University Amsterdam, Mimeo.

Gautier, P.A. (1998), *Unemployment and Search Externalities in a Model with Heterogeneous Workers and Heterogeneous Jobs*, Mimeo, Free University Amsterdam.

Gautier, P.A., G.J. van den Berg, J.C. van Ours and G. Ridder (1998), *Worker Turnover at the Firm Level and Crowding Out of Lower Educated Workers*, mimeo, Free University Amsterdam **49**.

Gautier, P.A. and M. Pomp (1999), 'Crowding Out in Two Equilibrium Models of Unemployment', CPB Report.

Hartog, J. and H. Oosterbeek (1985), 'Education, Allocation and Earnings in the Netherlands: Overschooling?', *Economics of Education Review* **7**, 185–94.

McCormick, B. (1990), *A Theory of Signalling during Job Search, Employment Efficiency, and 'Stigmatised' Jobs*.

Oi,W.Y. (1962) 'Labor as a Quasi-fixed Factor', *Journal of Political Economy*, 538–55.

Pfann, G.A. and F.C. Palm (1993), 'Asymmetric Adjustment Costs in Non-linear Labour Demand Models with Empirical Evidence for the Dutch and the U.K. Manufacturing Sectors', *Review of Economic Studies* **60**, 397–412.

Pissarides, C.A. (1994), 'Search Unemployment with On-the-job Search', *Review of Economic Studies* **61**, 457–75.

Thurow, L.C. (1975), *Generating Inequality*, New York: Basic Books.

Van Ours, J.C. and G. Ridder (1995), 'Job Matching and Job Competition: Are Lower Educated Workers at the Back of Job Queues?', *European Economic Review* **39**, 1717–31.

Venema, P.M. (1996), *Arbeidsvoorwaardenonderzoek in 1996*, Labour Inspectorate Ministry of Social Affairs, The Hague: Vuga.

ACKNOWLEDGEMENTS

The author would like to thank the Department of Social Affairs for kindly letting me use the AVO data; L. Borghans, G.J. van den Berg, A. de Grip, J.C. Van Ours, M. Pomp, and G. Ridder, for their useful comments and discussions. Any remaining errors are mine.

11. Job Competition in the Dutch Labour Market

Loek Groot and Albert Hoek

1 INTRODUCTION

Human capital theory and job competition theory contest the relationships between the steadily rising educational level of the labour force on the one hand and changes in wage differentials and unemployment rates between educational categories on the other. On the basis of their empirical findings, Van Ours and Ridder (1995) conclude that 'bumping down' is not a likely explanation for the fairly high unemployment rates among the lower educated in The Netherlands during the 1980s. We will argue that their test is seriously flawed and inadequate for testing the bumping-down hypothesis in a proper way.

In order to clarify the issue at hand, in Section 2 we will discuss Thurow's job competition theory in comparison with the human capital theory and list a number of considerations that are important for bumping-down processes in general. Section 3 then illustrates the working of a fictitious labour market under assumptions of the human capital theory and the job competition theory, respectively. This exercise enables us to clearly demonstrate the differences between the two theories regarding assumptions and predictions. It will be shown that an exogenous and sudden increase in the average level of education gives rise to different outcomes. According to the human capital theory, the average wages of the lower educated will increase as a result of decreased supply, while those of the higher educated will decrease as a result of an increased supply. This amounts to a reduction in wage inequality between higher and lower educated workers. According to the job competition theory, however, average wages of both higher and lower educated will decrease, but wage inequality between educational categories increases. In Section 4, we survey recent empirical studies conducted in The Netherlands concerning job competition. In this section we also present our findings about whether (i) the increase in the average level of education of the labour force have led to a rise in wage inequality between higher and lower educated and whether (ii) schooling programmes for the lower educated can reduce unemployment among the lower educated workforce. The empirical evidence collected so far proves to be mixed. After this survey, we will discuss in detail in Section 5, the flaws of both the theoretical model and the empirical test conducted by Van Ours and Ridder (1995). Lastly, using the same data as Van Ours and Ridder, we present an alternative way to test whether (iii) job competition increases if unemployment (or the V/U-ratio) among higher educated workers increases. Contrary to their findings, our results suggest that job competition mainly occurs between higher and middle educated workers.

2   WHAT DOES THE JOB COMPETITION THEORY SAY?

The number of articles on the job competition theory is only a small fraction of the enormous stream of articles inspired by the human capital theory. The two theories give different explanations of the relationships between education, wage differentials and unemployment rates. According to the human capital theory, education is first of all an investment in productive and marketable assets.[1] The monetary benefits of these investments are higher future wages, which in general are higher the higher the educational level. The costs of human capital investments are mainly determined by forgone earnings while in school, and the direct costs of schooling, such as tuition fees. In this framework, wages have an important signalling function. The investment decisions of individuals are influenced by a comparison of the costs and benefits. If a particular educational category is in short supply (e.g., computer scientists and IT specialists in the 1990s), its relative wage will rise and more students will choose such a career (see e.g. Topel (1997, Figures 3 and 4, pp. 70–71) for the close link between wage ratios and enrolment rates). In the long term, wage differentials serve to mediate demand and supply. Note that not all students need to make their schooling decisions on the basis of costs and benefits: it is sufficient that only a fraction of all students, particularly those on the margin who hesitate between one or the other study, switch to those educations with relatively, and temporarily, high wages and low unemployment rates to ensure an equilibrium in the long term.

The fact that individuals weight the costs and benefits and pros and cons of different educational careers against each other is not contested by Thurow (1979) in his job competition theory. However, different assumptions are made regarding the processes of wage determination and the matching process of workers and jobs taking place in the labour market. These are summarized in Table 11.1.

Table 11.1 The main differences between the human capital theory and the job competition theory

	Human capital	Job competition
Adjustment mechanism	Wage levels	Number of jobs
Productivity	Person-linked	Job-linked
Wages	Flexible	Fairly stable
Job chance determined by	Absolute educational level	Relative educational level

According to the job competition theory, wages and productivity are linked to jobs rather than to persons. The matching of demand and supply of labour is not so much a process in which employers try to get trained workers as cheap as possible (by adjusting wages to the state of the labour market), but one in which they try find workers who can perform the job at the lowest training costs:

> Thus the labor market is not primarily a market for matching the demands and supplies of different job skills, but a market for matching trainable individuals with training ladders. Except for background characteristics, the demand for job skills creates the supply of job skills since the demands for labor determine which job skills are taught. In marginal productivity terms, marginal products are associated with jobs and not with individuals. The operative problem is to pick and train workers so that they can generate the desired marginal product of the job in question with the least investment in training costs. For new workers and entry level jobs, background characteristics form the basis of selection. (Thurow, 1979, p. 18).

Since training costs are not observable, employers will rank potential workers according to their background characteristics such as age, sex and education. Younger workers are more mouldable than old ones. Education is probably the most important indicator of future training costs, because it is a good predictor of workers' disciplinary and learning capacities. Gender characteristics can be used by employers to maximize the pay-off of training costs.[2] Moreover, age, sex and educational level are the easiest indicators of training costs to assess.

It is implicitly assumed that higher educated job applicants within the same educational field (e.g., technical, socio-cultural, etc.) can do the work of the lower educated workers at lower training costs. Employers are prepared to make higher training costs as the labour market tightens (longer job queues). As a consequence, the potential workers at the end of the labour queue will also find work. In a slack labour market (longer labour queues than job queues comprised of vacancies to be filled), workers at the lower end of the labour queue become or remain unemployed. It is not so much the wages that fluctuate at economic up- and downturns, but the number of jobs and vacancies. If the job queue does not change, an exogenous increase in the educational level of the workforce will make it easier for employers to lower training costs by recruiting higher educated workers for jobs which were previously done by workers of lower educational rank. Strictly speaking, this is what is understood by job competition, bumping down or crowding out proper: lower educated workers are replace by higher educated workers in jobs, without a change in job description. Contrary to what is sometimes argued, non-neutral or extensive skill-biased technological change,[3] shifting the demand curve for higher educated labour to the right and for lower educated labour to the left, is not a factor that can explain job competition proper since this will also change the job contents. If anything, it increases the number of jobs requiring a high level of education and reduces the number of low-skilled jobs. On the same footing is increased trade between developed and developing countries: in so far as this can explain the reduced demand for low-skilled labour (because products which are relatively intensive in low-skilled labour are now imported), it causes a reduction of the number of low-skilled jobs in developed countries, but not necessarily a replacement of low-skilled workers by high-skilled workers in low-skilled jobs. If the latter process takes place, it becomes a defensive strategy for individuals to raise their educational level. If job competition occurs due to an increase in the supply of higher educated labour, then others must improve their educational level 'simply to defend their current income position. If they don't, others will and they will not find their current job open to them' (Thurow, 1979, p. 30).

Before we go on to a brief discussion of relevant circumstances for job competition to take place, two issues need to be addressed. First, why do employers rank workers according to expected training costs? Second, why does Thurow believe that wage flexibility and competition among workers cannot do the job it is supposed to do? Minimizing training costs is important because every job requires job-specific and company-specific human capital for which the employer bears at least part of the costs. These skills can to a large extent only be learned at work. Crucial in this process of recruiting workers according to training costs is the importance of on-the-job training (OJT), and the distribution of costs and benefits of training between employer and employee (see Thurow, 1979, pp. 18–19). Regarding the second issue, stimulating the transfer of knowledge among workers and especially between trained and untrained workers, employers are reluctant to make use of direct wage competition and limit job competition to entry-level jobs.[4] An additional reason is the interdependency of marginal productivity of different factors of production.[5] In the end, the theory stands or falls with the importance of non-costless OJT and skills that cannot be learned outside the job: 'More potential plumbers will not lower the wages for plumbers since the market is structured in such a manner that individuals cannot learn plumbing skills unless there is a job opening available' (Thurow, 1979, p. 23).

There are some considerations that are of interest for the process of job competition or crowding out of lower educated by higher educated workers. First of all, it depends on demand and supply conditions on the labour market. The Netherlands, for example, had an extraordinary growth of the potential workforce during the 1970s and 1980s due to the baby boom after World War II and rapidly increasing female labour participation rates (starting from a very low level at the end of the 1960s). Both factors lengthen the labour queue, which may partly explain why the Dutch economic literature has so many publications on job competition compared to the rest of Europe. Second, a compressed wage structure (i.e. modest gross wage inequality) makes it less expensive for employers to select higher educated workers than is strictly required to do (lower level) jobs properly, and still pay them according to their educational level. Third, modest net wage inequality reduces the opportunity costs for overschooled workers. Searching for a job below one's own level probably shortens the duration of the search process, and the loss in forgone income by accepting a lower qualified job is small if net wage inequality is modest. Fourth, the conditions under which welfare benefits can be obtained can exert a significant impact on crowding out. Over the past few years, more austere conditions have been introduced in The Netherlands for the unemployed on welfare benefits with respect to their obligation to accept job offers. The criterion is no longer whether the work is suitable (i.e. at one's own level), but whether it is common, current, going work. If the labour market is slack, this may increase the level of crowding out, especially among those who have just left school.

The different views of the human capital and the job competition theory on the relationship between rising educational levels and the incidence of unemployment at the bottom end of the labour market have some policy relevance. If the human capital theory is right, this suggests measures which enhance the flexibility of the labour market such as abolition or reduction of minimum wages, abolition of the legal extension of collective wage agreements on whole sectors of industry, more schooling for the unemployed, reduction of social benefits levels or the replacement ratio, reduction of the tax wedge, a reform towards employment programmes, etc. If the job competition theory is right, employment programmes and the schooling instrument cannot reduce macro-unemployment. Providing additional training to one group of unemployed individuals lifts this group to a higher rank on the labour queue, but other groups will take over their positions. To reduce unemployment at the bottom end, the government must devise special job programmes for those with the least favourable background conditions.[6]

3 BECKERISTAN AND THUROWIA

So far we have presented the two theories as each other's counterparts. In the real world, both theories have some relevance: 'Readers can judge for themselves exactly where they would place the American economy on such a continuum and whether they think a job competition model can aid in answering the relevant questions and puzzles' (Thurow, 1979, p. 25). To flesh out the adjustment process of a sudden increase in the educational level of the workforce, we distinguish two initially identical imaginary countries, *Beckeristan* and *Thurowia*. The workforce is set equal to 100, and three educational levels are distinguished. The exogenous increase in the educational level of the workforce changes the distribution over lower, middle and higher educated in both countries from 50 : 30 : 20 to 25 : 50 : 25. The two theories differ in the way the labour market adjusts to a new equilibrium. For simplicity, we concentrate on relative wage levels and abstract from (the occurrence of) unemployment.

In *Beckeristan* wages are flexible. Since the number of lower educated workers is halved, while the number of middle and higher educated workers increases, the labour supply curve of the former shifts inward, and those of the latter outward, as illustrated in Figure 11.1. Changes in technology over time, which may change the relative demand of educational categories, do not play a role here since we have assumed an instant (overnight) change in the educational structure of labour supply. Moreover, substitution elasticities between workers of different educational levels are already implicit in the slopes of the labour demand curves. The easier it is for employers to substitute a certain educational category of workers, the flatter the slope of the labour demand curve. In Figure 11.1, the lower and middle educated workers are easily substitutable, while the demand for higher educated workers is rather inelastic. Table 11.2 summarizes the core data for the new equilibrium, in which nominal National Income (although National Income in real terms may have changed

Figure 11.1 The main difference between human capital and job competition theory

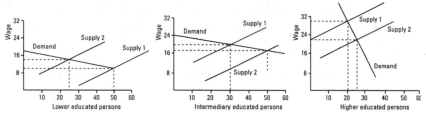

Table 11.2 The equilibrium wage levels according to the human capital theory

Old Educational level	#	y	New Educational level	#	y
Lower	50	10	Lower	25	14
Middle	30	20	Middle	50	16
Higher	20	30	Higher	25	22
Total	100	N.I.=1700	Total	100	N.I.=1700

= number of jobs; y − average income; N.I. − National Income

due to the inflow of better trained and more productive workers) has not changed.

In *Thurowia* the job queue does not change as a result of the change in the educational distribution of the labour queue. Moreover, wages are tied to jobs, and the only effect of the sudden flood of higher educated workers is that employers aggravate entry level job requirements. As a consequence, the higher educated take the better paid jobs previously held by middle educated workers, who in turn take over the better paid jobs of the lower educated workers (see Table 11.3). Table 11.4 summarizes the average wages received by workers with different educational levels.

Comparing Tables 11.4 and 11.2, we see that wage inequality between educational levels has decreased in *Beckeristan* from 3 : 2 : 1 to 1.6 : 1.1 : 1, while in *Thurowia* it has risen sharply to 4.1 : 2.3 : 1. Moreover, wages of the lower educated in *Beckeristan* have risen from 10 to 14 (since the supply of lower educated is reduced, their scarcity price increases), while in *Thurowia* they have declined from 10 to 7, so in both countries the rise and decline is absolute as well as relative. These diverging outcomes are similar to the way

Thurow (1979) tested his theory against the predictions of the human capital theory. This imaginary experiment gives us a clue as to how we can discriminate between job competition and human capital theory predictions with respect to the relationship between the educational distribution of workers and relative wages.

Table 11.3 The distribution of workers and jobs over wage levels according to the job competition theory

Old #	# jobs	x y		New #	# jobs	x y		
L = 50	15 × 5	20 × 10	15 × 15	L = 25	15 × 5	10 × 10		
M = 30	7 × 15	16 × 20	7 × 25	M = 50	10 × 10	22 × 15	16 × 20	2 × 25
H = 20	6 × 25	8 × 30	6 × 35	H = 25	11 × 25	8 × 30	6 × 35	

= number, y = income

Table 11.4 The equilibrium wage levels according to the job competition theory

Old Educational level	#	y	New Educational level	#	y
Lower	50	10	Lower	25	7
Middle	30	20	Middle	50	16
Higher	20	30	Higher	25	29
Total	100	N.I. = 1700	Total	100	N.I. = 1700

= number of jobs; y = average income; N.I. = National Income

4 EMPIRICAL RESEARCH ON THE JOB COMPETITION THEORY IN THE NETHERLANDS

Hartog and Oosterbeek (1985) investigated the relation between education, job level[7] and gross wages. They estimated the following two equations:

$$\ln Y_i = \alpha_0 + \alpha_1 s_i \tag{1}$$

Y_i = individual income

s_i = educational level

$$\ln Y_i = \beta_0 + \beta_1 r_i \qquad (2)$$
$$r_i = \text{required educational level}$$

The issue here is the question of whether job levels or educational levels have the higher explanatory power with regard to wage levels. Their conclusion is that equation (1), which is more directly in line with the human capital theory, performs better than equation (2), which is more in line with the job competition theory.[8] This conclusion has to be qualified. First, the data only contained information on the employed. The unemployed, including those with high educational levels, probably have a low income. Including them in the estimation, by assigning the unemployed an arbitrary job title, will certainly reduce the explained variance, and hence the explanatory power, of equation (1) and increase the explanatory power of equation (2). Second, Netherlands Statistics (CBS, 1995, p. 94) finds exactly the opposite for similar regressions on a different data set.

Teulings and Koopmanschap (1989) concluded that the high incidence of unemployment among the lower educated is due to crowding out by middle and higher educated workers. The alternative explanation, an increase in the required educational level either within or across occupations (e.g., due to rapid technological developments that may shift the labour demand curve for the higher educated to the right, and for the lower educated workers to the left), is rejected. In their model, they simulated the effects of a 3 per cent fall in overall labour supply. Although the unemployment rate among those with middle and higher education does not change significantly, the unemployment rate of the lower educated would fall from 11.8 to 4.9.

De Beer (1995) investigated whether the decrease in low wage jobs between 1979 and 1993 is the main cause of the shortage of jobs for the lower educated. Only if the job requirement level is taken as the relevant criterion, can it be concluded that from the mid-1970s onwards the number of 'bad jobs' has fallen. However, in the same period the educational level of the workforce rose sharply, so that the number of the lower educated decreased at least pro-portionally. Taking working conditions or wages as the relevant criteria shows that the number of 'bad jobs' has even increased. De Beer's conclusion is in accordance with what can be expected from the job competition theory: with an overall shortage of jobs, the higher and middle educated crowd out the lower educated workers, which is the reason why unemployment is concentrated among the lower educated.

In the remainder of this section we present some empirical evidence for the following two hypotheses formulated in line with the job competition theory, and contrary to what could be expected in line with the human capital theory:

(i)   an increase in the average level of education of the labour force causes a rise in wage inequality between higher and lower educated workers;
(ii) schooling programmes for lower educated unemployed workers do not reduce overall unemployment.

4.1 Educational levels and wage inequality

Table 11.5 shows that between 1975 and 1993 the enrolment rates at the lower educational levels decreased, while it increased at the middle and higher educational levels. According to the human capital theory, a higher supply of higher educated workers and a lower supply of lower educated workers will, *ceteris paribus*, reduce wage inequality between higher and lower educated workers. According to the job competition theory, a higher supply of higher educated workers without a corresponding change in the job queue will 'force' these workers to take jobs of a lower rank, which results in a decrease in the average wages received. Both theories therefore predict a decline in wages of higher educated workers if the supply of these workers rises rapidly. Figure 11.2 illustrates that this is indeed the case for the period 1969–1993. Higher educated workers have experienced a decline in their wages compared to the average wages of all workers.

Table 11.5 Indexed educational participation between 1975–1993 (1975=100)

	PVE	LGSE	HGSE	PUE	IVE	HVE	UE
1975	100	100	100	100	100	100	100
1980	98	102	113	106	142	106	116
1985	91	93	115	118	250	111	125
1990	76	91	121	128	282	145	133
1993	71	86	119	130	328	183	150

Notes:
PVE = Preparatory Vocational; LGSE = Lower General; HGSE = Higher General; PUE = Pre-University; IVE = Intermediate Vocational; HVE = Higher Vocational; UE =University.
Source: Sociale en Culturele verkenningen, 1995

More important is the development of the relative wage of the higher educated compared to the lower educated workers. As outlined in Section 2, the human capital theory predicts a decline in wage inequality due to the large increase (decrease) in supply of higher (lower) educated workers in the past decades, whereas the job competition theory predicts a rise in wage inequality.[9] As can be seen from Figure 11.3, the wage differential is quite constant for the interval

1969–1980, and decreases between 1980–1985. The data do not show a rising wage inequality between higher and lower educated workers. A closer look at the figures reveals that the decreasing segment of the wage differential is not so much due to higher wages of the lower educated, but rather to lower wages of the higher educated. However, there are some factors that may hide the deterioration of relative wages of the lower educated workers as predicted by the job competition theory. First, the data presented in Figures 11.2 and 11.3 do not relate to the total labour force, but only to those who are employed. The incomes of the unemployed are not taken into account. However, the lower educated are more severely hit by unemployment than the higher educated. Not taking into account the higher unemployment rates among the lower educated, results in an upward bias in the relative wages of lower educated workers. It is therefore not unlikely that the high overall unemployment rates of the 1980s have decreased the relative wages of the higher educated because many of these

Figure 11.2   Relative wages (compared to the average wage of all workers) by educational level, 1969–1993

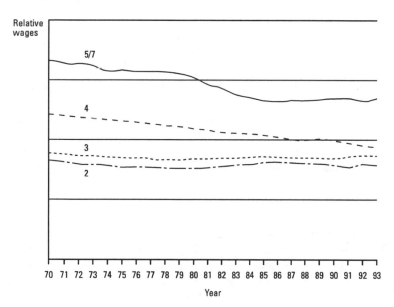

2   = Primary
3   = Lower (vocational & general)
4   = Intermediate (vocational & general)
5/7 = Higher vocational + academic

Figure 11.3   Relative wages of higher compared to lower educated workers,
1969–1993

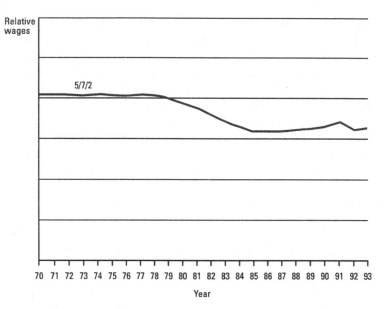

higher educated workers took jobs below their own level and the relative wages
of the lower educated workers did not decrease because relatively many of them
became unemployed, which remains outside the scope of the data presented in
the above figures. Second, minimum wage legislation may have precluded the
decline in the relative wages of lower educated workers. Without minimum
wage legislation, the relative wages of the lower educated might have decreased
as unemployment increased. If this indeed would have happened the evidence
would be in line with job competition theory.

4.2 The schooling instrument
According to the job competition theory, high unemployment among lower
educated workers is caused by crowding out. Alternatively, the human capital
theory asserts that high unemployment is partly due to insufficient productive
skills among the lower educated. Raising the set of marketable productive skills
of lower educated unemployed individuals is then the most direct way to reduce
unemployment.

     To reduce unemployment among the lower educated, it is necessary that
sufficient jobs or vacancies are available at levels just above the lower

educational levels. The schooling instrument to reduce unemployment can be successful only if vacancy rates (or V/U ratios) at higher levels are such that the lower educated unemployed workers have better prospects of finding work at these higher levels if they participate in additional schooling. If the number of vacancies is insufficient (or low V/U ratios) at all levels, opening up the possibility of job competition, skill upgrading of one particular group will only redistribute unemployment from this group to another.

Figure 11.4   Number of unemployed and number of vacancies by educational level

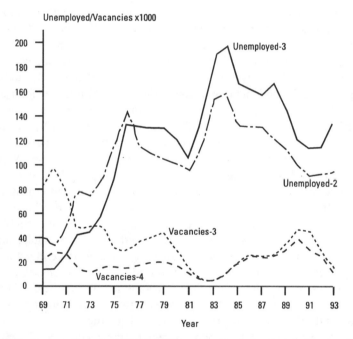

The CBS time series for 1969–1993 contain data about the number of unemployed persons as well as the number of vacancies, distinguished by educational and job requirement levels. Figure 11.4 shows the number of unemployed at levels 2 and 3 compared to the number of vacancies at levels 3 and 4 (see the legenda of Figure 11.2). Between 1973–1985, the number of unemployed with only primary education increased sharply, while the number of vacancies one level higher decreased. The divergence of the number of unemployed at level 3 and the number of vacancies at level 4 is even stronger. A significant reduction of unemployment by means of training programmes for the lower educated unemployed workers is therefore not very likely. Admittedly, this is a very static way to look at a dynamic labour market. Selective training programmes to remove temporary discrepancies on the labour market can be effective, but to reduce overall unemployment by means of an *en masse* schooling programme for the unemployed seems unlikely.

5   WAGE INEQUALITY, SCHOOLING AND JOB COMPETITION

Van Ours and Ridder (1995) try to explain the widely diverging unemployment rates over educational categories (see also Table 11.6). Whether an unemployed worker with educational level i searches for jobs at his own level or a level below $(i - 1)$, depends on both the wage differential and the unemployment-vacancy (V/U) ratios. Only if V_{i-1}/U_{i-1} is much higher than V_i/U_i, and hence average expected search duration is much shorter, is it profitable for a worker with level i to search for a job at level $i - 1$. In equilibrium, the lower wages received by accepting a job at level $i - 1$ are compensated by the shorter unemployment duration.[10] To our knowledge, this is the first time that Thurow's job competition theory has been modelled in a formal way. However, Van Ours and Ridder make a rather untenable assumption, especially if one aims at formalizing and testing the incidence of job competition and crowding out, namely: 'If he searches for a job at level $i - 1$, he is part of the pool of unemployed workers searching for jobs at level $i - 1$' (Van Ours and Ridder, 1995, p. 1722). As a consequence, unemployed workers searching for jobs below their own educational level do not have *any advantage* in getting jobs over those who have merely the required educational level for these same jobs, that is, the average search duration for those applying for jobs below their own educational level is assumed to be exactly equal to the search duration of lower educated workers looking for the same jobs. The crucial ingredient brought forward by Thurow – that employers prefer higher educated above lower educated workers in order to minimize training costs – is missing in this framework. If one takes Thurow seriously, one should at least leave open the possibility that the expected average search duration of unemployed workers merely seeking employment below their own level is much shorter than the average search duration of unemployed workers merely seeking jobs with educational requirements equal to their educational status. Moreover, as Table 11.6 illustrates, the rate of unemployment among college graduates and higher vocational workers is lower than among intermediate vocational workers, which in turn is lower than among those with a lower vocational educational background or just primary education. According to Van Ours and Ridder,[11] for a process of bumping down to take place at all, would require that the number of vacancies relative to the number of unemployed is much higher at lower level jobs than at higher level jobs,[12] which is very unlikely given the high unemployment at the bottom end of the labour market.

Table 11.6 Shares in the labour force and in the unemployed by educational level, 1990 and 1994, %

Education	1990 Labour force	Unemployed	1994 Labour force	Unemployed
Primary	12	24	9	19
LGSE/PVE	25	29	23	28
HGSE/PUE/IVE	41	31	43	35
HVE	15	10	17	12
UE	7	6	8	6
Total	100	100	100	100

Source: CBS, Working Population Survey 1994 (converted to the share in the relevant population group).

The challenged assumption, that workers seeking jobs below their educational degree have an equal search duration to lower educated workers seeking these same jobs, is the real culprit here. This assumption is crucial for the rational behaviour that Van Ours and Ridder ascribe to job seekers: they only bump down if the shorter search duration compensates them for the lower wages of jobs at lower levels.[13] However, if those workers who bump down can obtain a job at a lower level fairly quickly,[14] whereas they would experience a much longer search duration for a job at their own level, then the condition of whether bumping down is likely to take place becomes much weaker. For instance, if one assumes that unemployed workers can get a job below their own level immediately, then bumping down will take place if (1) the number of vacancies at higher levels falls short of the number of unemployed at higher levels and (2) the present value of life-time earnings when initially taking a lower level job is higher than or equal to that when continuing to search for a job at one's own level.[15]

Basically (for simplicity, we assume only two levels of education i and $i-1$), Van Ours and Ridder estimate the following equation:

$$F_i = k \left((1-\lambda_i)U_i\right)^\alpha (V_i)^{1-\alpha} \tag{3a}$$

$$F_{i\text{-}1} = k \, (U_{i\text{-}1} + \lambda_i U_i)^\alpha \, (V_{i\text{-}1})^{1-\alpha} \tag{3b}$$

In the first (Cobb-Douglas) matching function,[16] the number of filled vacancies (F) at job level i is dependent on the number of unemployed workers seeking employment at their own level $((1- \lambda_i)U_i)$ – with λ_i the fraction of unemployed with level i seeking employment below their own level – and the number of vacancies at level i. In equation (3b), the number of filled vacancies at level $i-1$ is dependent on the number of vacancies and the number of unemployed at that level plus the number of unemployed from a higher level seeking employment here. However, in just summing up (i.e. *pooling*) the number of unemployed (whatever their educational level) who are seeking employment in jobs at level $i-1$ by the term $(U_{i\text{-}1} + \lambda_i U_i)$, the advantage that higher educated unemployed workers might have compared to lower educated ones for the same jobs, is not taken into account.

If we made the rather extreme, and opposite, assumption that the higher educated can find employment at a lower level *immediately*, due to their lower training costs, we would get the following equation:

$$F_{i\text{-}1} = k(U_{i\text{-}1})^\alpha (V_{i\text{-}1} - \lambda_i U_i)^{1-\alpha} \tag{3b'}$$

According to (3b'), the number of vacancies available for the unemployed workers with educational level $i-1$ is reduced by the number of unemployed workers of a higher educational level who have chosen to work below their own level. The LHS of (3b') must then be interpreted as the number of filled vacancies at level $i-1$ by workers with educational level $i-1$. Alternatively, the number of overeducated $\lambda_i U_i$ finding employment at level $i-1$ can be subtracted from $F_{i\text{-}1}$.

If there is some truth in the notion that employers select workers according to the expected training costs, and if these costs vary inversely with the educational level, then the V/U ratios at different levels become much less important. For high-skilled workers, the V/U ratio at lower levels is not of overriding importance, as long as they have a clear advantage in finding employment below their own level.[17] Still, it remains true that it is only rational for workers to seek jobs below their own level if the net present value of doing so is at least equal to the net present value of seeking jobs at their own level (with a longer search duration, but higher wages). The effects of wage differentials are, however, not taken into account in the empirical estimation model of crowding out in Van Ours and Ridder (1995), although much effort is spent in the very elegant theoretical model of job competition to include the effects of wage differentials.

Unfortunately, the data used by Van Ours and Ridder neither allow a distinction between filled vacancies by educational levels of workers, nor the inclusion of the effects of wage differentials. They find no evidence of job competition at the lower educational levels, but they do find some job competition between academically educated workers and workers with a higher vocational education (which is also the only combination for which their condition is fulfilled). In the remainder of this chapter we will present an alternative, albeit indirect, test of job competition based on the same data as used by Van Ours and Ridder (1995).

6 AN INDIRECT TEST ON JOB COMPETITION

The hypothesis that we want to test is whether job competition at level i–1 will increase if the V/U ratio at a higher level i decreases. A direct test on the job competition theory would at least require data of filled vacancies distinguished by job level requirements as well as the educational levels of workers who have filled these vacancies. However, besides the number of vacancies and the number of unemployed distinguished by levels, we only have data on filled vacancies distinguished by job level. The problem is therefore that vacancies can be occupied by workers with the required or a higher level of education.[18] Using the same data as Van Ours and Ridder (1995),[19] we propose the following indirect test based on the following causal chain:

$U_i\uparrow$ or $V_i\downarrow \rightarrow (V_i/U_i)\downarrow \rightarrow$ vacancy-flow duration at level $_{i-1}\downarrow \rightarrow F_{i-1}\uparrow$

If the (U_i/V_i)-ratio deteriorates, it becomes more attractive for those with educational level i to search for jobs at level $i - 1$. According to the Cobb-Douglas matching technology, a larger pool of unemployed workers searching for jobs at this lower level will reduce the time for employers to find suitable candidates, especially if part of the pool of applicants have a higher educational level than strictly required to do the job properly. Therefore, if job competition occurs, we can expect that a lower V/U ratio at level i will increase the flow of filled vacancies with job requirement level $i - 1$ (by reducing the average vacancy-flow duration level for employers). In the absence of job competition, we would expect that the flow of filled vacancies at one particular level not be influenced by the scarcity conditions reflected in V/U ratios at a lower level. We therefore estimated the following equation:[20]

$$F_{i-1j} = \beta_0 + \beta_1 (V_{i-1j}/U_{i-1j}) + \beta_2 (V_{ij}/U_{ij})$$

F_{ij} indicates the number of filled vacancies at educational level i (1 = lower, 2 = intermediate, 3 = higher vocational, 4 = university) and educational field j (1 = technical, 2 = medical, 3 = clerical, 4 = socio-cultural). According to this equation, the flow of filled vacancies depends on the V/U ratio at this level as well as on the V/U ratio at a higher level. We may expect a positive sign for β_1,

Table 11.7 Estimation results of the indirect test on job competition

	Technical	Medical	Clerical	Social cultural
Higher	R^2= 0.83	R^2= 0.58	R^2= 0.75	R^2= 0.38
	β_1= 0.96 (2.3)*	β_1= 1.20 (2.0)	β_1= 0.94 (3.4)**	β_1= 1.03 (1.5)
	β_2= -0.06 (-0.2)	β_2= -1.42 (-2.3)*	β_2=-3.55 (-1.3)	β_2= -1.07 (-1.5)
Interm.	R^2= 0.60	R^2= 0.76	R^2= 0.93	R^2= 0.96
	β_1= 1.01 (1.4)	β_1= 1.16 (3.5)**	β_1= 1.72 (4.2)***	β_1= 1.01 (8.3)***
	β_2=-2.69 (-0.4)	β_2= -0.89(-2.7)**	β_2= -0,85 (-2.1)*	β_2 =-0.94 (-7.7)***
Lower	R^2= 0.33		R^2= 0.80	R^2= 0.58
	β_1= 0.49 (0.6)		β_1= -0.40 (-0.67)	β_1= 0.83 (1.6)
	β_2= 0.09 (0.1)		β_2= 1.26 (2.1)*	β_2= -0.10 (-0.2)

• t-values in brackets. *= significant at 10%, **= significant at 5%, ***= significant at 1%.
• Because 'medical'at the lower level does not exist, no results are reported.

since more vacancies relative to the number of unemployed at this level will increase the chance for each unemployed worker to get a job (there are simply more job openings (vacancies) available). For β_2, we expect a negative sign: as the number of vacancies at a higher level is higher, or the number of unemployed workers is lower, fewer higher educated unemployed workers have reason to look for jobs below their own level. Table 11.7 summarizes the results.

Ten out of eleven values for β_1 have the expected positive sign, five being statistically significant at the 10% level. For β_2, nine out eleven have the expected negative sign, four being significant at the 10% level. These results suggest that job competition occurs mainly at the intermediate level for medical, clerical and social-cultural occupations. At this level, it seems that the ratio of vacancies to the number employed at the higher vocational level influences the flow of filled vacancies at the intermediate level.

Just like Van Ours and Ridder (1995), we did not find evidence that job competition occurs at all levels. Because we used the same data, it is remarkable that we found no evidence for job competition between academics and higher vocational workers which they did. For this reason, the difference in outcomes must be traced back to different assumptions made and the way of testing.

7 CONCLUSION

To what extent job competition and displacement of lower educated by higher educated workers prevails, is still a matter of controversy in the economic literature. In this chapter we discussed the explanatory power of two competing theories of the labour market, the job competition theory and the human capital theory. Using two fictitious economies, we were able to illustrate clearly the major implications of the two theories in the case of an exogenous rise in the educational level of the labour force. Empirical research on job competition and displacement for The Netherlands shows ambiguous results. Both theories can explain why unemployment is concentrated among the lower educated. Therefore, the empirical fact of the heavy incidence of unemployment among lower educated workers is not sufficient to discriminate between the two theories. High unemployment rates among the lower educated workers, the female labour force and older workers do not necessarily imply that at the micro-level their jobs are occupied by higher educated males and young workers. A truly discriminating test of the two theories, if possible at all, would require a much richer data set than the one used in this chapter or as used in Van Ours and Ridder (1995). For this reason, the evidence provided here is only circumstantial.

NOTES

1. There are, broadly speaking, two approaches that try to explain the demand for education. First, education can be seen as a *consumer* good. This approach stresses the intrinsic value or worth of education as a means for personal development, to broaden one's horizons, etc. Second, education can be seen as an *investment* good for which one first has to incur effort and costs, but which yields a higher income and a better job in the future (Becker, 1964). This approach stresses the instrumental value of education as a means to acquire productive skills and hence earning power, although it does not weaken the intrinsic worth (these are subsumed under immaterial benefits of education). Here we want to add a third approach: the demand for education can be seen as a 'demand for postponing paid work'. In this approach a student is not so much interested in what can be learned at school, nor in the expected higher earnings in the future due to accumulated human capital, but only to postpone the duty to perform paid work. To enrol as a student in university gives one the opportunity to postpone paid work for about six years.

2.	The theory of statistical discrimination developed by Phelps (1972) says that evaluations that employers make of candidates or job applicants in situations of incomplete information are partly based on easy to assess individual characteristics and partly based on group characteristics. Group characteristics are better known and generally easier to determine than the possible individual deviations from the overall group characteristics. *On average* women interrupt their labour market career more often and for longer spells than men, although this does not necessarily apply to *each* individual woman. As a consequence, in occupations with high training costs and where interruption is costly, employers prefer men to women, even if some women do not wish to interrupt their careers and have the required education for the jobs available. So men and women with identical characteristics (education, age, work experience, etc.) are at different places in the labour queue. Job competition is thus not only limited to educational categories, but also to gender.

3.	Johnson (1997, pp. 47–8) makes a distinction between *extensive* skill-biased technological change, such as the use of robots replacing routine work, where higher educated workers become more productive in jobs usually allocated to lower educated workers, and *intensive* skill-biased technological change, such as the advancement of computer software and the widespread use of computers, where higher educated workers become even more productive in the jobs they already perform.

4.	'If workers feel that they are training a potential wage or job competitor every time they show another worker how to do their job, they have every incentive to stop giving such informal training. Conversely, in a training system where no one is trained unless a job is available (this is what on-the-job training means), where strong seniority provisions exist, and where there is no danger of some competitor bidding down your wages, employees can more freely transmit information to new workers and can more readily accept new techniques. Here wage and job competition (above the entry level) becomes counterproductive' (ibid., 22–23).

5.	'The marginal product of capital depends on the quantity and quality of labor with which it is working. Consequently, employers will want to generate more job skills, general or specific, than individuals will be willing to buy. Individuals simply are not able to appropriate all of the indirect benefits of the additional skills' (ibid., 19).

6.	Another policy could be what is known as 'smoking the chimney': by stimulating employment growth at middle and higher levels, job competition at lower levels will be reduced.

7.	Information about job levels was obtained in a qualitative-subjective way, asking workers which educational level they think is required to do the job properly. Hartog (1985) comes to the same conclusions using a more objective method by using ARBI codes to assess job levels.

8.	Apart from that, the so-called *assignment* model, which focuses on the optical match between the characteristics of workers and jobs, had the best performance, but this goes beyond the scope of this chapter.

9.	In contradiction to the job competition model presented in Section 2, a changing economic environment such as increased trade and non-neutral technological change may have shifted the demand curves for higher and lower educated workers. The results of this test are therefore only tentative, at best.

10.	'So an equilibrium situation with search at level i–1 by unemployed workers at level i requires the average search duration at level i to be longer than that at level i–1. Furthermore it follows that the larger the wage differential between the educational levels, the larger the difference between the average search duration must be' (*ibid.*, p. 1722).

11.	In particular their equation (12): there is job competition if
	$U_i/V_i > (1/\phi)U_{i-1}/V_{i-1}$ with $0 < \phi < 1$ if $W_{i-1} < W_i$.

12.	Van Ours and Ridder (1995, 1724) show that this condition is only satisfied in the 1980s for academically trained workers *vis-à-vis* higher vocational workers.

13.	In their theoretical framework they further assume that workers with jobs below their educational level stick to these jobs (and wages) forever, which is also unlikely.

14. Indeed, if Thurow is right that employers prefer higher educated workers to minimize training costs, then the chance of success of applying for a vacancy is higher if the educational level of the job applicant is higher than the required level.
15. Moreover, for workers with a strong work ethic even (2) need not be fulfilled.
16. In this function k is an efficiency parameter that is assumed not to vary with the job level. Parameter α is a measure for the relative importance of the number of unemployed versus the number of vacancies in determining the flow of filled vacancies. In Van Ours and Ridder (1995), this parameter is around 0.30.
17. Therefore, the claim of Van Ours and Ridder that for job competition to occur 'a necessary but not sufficient condition for an unemployed worker at level i to search below his educational level is that the UV-ratio is lower at the lower level of education' (ibid., 1724) is not true. This claim is the logical outcome of the challenged assumption made.
18. In principle, it is possible that workers with a lower level of education than required are selected from a pool of applicants. However, this is very unlikely in a slack labour market and even more unlikely if employers prefer higher educated above lower educated workers to minimize training costs (see also Van Beek and Van Praag, 1992).
19. At this place we want to thank Van Ours and Ridder for making available these data, which enabled us to do the indirect test discussed below.
20. Admittedly, this equation is not consistent with a Cobb-Douglas matching technology (in which both the number of unemployed and the number of vacancies would determine the number of filled vacancies positively).

REFERENCES

Becker, G.S. (1964), *Human Capital*, New York.

CBS (Centraal Bureau voor de Statistiek) (1995), *Tijdreeksen Arbeidsrekeningen 1969–1993, Ramingen van het Onderwijsniveau, een Tussenstand*, Voorburg.

De Beer, P. (1995), 'Werk aan de Onderkant', *Economisch Statistische Berichten* **80** (4033), 1038–40.

Hartog, J. (1985), 'Overscholing?', *Economisch Statistische Berichten* **70** (3493), 152–6.

Hartog, J. and H. Oosterbeek (1985), *Education, Allocation and Earnings in the Netherlands: Overschooling?*, Research Memorandum no. 8523, University of Amsterdam, Amsterdam.

Johnson, G.E. (1997), 'Changes in Earnings Inequality: The Role of Demand Shifts', *Journal of Economic Perspectives* **11** (2), 41–54.

Phelps, E.S. (1972), 'The Statistical Theory of Racism and Sexism', *American Economic Review* **62**, 659–61.

Teulings, C. and M. Koopmanschap (1989), 'An Econometric Model of Crowding Out of Lower Educational Levels', *European Economic Review* **33** (8), 1653–64.

Thurow, L.C. (1979), 'A Job-competition Model', in M. Piore (ed.), *Unemployment and Inflation*, New York, 17–31.

Topel, R.H. (1997), 'Factor Proportions and Relative Wages: The Supply-side Determinants of Wage Inequality', *Journal of Economic Perspectives* **11** (2), 55–74.

Van Beek, K.W.H. and B.M.S. van Praag (1992), *Kiezen uit Sollicitanten, Concurrentie tussen Werkzoekenden zonder Baan*, WRR, The Hague.

Van Ours, J.C. and G. Ridder (1995), 'Job Matching and Job Competition: are Lower Educated Workers at the Back of Job Queues?', *European Economic Review* **39**, 1717–31.

Index

A-level qualifications, cumulative
  percentage of workers with 170
Abowd, J. 136
adjustment costs 205
Adler, P. 27
aggregate skill trends (1950–1995)
  29–38
Aigner 228
Alba-Ramirez, A. 14, 73, 193
allocation theory 7–8, 10
Alpin, C. 14
Anderson, B. 75
Angrist, J.D. 186
apprenticeship level qualifications,
  cumulative percentage of workers
  with 167
ARBI code 13
Arrow, K. 28
Ashenfelter, O. 136, 153
Ashton, D. 18, 79
Asplund, R. 14, 17, 18
assignment theory 6
AVO (Arbeids Voorwaarden
  Ontwikkeling) 212

Bartel, A.P. 28, 53
Battu, H. 12, 14, 19, 74, 158
Baumol, W.J. 53
Bazen, S. 198
Becker, G.S. 129, 194
Belgium
  earnings profiles 182, 183
  sample selection effects, earnings
    function 184
Bell, B. 153, 158
Benassy, J.P. 153
Berman, E. 41
binary probit model 181
Blackburn, M. 153, 162

Blackburn, M.L. 186
Blanchard, O. 135, 153
Blanchard, O.J. 129
Borghans, L. 4, 11, 20, 74, 198
Borjas, G. 133, 134
Bound, J. 4, 133, 134
Bradley, M. 80, 104
Brauer, D. 133
Britain
  education 79
  exclusion from skill rises 96–8
  occupational structure 90
  overeducation 85–7, 157–74
  productivity 79
  qualifications 104–5
    demand for qualifications (1986 and
      1997) 85
    educational qualifications 157–8
    qualification levels across three data
      years 164
    qualifications required (1986 and
      1997) 84
    of the workforce 83
  skills 78–81
    type of work skill changes 1992 to
      1997 95
British Household Panel Study (BHPS)
  160
Bruinshoofd, A. 20
Bruinshoofd, W.A. 126
bumping down 3, 5, 11, 12, 18, 231
  consequences 20
  effect on wages 175–202
  Finland 57–76, 69
  measurement 175–6
  and reservation wages 176–8
bumping rights 158
Burchell, B. 18
Burdett, K. 129

Cain 228
CBA (Centraal Bureau
    Arbeidsvoorzieningen) 110
CBS (Statistics Netherlands) 110, 239
Chamberlin, E. 135
clerical workers 93-4
Cohn, E. 73, 111
college enrolment 109
commercial qualifications, cumulative
    percentage of workers with 167
competition
    in the labour market 135
    monopolistic competition 143-8
competitiveness 3-4, 48
computerization 50
Constant Returns to Scale (CRS)
    matching function 208
credentialism 10, 14, 83-5, 93-4
crowding out 3, 175, 186, 192, 203-5, 211
    different probabilities based on stock
        of 1995 sample 222
    framework for analysis 206-12
    measuring importance 213-26
    probabilities based on ordered logits
        for different years and education
        groups 221
    testing with micro data 213-15
crowding out model 207

Davies, B. 18
Davis, D.R. 4
Davis, S. 134, 153
De Beer, P. 110, 128, 239
De Grip, A. 11, 15, 20
De Koning, J. 110
de Neubourg, C. 129
deskilling 52
Diamond, P.A. 129
Dictionary of Occupational Titles 13, 17,
    28
differential overqualification theory 170
Dixit, A. 148, 150, 153
Doeringer, P.B. 158
'drawing chimney policy' 204
Duncan, G.J. 73
Dutch Department of Social Affairs 13

earnings
    direct and indirect effects of education
        185

see also wages
earnings function, sample selection
    effects 184
earnings profiles
    by level of education (men) 182
    by level of education (women) 183
Economic and Social Research Council
    (UK) 78
ECVT 14
EDUC - 1970 (Median Years of
    Schooling - 1970) 30, 40, 45, 52
education
    average schooling by occupational
        category 60-61
    Britain 79
    direct and indirect earnings effects 185
    earnings profiles, by level of education
        182, 183
    and employment 191
    indexed educational participation
        between 1975-1993 240
    least educated workers, labour market
        transitions 61-3
    and occupational prestige
        (1986-1995), Britain 164-70
    returns to 28
    skills and productivity, growth by
        decade (1950-1990) 47
    and unemployment, Netherlands 110
    and wages 191-2
education-wage profile, and
    occupational productivity profile
    6-10
educational attainment, and skills 35
educational levels
    and job complexity 227-8
    and wage inequality 240-42
educational qualifications
    Britain 157-8
    distribution 14
    of the unemployed 169
    see also qualifications
educational structure of occupations
    59-61
Eide 4
employment
    distribution by industry 42
    distribution by occupational group
        (US) 33
    and education 191

industry employment, changes 42-3
equilibrium, and overeducation 122-3
equilibrium wage levels, job competition
    theory 238
European Commission 4
European Union Labour Force Survey
    124
exclusion from skill rises, Britain 96-8,
    101

Felstead, A. 18, 104
Finland
    bumping down 57-76, 69
    labour force and employment
        (1975-1995) 58
    labour market 61
    ·labour market transition patterns
        66-70
    overeducation 63-6, 69
Frank, R.H. 170
Freeman, R. 133
Freeman, R.B. 3

Gallie, D. 80
Gautier, P.A. 12, 20, 210, 211, 213, 228,
    229
GDP per Full-Time Equivalent
    Employee (FTEE) 47
Gelderblom, A. 110, 128
gender differentiation, in skills 87
General Educational Development
    (GED) 29
Gill, I.S. 28, 53
Glyn, A. 158
Goldthorpe, J.H. 160
Gottschalk, P. 109
Goux, D. 124
Green, A. 79
Green, F. 5, 10, 13, 18, 79
Greene, W.H. 180, 183
Grogger 4
Groot, L. 12, 20, 111, 128, 129
Groot, W. 165, 193

Halaby, C. 15
Handbook for Analysing Jobs 13
Harmon, C. 186
Hartog, J. 6, 13, 14, 15, 73, 74, 111, 128,
    192, 193, 195, 238, 250
health sector, Britain 90

Heckman, J.J. 176
'Heckman's Lambda' 180
Heijke, H. 111
Hernstadt, I. 31
Hersch, J. 73
Hickok, S. 133
Higuchi, Y. 28, 53
hiring and firing rates, for different job
    complexity levels 226
Hirschhorn, L. 31
Hoek, A. 12, 20, 129
Hoffman, S.D. 73
Hollanders, H. 129
Hope, K. 160
Hope-Goldthorpe scale 160, 163, 170
    cumulative percentage of unqualified
        workers 166
    means core across education groups
        167
Horowitz, M. 31
Howell, D.R. 53, 124
human capital 135, 136, 138, 180, 181,
    192
    neo-classical theory 194
human capital model 178
human capital theory 111-12, 118, 175,
    231, 232, 235-6
    equilibrium wage levels 237
    and job competition theory, main
        differences 233, 236-7

income inequality 109
industry
    changes in employment 42-3
    distribution of employment 42
    effects on aggregate skill growth
        43-6
    skill trends 92
interactive skills 30, 40, 45, 46

job competition
    in the Dutch labour market 231-52
    indirect test 247-9
        estimation results 248
    schooling, and wage inequality 244-7
    versus wage competition 11-12
job competition models 11, 112, 206
job competition theory 231, 232-6, 236
    distribution of workers and jobs over
        wage levels 238

empirical research in the Netherlands
238–44
equilibrium wage levels 238
and human capital theory, main
differences 233, 236–7
job complexity level 215, 216
classification 227–8
different job complexity levels, for
hiring and firing rates 226
and education levels 227–8
estimates 217–22, 222–3
shifts in distributions 224, 225
simulated probabilties of being
employed at a certain level 220
Johnson, G.E. 4, 133, 134, 250
Jonker, N. 6, 193
Juhn, C. 153

Kahn, S. 73, 111
Kato, T. 158
Katz, L. 4, 133, 134
Keep, E. 79
Keese, M. 191
Kettunen, J. 129
Kiker, B.F. 14
Kiyotaki, N. 135, 153
Kleinknecht, A. 130
Knight, J.B. 6
Koeman, J. 130
Koopmanschap, M. 239
Kraft, A. 159
Krueger, A. 153
Krueger, A.B. 186

labour demand 136–8
labour force, shares by educational level
245
Labour Force Survey (Britain) 79, 87,
157, 159
labour market 112–13
changes over time in exogenous
variables 123–6
competition 135
condition in 1993 and 1995 214–15
matching process 113–14
Netherlands 235
tightness, wage and duration 117
labour market flows 207
labour market transition patterns 66–70
labour market transitions

multinomial logit estimation results
between 1975 and 1985 72
multinomial logit estimation results
between 1985 and 1995 72
labour queue theory 111, 112, 120
labour skills, measures 29–32
Lam, A. 13
Lang, K. 4
Layard, R. 112, 129, 136, 153
'learning society' 97, 101
'The Learning Society' 78
learning time measures 87–8
learning-by-doing 28
least educated workers, labour market
transitions 61–3
Leontief, W. 4
Lever, M.H.C. 130
LFS, comparison with SCELI 1986
102–5
Lichtenberg, F.R. 28, 53
lifelong learning 97
Lilja, R. 14, 17, 18
Lindbeck, A. 126
logit equations, for overeducation 171
Longitudinal Census Data Set (1970–95)
59
low skilled workers 5
overeducation and crowding out
109–32
unemployment 211
unemployment rate 203, 205
low skills and low pay 98–9
low wage employment, and
overqualification 133–56
low wage jobs, decrease 239

McCormick, B. 208, 228
Machin, S. 80
Manacorda, M. 79, 93, 157, 159, 160,
162
management efficiency 78
Marsh, C. 103
Marshall, R. 77
Mason, G. 13, 79
Massen van den Brink, H. 128
matching process 119–20
labour market 113–14
and schooling 124–6
matching theory 6
Matsuyama, K. 135, 153

Maurin, E. 124
Mayhew, K. 79
Median Years of Schooling - 1970
    (EDUC - 1970) 30, 34, 40, 45, 52
Meijers, H. 129
Meyer, B.C. 75
Miller, A.R. 30, 53
Mincer, J. 28, 53, 152, 153, 194
minimum wage 152-3
    reduction 149
monopolistic competition 143-8
motor skills 30, 40-41, 46
    decline 52
    growth 47
Murphy, K. 4, 133, 134
Murray, A. 87
Muysken, J. 12, 18, 129

Nash-bargaining process 115
negative signalling effect 208
Nelson, R.R. 28
Netherlands 126
    education and unemployment 110
    job competition 231-52
    job competition theory, empirical
        research 238-44
    labour market 235
    percentage of workers with excess
        education 110
    returns to human capital 111
    unemployment, rates for different
        education classes 204
    unions 124
    wages
        mean and standard deviation of
            wages for IVR graduates 199
        predicted incidence of low wages
            200
        wage equation for school leavers
            192, 193-8
Netherlands Statistics 239
Neumark, D. 186
Nicaise, I. 4, 19, 181, 186
Nickell, S. 153, 158
Nielsen, S. 135, 153
Nishimura, K. 135, 153

O-level qualifications, cumulative
    percentage of workers with 169
occupation, skill trends 91

Occupational Outlook Handbook 7
occupational prestige, and education,
    Britain (1986-1995) 164-70
occupational productivity profile, and
    education-wage profile 6-10
occupational structure, in Britain 90
occupational trends 32-3
occupations
    educational structure 59-61
    and skill changes 89-90
OECD 4, 124
OECD countries, wages 191
Oi, W.Y. 211
on-the-job-training 234-5
Oosterbeek, H. 13, 73, 111, 128, 238
opportunity cost hypothesis *see*
    reservation wages
optimal skill level 8
ordered logit estimates 217-22
    results 220
Ordinary Least Squares (OLS)
    regressions 176, 177, 181
The Overeducated American 3
overeducation 3-6, 9, 57-8, 127
    Britain 85-7, 157-74
    changing definitions 66
    determinants 170-72
    and equilibrium 122-3
    extent of mismatch 165
    Finland 63-6, 69
    logit equations 171
    measurement 161, 162
    transition probabilities 70
overqualification 145-6
    and low-wage employment 133-end
        chap
    reduction 152
overschooling 109-10

Palm, F.C. 211, 226
part-time work 124
Pfann, G.A. 211, 226
Phelps, E.S. 28, 112, 250
Piore, M.J. 158
Pissarides, C.A. 18, 112, 127, 129, 228
Pomp, M. 228
productivity 5, 6, 211
    Britain 79
    education and skills, growth by decade
        (1950-1990) 47

measures of growth 47
productivity-wage-ratio 7, 8, 9
professional qualifications, cumulative
    percentage of workers with 172

qualifications
    Britain 104–5
    demand for, in Britain 85
    and employment 79–80
    required in Britain (1986 and 1997)
        84
    of workforce, Britain 83
    see also educational qualifications

R&D intensity 50
Ramey, V. 134
Real Estate industry 94
redundancy rates 211
Reeve, T.A. 4
Reich, R.B. 77
relative employment 158
reservation wages, and bumping down
    176–8
reservation wages hypothesis 182, 185
Ridder, G. 21, 128, 152, 207, 231, 232,
    244, 246, 247, 248, 249, 250, 251
Robinson, P. 79, 93, 157, 159, 160, 162
Romer, D. 129
Romer, P.M. 4
Roos 30
Roy, A.D. 6
Rumberger, R.W. 13, 15, 28, 32, 74

Saint-Paul, G. 159
sales assistants 93
SCELI (Social Change and Economic
    Life Initiative) 80, 83–94, 158, 160,
    165
    comparison with LFS 1986 102–5
Schmitt, J. 162, 163
schooling
    average schooling by occupational
        category 60
    and the matching process 124–6
    returns 53
    and supply of skills 116–18
    wage inequality, and job competition
        244–7
    see also education
schooling instrument 242–4

Schultz, T.W. 129
screening theory 4, 119
search theory 175, 177
Shockey, J.W. 12
Sicherman, N. 73, 111, 159, 170
skill changes
    at industry level 38–46
    regressions 49–50
skill growth, and technology 46–51
skill levels 27
    and wages 192
skill trends
    Britain 81–2
        comparing 1997 with 1986 83–94
    by age 89
    by industry 92
    by occupation 91
    measures 88
skilled workers 113, 133, 151–2
    equilibrium on the skilled labour
        market 118–19
skilled-to-unskilled wage gap 4
skills
    aggregate skill levels, trends 33–8
    aggregate skill trends (1950–1995)
        29–38
    annual rate of change 36
    Britain 78–81
    change in skill levels, decomposition
        44
    changing skills of the lowest paid
        quintile 99
    education and productivity, growth by
        decade (1950–1990) 47
    and educational attainment 35
    effects on aggregate skill growth,
        industry 43–6
    growth 38
    impact 119–23
    importance 77–8
    labour skills, measures 29–32
    low skills and low pay 98–9
    and low wages 191–202
    measurement 5
    supply of skills 121–2
        and schooling 116–18
    and technology 27–56
    trends in particular job skills 1992–97
        94–6
    underutilization 10, 11, 12, 191–202

defined 12
measurement 12–16
wage-reducing effect 193
'Skills Survey' (Britain) 81–2
findings 83–94
Sloane, P. 12, 14, 19
Sloane, P.J. 73, 111, 158, 164, 165, 173
Smith, E. 129
Smith, H. 15
Smits, W. 193, 198
Snower, D. 135, 153
Snower, D.J. 126
'Social Change and Economic Life
Initiative' (SCELI) 80, 83–94,
102–5, 160, 165
social planner solution 148, 150
sorting hypothesis 111
Spanish Living and Working Conditions
Survey 14
Spearman rank correlation coefficient
93
Spence, A.M. 119
Spence-Dixit-Stiglitz utility function
137
Spenner, K.I. 27, 31, 53
Stasz, C. 13, 16
Statistics Finland 59
Statistics Netherlands 194, 204, 213
Steedman, H. 79, 87
Stiglitz, J. 148, 150, 153
substantive complexity 30, 37, 38–9, 45,
46
substitutability hypothesis 171
Sweden 109

technological advance, and skill change
48–51
technology
and demand for skills 27–56
and skill growth 46–51
technology change 27–8, 79
ter Weel, B.J. 12, 18, 126, 129
Teulings, C. 239
Thurow, L.C. 111, 120, 128, 206, 231,
232, 233, 234, 235, 236, 238, 244
Tinbergen, J. 6
Tirole, J. 148, 150, 153
Topel, R. 4, 133, 153
Topel, R.H. 109, 232
training 12

training costs 233, 234, 246
training time 87–8
Treiman 30
Tucker, M. 77

UK National Survey of Graduates and
Diplomates 14
undereducation 57
underemployment, and wage formation
114–16
underutilization of skills 10, 11, 12
defined 12
empirical method of measurement 14,
16
measurement 12–16
objective measure 13
subjective assessment 13–16
unemployment 58–9, 64, 69, 120, 127,
143, 147, 168, 239, 242, 249
and education, Netherlands 110
educational qualifications of the
unemployed 169
hysteresis 126
and low-skilled workers 211
number of unemployed and number of
vacancies by educational level
243
unemployed workers, shares by
educational level 245
voluntary 177
unemployment rates 241, 244
for different education classes,
Netherlands 204
unions 51, 53, 124, 133, 143
United States
economy 27
employment, distribution by
occupational group 33
farming 28
predicted incidence of low wages 200
skill requirements 38–41
trade patterns 4
unskilled workers 159
upgrading 4, 9, 11, 12
upskilling 80–81, 88
in industries 90
US Bureau of Labor Statistics 7

Van Ark, B. 79
Van Beek, K.W.H. 251

Van den Berg 229
Van der Geest, L. 130
Van der Meer, P. 157, 159, 162, 171
Van der Velden, R. 111
Van Eijs, P. 111
Van Lede, C.J.A. 130
Van Ours, J.C. 21, 128, 129, 152, 207,
    231, 232, 244, 246, 247, 248, 249,
    250, 251
Van Praag, B.M.S. 251
Van Reenen, J. 80
Van Smoorenburg, M. 111
Van Zon, A. 129, 153
Venema, P.M. 213, 227
Verdugo, N.T. 14, 74
Verdugo, R.R. 14, 74
Vernon, R. 51
Vogler, C. 103

wage competition, versus job
    competition 11–12
wage competition models 11
wage equation, for school leavers in the
    Netherlands 193–8
wage formation 118–19, 121, 123–4
    and underemployment 114–16
wage inequality
    and educational levels 240–42
    schooling and job competition 244–7
wages 137, 141, 159, 175
    and education 191–2
    effect of bumping down 175–87
    gross hourly wages 218
    low wages
        definition 192, 198–9
        predicted incidence for different
            educational groups 201

        predicted incidence for Netherlands
            200
        predicted incidence for US 200
        skill-related causes 199–201
        and skills 191–202
    relative wages by educational level
        1969–1993 241
    relative wages of higher compared to
        lower educated workers
        1969–1993 242
    see also earnings
Walker, I. 186
WBEAA 194
Webbink, D. 111, 128
Weiss, A. 128
Welch, F.R. 28, 134
White, H. 48
wholesale industry, Britain 90
Wielers, R. 157, 159, 162, 171
Willems, E. 193
Willis, R. 135
Wolff, E.N. 13, 17, 53, 124
work skill changes, Britain, 1992 to 1997
    95
workers
    allocation over different jobs
        1992–1993 216
    allocation over different jobs for 1993
        and 1995 215
    allocation over different jobs
        1994–1995 216
workers' surplus 138–40, 141
workplace skills 34–5
    growth (1950–1995) 37

Zuboff, S. 22, 31
Zwick, T. 12, 18, 19